Wakefield Press

Europe @ 2.4 km/h

Ken Haley is one of Australia's most widely travelled authors. He became a paraplegic in 1991, but so far as Ken is concerned the only difference that has made is that he now observes the world from a seated position. A journalist by profession, he has had stints on the foreign desk of *The Times*, *Sunday Times* and *Observer* in London, the *Gulf Daily News* in Bahrain and the *South China Morning Post* in Hong Kong. He has also worked at the *Age*, Melbourne, and as a newspaper sub-editor in Athens, Hong Kong and Johannesburg. Until recently he was the editor of the *Dimboola Banner*.

Also by Ken Haley

Emails from the Edge

Europe @ 2.4 km/h

KEN HALEY

Wakefield
Press

Wakefield Press
1 The Parade West
Kent Town
South Australia 5067
www.wakefieldpress.com.au

First published 2011

Cover design by Stacey Zass, Page 12
Edited by Julia Beaven, Wakefield Press
Typeset by Wakefield Press
Printed in China by the Opus Group

National Library of Australia Cataloguing-in-Publication entry

Author:	Haley, Ken, 1954– .
Title:	Europe @ 2.4 km/h / Ken Haley.
ISBN:	978 1 86254 917 3 (pbk.).
Notes:	Includes bibliographical references.
Subjects:	Haley, Ken, 1954 – Travel – Europe.
	Journalists – Australia – Biography.
	Paraplegics – Australia – Biography.
	Europe – Description and travel.
Dewey Number:	070.92

Publication of this book was assisted by the Commonwealth Government through the Australia Council, its arts funding and advisory body.

Contents

PROLOGUE	Which Europe Would That Be?	xi
CHAPTER 1	Magnetic North RUSSIA	1
CHAPTER 2	True North (Refilling the Ocean) NORWAY and NORRLAND, CENTRAL SWEDEN	31
CHAPTER 3	Our Bicycles Have Seats SOUTHERN SWEDEN, OSLO and DENMARK	50
CHAPTER 4	The Past is a Foreign Country COPENHAGEN, NYKØBING and BREMEN	69
CHAPTER 5	Fellatio at Eleven THE NETHERLANDS	79
CHAPTER 6	Why is there a Belgium? FLANDERS and WALLONIA	102
CHAPTER 7	Close to Civilisation GERMANY	123
CHAPTER 8	French Impressions THE NORTH OF FRANCE	164
CHAPTER 9	*Chic* Just Happens THE SOUTH OF FRANCE and MONACO	196
CHAPTER 10	An Avalanche Without Snow ANDORRA	224
CHAPTER 11	Broken Railway, Smokin' Bar NORTHERN IBERIA (NORTHERN SPAIN, NORTHERN PORTUGAL)	232
CHAPTER 12	The End of Europe SOUTHERN IBERIA (SOUTHERN SPAIN, SOUTHERN PORTUGAL)	256
EUROPILOGUE		280
NOTES		285
BIBLIOGRAPHY		289
ACKNOWLEDGEMENTS		291

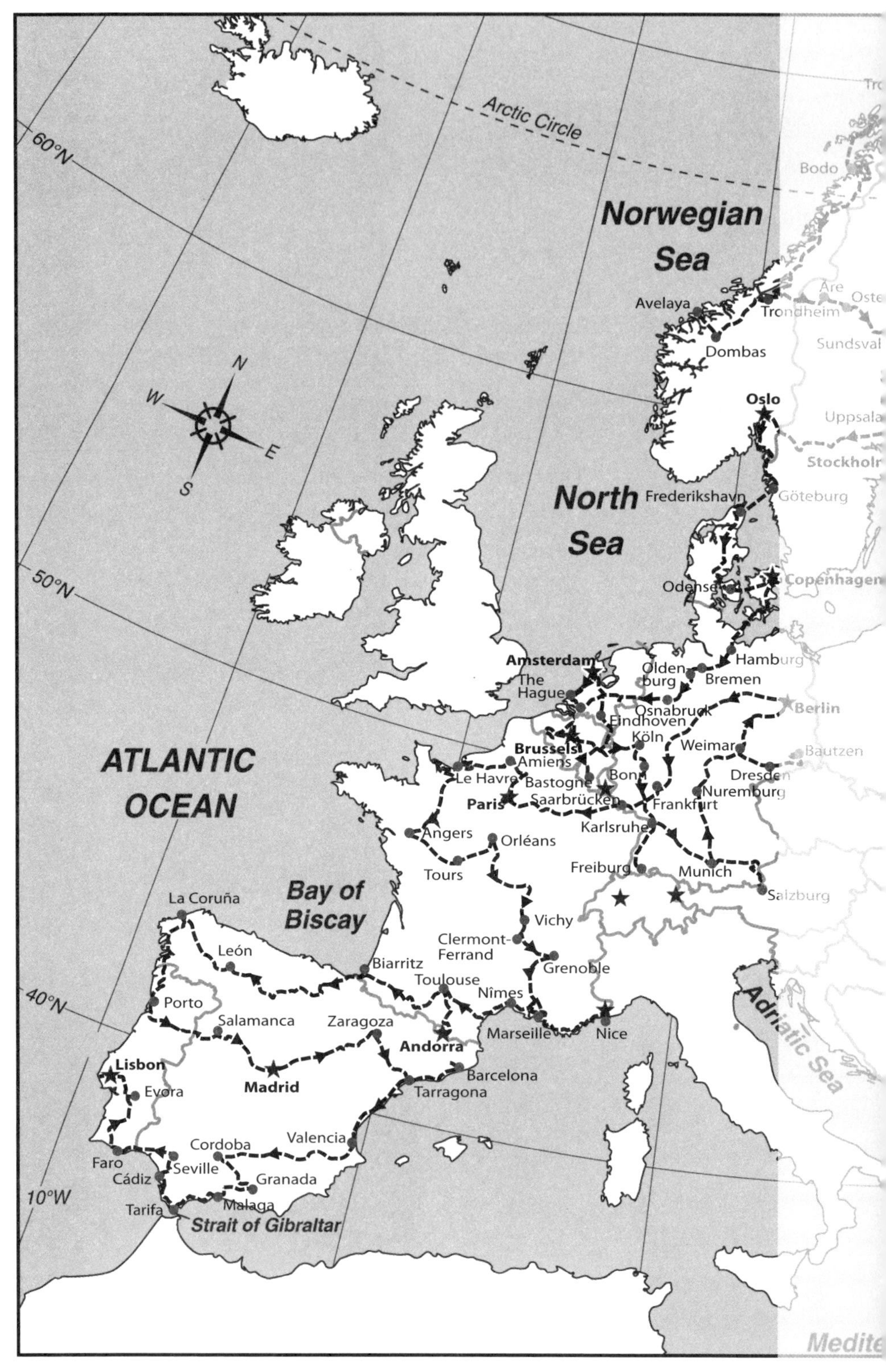

Arctic Circle
60°N
50°N
40°N
10°W
Norwegian Sea
North Sea
ATLANTIC OCEAN
Bay of Biscay
Strait of Gibraltar
Adriatic Sea
N
W
E
S
Bodo
Avelaya
Trondheim
Dombas
Sundsval
Oslo
Uppsala
Göteborg
Frederikshavn
Odense
Copenhagen
Amsterdam
The Hague
Hamburg
Oldenburg
Bremen
Osnabruck
Eindhoven
Berlin
Brussels
Köln
Weimar
Bautzen
Amiens
Le Havre
Bonn
Dresden
Bastogne
Paris
Saarbrücken
Nuremburg
Frankfurt
Karlsruhe
Angers
Orléans
Tours
Freiburg
Munich
Salzburg
Vichy
Clermont-Ferrand
Grenoble
La Coruña
León
Biarritz
Toulouse
Nîmes
Porto
Salamanca
Zaragoza
Marseille
Nice
Andorra
Lisbon
Madrid
Barcelona
Evora
Tarragona
Valencia
Cordoba
Faro
Cádiz
Seville
Granada
Tarifa
Malaga

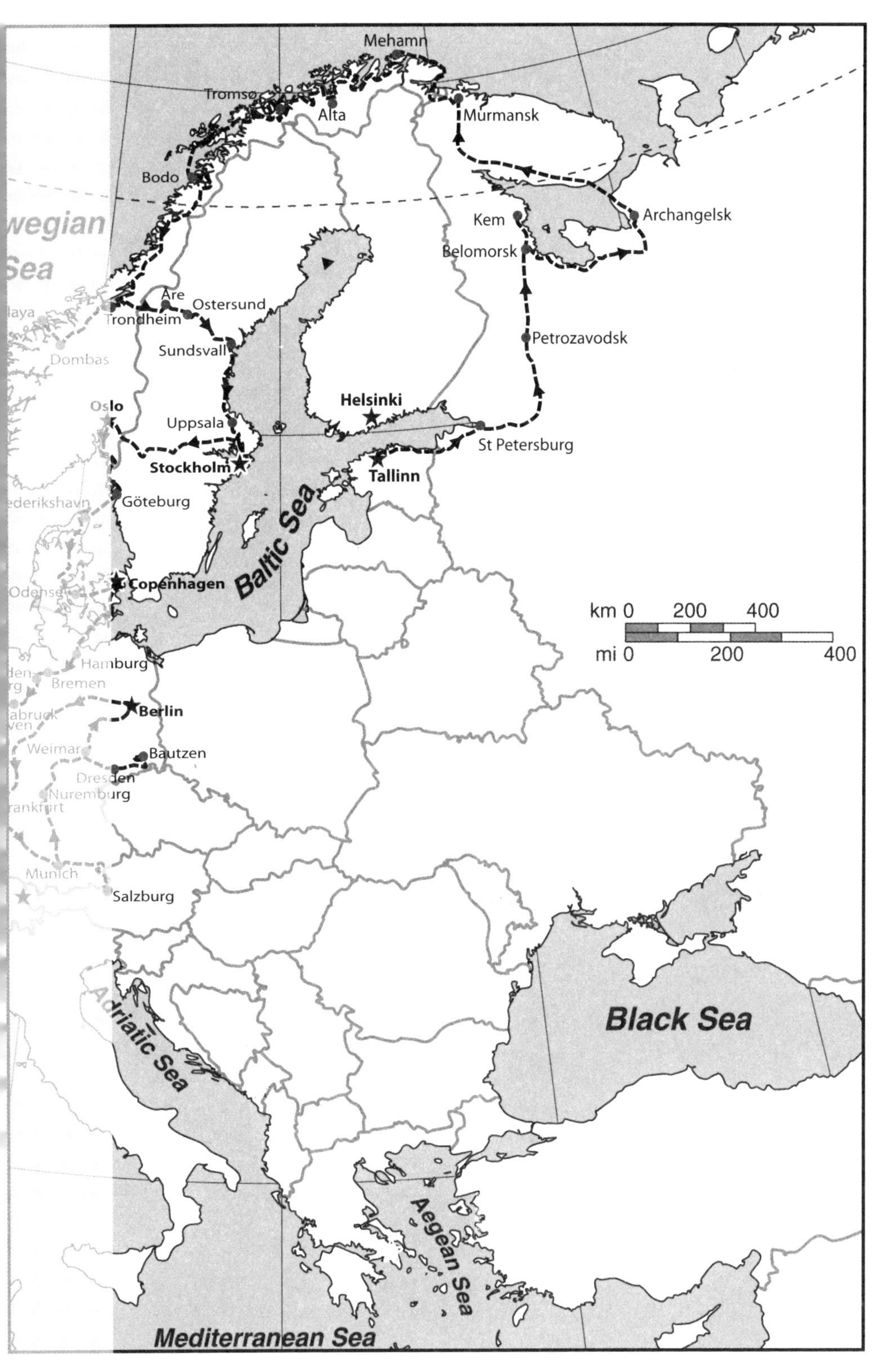
Mehamn
Tromsø
Alta
Murmansk
Bodo
Archangelsk
Kem
Belomorsk
Are
Ostersund
Trondheim
Sundsvall
Petrozavodsk
Helsinki
Oslo
Uppsala
St Petersburg
Stockholm
Tallinn
Göteburg
Baltic Sea
Copenhagen
km 0 200 400
mi 0 200 400
Hamburg
Bremen
Berlin
Weimar
Bautzen
Dresden
Nuremburg
Munich
Salzburg
Adriatic Sea
Black Sea
Aegean Sea
Mediterranean Sea
Dombas
Odense
wegian
Sea

Nous voulons voyager sans vapeur et sans voile!
Faites, pour égayer l'ennui de nos prisons,
Passer sur nos esprits, tendus comme une toile,
Vos souvenirs avec leurs cadres d'horizons.

We long to travel not by steam or sail,
For here in prison every day's the same.
Oh, paint across the canvas of our soul
Your memoirs, with horizons as their frame.

Charles Baudelaire,
Les Fleurs du Mal,
Part III, Verse 2
LE VOYAGE

To Nin,
for all your love in the unconditional past, perfect.

Prologue

Which Europe Would That Be?

What am I doing here in Europe? You might well ask; I ask myself. Surely there can be nothing new under the European sun, you say, nowhere on the face of the globe will you find real estate more tramped over, fought over, written about. Even the ancients called it 'the known world'.

At school, 'European' was often bracketed with 'explorer'. The first pictures we received of these mavericks from the other end of the world portrayed them as heading out to the lands of 'lesser breeds', discovering societies that didn't have enough sense to know they were lost. Well, the Europeans' world might be 'known' to them but, 400 years later, we in their Antipodes have our own 'known world'. So, I tell myself, perhaps it's time to return the compliment and go exploring the Old World anew.

The European explorers set off in search of spice and riches. If my only spice turns out to be the piquancy of human behaviour, my only riches the joy of the journey itself and of witnessing the cultures I roam among, so be it. We live in different times, or so we like to believe. I come in peace, O Father of Continents, and have no desire to conquer you. Let others treat you as a glittering bauble, your attractions all obvious, all external. For me, Europe is a magic box. I yearn to know what's inside, and to find out I will try to grasp it at both ends, north and south, to turn it round, shake it a little.

Four years since my last European landfall, I am picking up where I left off – Tallinn, Estonia – and tomorrow will ring in the grandeur of St Petersburg. After traipsing across that vastness of 'European Russia' which goes by the name of Karelia, I will light out for the northernmost reaches of the only continent we call the Continent before pursuing a host of detours that land me, finally, on the road to Portugal.

It's fair to say I'm on a quest. But as I hurtle 39,000 feet over the Urals, in an arc that will touch down at Frankfurt, the object of that quest appears as insubstantial as the clouds outside my window.

A week before leaving Australia I was having a drink with two colleagues during a mid-shift break and found myself hard pressed to say what was so special, uniquely European, about Europe. When I suggested that Europe stood for the idea that humans were destined to subdue or govern the natural world rather than coexist passively with it, one of my colleagues scoffed, 'You could say the same about Australia or America'. Conceding his point – perhaps too readily, given that Australia and America are 'European' societies, too – I found myself back at square one. Not to worry, I would have plenty of time to ponder the question further: seven-and a-half months of it.

In a direct line, the northern point of this landmass lies about 5000 km from its southern tip. But this will be a journey of tangents, not short cuts. By visiting its northern, southern and western extremities, I aim almost literally to comprehend the whole, to encompass what lies between the extremities, to open the lid on this magic box of Europe. How much room can there be inside for secrets? Next to my homeland, Australia, it is the smallest as well as the oldest-named of all those pieces of the terrestrial jigsaw we call continents. Surely, when the shaking has stopped, I will know what enticed me here: the culture, the scenery, the 'European spirit' (if such a thing exists), the people themselves. Or all of the above and then some.

In Hong Kong, a couple of days before my flight to Europe, I read in the *South China Morning Post* an article about Sierra Leonean ex-child soldiers being educated in a Spanish college, prompting the thought that one thing Europe must stand for is the belief its values are universal. Sometimes this presumption has been put to questionable use, as in the exploitative aspect of colonialism; and sometimes to benign use, as reflected in the inclusiveness and generosity of spirit exhibited in that Spanish initiative.

Yet, when six months later I reach the European town closest of all to Africa, I will find this shaft of illumination blotted out by a much darker, indeed shameful, facet of the Continental character.

To complicate my attempts to get to grips with Europe – which is, after all, where we Westerners hail from – I reminded myself that the clarity provided by maps was always going to be too vague to be universally acceptable. As I'd noted years ago, if you use Europe as a geographical label one glance at an atlas will suffice to establish that almost all of Turkey (97 per cent, in case you were wondering) is in Asia and, whatever the Cypriots think, their island is wholly non-European. (Eight months later, in *The Economist's* annual review of the world,[1] I read with astonishment that the new €1 coin entering the union's currency in 2008 shows Cyprus due south of Italy, many kilometres west of its true location.)

To be fair, some people have argued that Europe is not a continent at all – and technically they are right. It is a trio of peninsulas at the pointy end of Eurasia (now that's a *real* continent) as much as a set of values, a cultural legacy or an economic club.

If it's any of these three, the question immediately arises: can anyone join? No one can rightly dispute the contribution that Jewish culture has made over many centuries to European ideals, most obviously in the religious sphere. And maybe it is because so many of Israel's settlers came from Europe that, to take what might on the surface seem a trivial example, the Israeli national football team takes part in the European competition.

Truly, the closer I get to Europe – and, with the Urals a receding memory, my plane is now over Warsaw, beginning its descent – the further I seem to be from understanding the mysterious contents of this 'known world' spread out beneath my feet. The magic box conceals its treasures well. As I am soon to discover, the meaning of Europe has bamboozled sharper intellects than mine. For all I know, most Europeans share my bafflement. Perhaps, it occurs to me, there is no such entity, in the sense Margaret Thatcher had in mind when she said there was no society. Or could it be that they are making it up as they go along?

Nor is the difficulty of pinning Europe down anything new. One of my favourite lines in 20th-century literature is uttered by a Damon Runyon character seated at a table in a Lower East Side diner when a mobster parks himself opposite and quietly informs him that 'the Boss' back in Chicago has a little job to be dispatched on the other side of the Atlantic, over in Europe. Our nervous hero, as Runyon records, not wishing to appear reluctant but equally anxious to play for time, replies, 'And which Europe would that be?'

My question, my quest, exactly.

Then again, I tell myself, maybe I'm missing the obvious point:

aren't Europeans all about activity (doing) while Asians are more contemplative (being)? I was contemplating just this point at Hong Kong International Airport before we boarded this flight when my meditation was interrupted by a young man ambling through the transit lounge, calling out to everyone in general and no one in particular, 'Hurry, hurry, hurry'.

This struck me as odd, since no one could go anywhere until the clearance for boarding was given. But his clarion call became more urgent by the second until everyone was listening to him.

'Hurry, hurry, hurry,' he repeated.

'*Hare, hare,* Krishna, Rama. *Hare, hare.*'

Europe this was not.

CHAPTER 1

Magnetic North

RUSSIA

Time spent:	28 days
Distance covered:	3102 km
Distance pushed:	136.8 km
Average speed:	2.399 km/h
Journey distance to date:	3102 km

Europe, we hardly know you. Yet we willingly fool ourselves into believing you are the most familiar of destinations. The mere sound of your name conjures up the Eiffel Tower, the Colosseum, the highest of high culture. To many minds, you are a byword for civilisation itself. But how many cheers can you raise for a civilisation that unleashed the greatest bloodletting in the history of the planet, not once but twice in as many generations?

'But,' I hear you plead, 'it's not fair to judge me by my worst moments.'

OK, we can do better than that, refusing to judge you at all – at least until we're better acquainted. So let's get a proper look at you, see how well we recognise you at closer quarters. Never interested in sightseeing for its own sake, I will nevertheless visit many of your 'unmissable' landmarks. But through the experience of travelling in many lands I have found certain principles that are likely to make any journey more memorable. And the greatest of these is the value of the unexpected encounter, the unforeseen episode, the uncommon character. If you're in it for the long haul, you have to be a voyager for all seasons, but there is bound to be more of the unknown lying in store if you go 'out of season'.

Armchair viewers of Discovery channel and readers of *National*

Geographic think they know what this part of the world is like, because they've seen the pictures – and a Mediterranean beach in summer is one cliché among many. But try to picture what it's like at latitude 70° N in summer, or imagine the Riviera in winter, and it's not so obvious. Even in the 'known world' you can find many a road less travelled.

The unfamiliarity principle is why, it seems to me, many of the best moments in a journey take the form of pleasant surprises. Others, more precisely termed epiphanies – when everything seems right with the world and it's beyond us to explain why – will also occur. If there's one thing to be expected from the long haul, it's the unexpected.

Since the beginning of May is the earliest time of year when you can go to Russia confident of not ending up icebound, it seems the most auspicious moment to embark on this crossing, which by the middle of December will have taken me across twelve countries.

Never staying long in one place, or in one type of place, is another defining feature of the way I travel. It is only half in jest that I tell inquirers this is a solo journey undertaken in the company of millions. This time out, I will spend just under two weeks in Amsterdam, and the same length of time in Paris, but at most halts just one or two nights. These 230 sleeps from May to December 2007 will nearly all be spent in 90 cities, towns or villages – not counting the nights spent on buses, trains or, literally, at sea – giving an average of less than two-and-a-half days per destination.

And where to lay my sorry head? Hostels (46 per cent of the time), hotels (38 per cent), guesthouses or private homes (13 per cent); and I will even get myself to the odd monastery or nunnery. It's one way to be sure of meeting a greater variety of people. Among this cast of thousands, though I could never have guessed it in advance, will be a Portuguese Buddhist restaurateur, the Governor of Gibraltar, and family I never knew I had – almost of all them Europeans who answer to another name.

My onward flight is about to touch down in Tallinn, a copybook landing. But for all the research and preparation carried out beforehand I'm on a collision course with this oh-so-familiar Continent that is truly incognito. Civilised, advanced, arrogant, self-entranced:

preconceptions exist to be modified, even shattered. The seatbelt sign is off. I'm ready for the adventure to begin.

This Baltic capital does its best to oblige. It is the evening of 27 April. Just a couple of hours ago, political tensions between Estonian Estonians and Russian Estonians erupted in the city streets. On my way into town I see every second plate-glass window smashed, where the wave of violence rolled out of town along the highway to Estonia's favourite seaside resort, Parnu.

So, are the Europeans back to their bad old ways? For what will prove to be the only time this year Estonia is making world headlines, confronting this fresh arrival with a textbook example of what is possibly the core issue gripping Europe today (and for as long back in history as you care to go): identity. Asked where they come from, as I will discover, few people count themselves as Europeans first and last. This stands in stark contrast with the answers you would get if you asked the same question of Americans, Australians or, for that matter, Chinese.

As the currency-exchange officer at the airport explains, a Soviet worker-hero statue that had been at the centre of contention between the Russian and Estonian communities was removed this morning (by the Estonian Estonians), infuriating Russian youths who 'trashed' the town. As I near the city centre, a police helicopter overhead exemplifies the menace in the air – and a quiet night in the suburbs suddenly seems appealing. I hear later from the Russian side that what inflamed their ire more was the simultaneous transfer of the remains of the Soviet soldiers buried under it.

Ask a Russian 'How are you?' and you may well get the answer '*Normalno*'. Tomorrow, one day closer to my departure for Russia, I will see a sign in the window of a Tallinn restaurant that reads CELEBRATING FRIENDSHIP. But right now the window itself, along with such pious hopes, has been shattered.

Kilometre Zero

May Day is always a good time to visit Russia. The bus from Tallinn heading due east to St Petersburg begins rolling just a minute after 6 am. Right on cue, the sun rises in a cloudless sky. Now the shards of glass have been swept away, everything is back to 'normal, no?'

On every budget trip I permit myself one small luxury. Last

time it was a GPS device; this time round, the gadget of choice is a speedometer, supplied by a bicycle shop in faraway Melbourne. At any hour of the day or night, all I will have to do to know how far I have gone, and how fast I am going, is to glance at this technological marvel perched on the side of my wheelchair.

Speed = distance ÷ time. A diary divided into days will not do: what marks my progress from one side of the Continent to the other will be how many kilometres I propel myself with two determined hands.

Of course, on a train or bus, or when my wheels are stationary, the speedometer will not register progress. But how far those vehicles take me is something I can estimate later, consulting maps. When I look down, it's the distance covered by my personal transport that captures my attention.

I look out the window at a white cloak of snow draped around the village of Aapsere. Half an hour down this road lies Russia, and just before 9 am this crisp, clean morning in the northern spring of 2007 I enter Churchill's well-wrapped enigma for the first time since 1985, when it was part of the Soviet Union.

To discover Europeanness, it stands to reason, all I have to do is meet Europeans, and here in European Russia seems as good a place as any to start. That notion collides with reality right away. Can 'my first Russian' be a typical European? I wonder.

At the Russian border town of Ivangorod I am 'greeted' by a woman in a pale-yellow sweater and blue parka whose face is a picture of surpassing sorrow, as if she has just stared Death in the face. It is a face that raises so many questions but answers none. Instinctively, I present my passport to a colleague with a visage less grim, the first and last time I'll need to do so, courtesy of the 'European idea' of integration, which clearly hasn't reached this corner of the continent. I even manage to winkle polite laughter out of this colleague by wishing a 'Happy May Day'. Luckily, he isn't plunged in gloom by the irony of working on the workers' holiday.

I didn't really expect to see any reminders of the communist era still standing, but on the border a sign announces that here, 148 km from St Petersburg, we are entering the district of Leningradskaya. Suddenly I find myself in one country but two universes, and they are evidently not parallel.

1 km

Half an hour of pushing myself around St Petersburg is enough to remind me why this civic gem appeals to the Russian imagination in a way that leaves Moscow for dead. Red, white and blue flags rest in holders yoked to light poles like troikas.

Then, just as I'm reflecting on the power of Russian patriotism, I spot a Mongol face among the crowd swarming down Nevsky Prospekt, the city's main boulevard, a vivid reminder that Russians are ethnically no 'purer' than that other glorious mongrel breed, the English. Students of English history know that the Danes and Norwegians invaded the Angles' land towards the end of the first millennium. Less familiar is the fact that, ever since the sixth century, Vikings raided, traded, and invaded the lands of the Slavs, where from the ninth century onwards they founded a series of city states.

Historians suspect that the name of the Viking clan that founded the mini-state of Kyiv (from which the Ukrainian capital, Kiev, derives its name) was Rus, the great-granddaddy of what we call 'Russia'.[2] In 1223 the fiefs that would form the core of today's state, foremost among them Muscovy, were overrun by the Mongols. Today, on Nevsky Prospekt, a face in the crowd has reminded me of that fact.

2 km

St Petersburg International, one of the few youth hostels in this city of five million, has a surprise or two in store. All the rooms are on the fourth floor, and there is no lift access. But the manager, a lateral or rather vertical thinker, arranges to bring a bed down from on high to the staff 'common room', which is generously vacated for the six nights of my stay. And – a bonus, this – the TV there has more channels than I've ever seen available on one set (300) so I venture into the world outside only after surfing from a concert in Kurdistan to a debate in Milan via al-Jazeera.

3 km

Meet Ivan Baranov, principal doorman at the Nevsky Palace Hotel, a five-star establishment on the boulevard of broken flagstones. All gold braid and broad smile, he greets me with a disclaimer, 'I am not from here. I come from a small town in Belarus, far to south'.

Introduction leads to revelation. 'This is my duty, guarding the door, but in the deep of my soul I am happy to remain a peasant.' And, once he learns where I am from, revelation extends to request. 'I want to ask you about farming in Australia. Could I get work in your country fleecing the sheep? This is my dream.

'From my early days I work on a farm. I know how to feed the pigs,' he assures me with wide-eyed trust. At a loss to know what to advise, I suggest Ivan contact the Australian Embassy in Moscow but, several steps ahead of me, he proceeds to display an expert's knowledge of Canberra's immigration points system.

4 km

I see I've spent one hour 40 minutes pushing the chair, 'progressing' a dismal 4.1 km. This works out at 2.46 km/h: I don't think I had any idea of how fast I would go, but this really is snail's pace (if you can picture a snail on wheels).

18 km

Time to check those must-see lists. Paris? Eiffel Tower. Tick. The Louvre. Tick. Berlin? The Brandenburg Gate. Tick. Berlin Wall remnant. Tick. St Petersburg? The Hermitage. Tick.

To see the world-famous museum opposite is no problem. Housed in the tsars' 250-year-old Winter Palace, it would be infinitely more difficult to avoid. But to see the Hermitage collection? Now that's impossible, for two reasons. You would need to visit every day for a month to see the fraction that is on display, and even then most of the treasures are locked away in storerooms. Still, nothing would have kept me away from following up my previous visit to its great galleries one bitter day 23 Februaries ago. And then, just as this visit begins, I in turn am visited by a great stroke of luck.

While I wait for the stair lift to be lowered, and explore my wallet for the admittance fee of 350 roubles (about A$17.50), an attendant approaches, face beaming, and says, 'Did you know that entrance is free on the first Thursday of every month?' I do a single take, thinking: Gosh, today's Thursday, and then a double: Hey, today's the third of May!

This is not an art book, but I must mention a few reasons why the Hermitage always leaves its visitors in awe. First, there is the grandeur of the green, white and gold palace itself. On the ceiling above the grand Jordan Staircase is a restored classical painting that shows the gods on Mt Olympus.

Unfamiliarity springs an early surprise in the form of a larger-than-life gilt diorama of a peacock atop a tree stump, flanked by an owl and a rooster that work this bizarre chronometer by hooting the minutes and crowing the seconds. Attributed to English horologist James Cox in the 1790s, the Peacock Clock was commissioned by minister Potemkin, more renowned for erecting village façades with nothing behind them to impress his lover, Tsarina Catherine, on her progress through rural Russia.

In Room 208 I make an early discovery in my European exploration, an anonymous work by a 15th-century Florentine painter that shows the baby Jesus with the whole world in his hands, an orb with Asia, Africa and – this is not a misspelling – Europia. I am intrigued by the suggestion of Utopia here, the notion that Europe – whatever else it may be – is an ideal called Europia to which the real-world entity only occasionally corresponds.

22 km

Inescapable on the way back to my hostel, lo and behold, Ivan, at his post in front of the Nevsky Palace. 'The quality of mercy is not strained,' he begins to recite, leaving me tongue-tied and strangely moved, as Portia's speech from *The Merchant of Venice* is one that my 87-year-old father knows by heart. Clearly, Ivan is beefing up his emigration pitch. I smile appreciation and make a mental note: if ever Australia is desperately short of peasant-minded doormen who can quote Shakespeare, he will go to the head of the queue.

40 km

Five days, 8 km a day (it would have been less but this city's underground railway, with no lifts down from street level, is off limits to wheelchair users). Tomorrow morning I head north to the boondocks.

It's 10 pm now, and I hope to slink back to my hostel for a few hours' sleep. Easy does it, if I can just avoid the drunks who swig from the bottle as they sway down the pavements on autopilot.

Uh-oh, there's Ivan under the Nevsky's awning, beckoning. No escape.

Patiently I listen as he tells me of his son, now nineteen, who was left deformed by an injury sustained during his birth. He says he just wanted to tell me one thing. 'I admire you. You do not' – and here he declaims in a manner worthy of Hamlet – 'surrender' – his arm is outstretched, statue-like – 'to despair'. How humbling. If only he knew ...

I could have told him quite a lot about succumbing to Despair but compliments come along rarely enough in life that no good purpose is served by showing those kind enough to offer them how undeserved they are. Those days were a different time, and too different a place in my life, to make it any part of Ivan's, and these days I hardly ever think of the time before and immediately after that fundamental divide in my life.

Still, the night you try to kill yourself is not one you're likely to forget. Nor is the state of mind that drove you to the brink of self-annihilation.

But how could I hope to convey the devastating damage to the certainties of everyday life wrought by Iraq's invasion of Kuwait on those working in 'the next emirate down', Bahrain, in the incandescent summer of 1990? How could I expect Ivan to comprehend the fear of that fight, and the pointlessness of flight when faced with a looming military threat just over the horizon?

To understand that, he would need a power of imagination to sense what it might be like to feel trapped and alone in the workplace but find no refuge at home from the menace abroad.

On the evening of August 19, the fuse to my suicide attempt was lit. Could Ivan, or anyone, appreciate why amid the disintegration of an entire society I snapped, and ran down the street yelling that this was the end of the world? Certainly he could understand why a police van would pick me up and its officers lock me up overnight – and even, perhaps with a shudder of horror, pity my reduced state, petrified and under near constant surveillance, in a Bahraini asylum for the next ten days where I was questioned, analysed and sedated, diagnosed 'borderline manic depressive', stabilised and at last released – not back to work but shipped home, a certified failure.

My decision to discard the lithium once out of any obvious external danger was logical enough, but no one apart from 'the wretched of the earth' can truly know the humiliating shame and naked dread that crippled my being as the ensuing months brought not recovery but a dousing of all the lights of hope, one by one.

You can't say I didn't put up a resistance. Whatever a 'nervous wreck' can do to restore himself to himself I did: seeking out psychiatric advice, the benefits of aromatherapy, relaxation and all manner of other cures for insomnia. When the fight had gone out of me, I turned to flight, quite literally. Year's end found me again in London, where I had last tasted happiness before the crash. But now it was a capital of desolation, bereft of work and hope alike. That round-the-world ticket from Melbourne permitted me to go in only one direction, from the east towards the setting sun. I could only flee so far.

Everywhere I travelled in thrall to my principal enemy, Despair. Could a friend have helped? No way I could think of. Some agonies are so private they cannot be shared, the loss of one's sanity above all.

Despair, to which Ivan does not see me surrendering now, had me comprehensively conquered then. I bowed my head to the counsel of Despair, 'Don't spread your Hell to others, you'll only drag them down'. Yet not until I arrived back in Melbourne at the end of February 1991 – after a brief unavailing stopover in Vancouver – did I realise for a certainty that I'd come home to die.

Exits there are aplenty. I might have found another had I not been staying with an old journalistic colleague and her friends in an East Melbourne mansion block and they not all gone out for the evening. I might have spied another road to extinction if so many of them, troubled souls, hadn't left a pharmacopoeia's worth of tablets on their various bedside tables.

Even after the mind has surrendered to Despair, dear Ivan, let me assure you, every sinew of the body strains against oblivion. Nevertheless, I might have called off that deed if one of my fellow guests had come back early. But my animal need to stop this interminable pain found a path through these converging factors, and in a trice the only possible thing I must do was as obvious as the night that follows day. In the quietest spell of a warm March night, after hours of restless pacing, I sat imperturbably still on a window sill, four floors up, steadied myself featherlight against the frame, and gently let go …

The thud as my body hit 15 metres below was heard by the friend whose hospitality I was grievously abusing, and who had arrived home just minutes before. Seven months in the world-class Austin Hospital set me back on the road to happiness, which for curious old me requires journeys such as the 2007 crossing of Europe that I have interrupted for your benefit – leaving Ivan at his revolving door.

Today strangers who blurt out, 'What happened to you?' almost never get a straight answer, because these days I won't waste my breath. But Ivan is far more perceptive than they. Language permitting, I tell myself, I might have disowned his compliment with an outpouring of revelations. Even that would have been a waste of breath, though, since a perfectly adequate response to his tribute 'You do not surrender to despair' would have been: No, Ivan, I most certainly don't. I live with the consequences of doing so once.

42 km

More than 440 km north-east of what has long been Russia's window on the world lies Petrozavodsk, the forgotten Petropolis, in the expanses of Karelia or, less grandly, the backwoods that Russians memorably term the *peripheria*.

Distance is not all that separates glitzy, go-getting Petersburg from Petrozavodsk – Peter's Factory, so called because the Great one founded it to make armaments for the Great Northern War he was bent on prosecuting against those not-yet-peace-loving Swedes.

An overnight train service links the two, saving me the cost of a night's lodgings. The fact that St Petersburg's Ladozhsky Station has been newly refurbished doesn't raise any expectation that it will have trains to match. Just as well, since it doesn't. But, to my mild surprise, given the carriages' Soviet-era vintage, an external hydraulic ramp is on the platform ready to winch me up onto night train No. 658. The *provodnik* (carriage attendant) – who remains a staple of long-distance Russian train travel, supplying everything from advice on connections to tea hot from the samovar – can barely wait to show his dexterity with the mechanical beast.

But once I'm on board his old habit of command and control reasserts itself. It is still forbidden for passengers to travel on intercity trains without producing identity documents (and in a couple of months a bomb will explode on the St Petersburg-Moscow train, so perhaps the authorities have reason on their side).

But now Andrei holds up a queue of passengers practised in the art of patience as he sets about wresting an internal door from its hinges. 'What are you doing that for?' I cry, oblivious to the fact he cannot understand a word I am saying. Over my protests, Andrei continues to play the vandal until he is left holding this door, casting about in vain for a place to put it down.

I knew from previous journeys on these old rattlers that my chair would be too wide for the corridor even after such an operation. 'The vestibule is good enough for me,' I tell Andrei, and this time he relents with a good-natured shrug, as if to say, Well, I tried. I stifle my satisfaction but know that tonight, covered by a thick blanket (provided by the *provodnik*, who else?), I will sleep fitfully but at least as well as the five other passengers in the compartment containing my assigned seat.

44–45 km

Sunday afternoon in a café on Karl Marx St. – where street names are concerned, there's been no revolution here since 1917 – and I fall into conversation with a couple at the next table. Fluent English-speakers are a rarity in the *peripheria*. Rustig and Angela Rstislav are both professors of European law at the University of Petrozavodsk: help is at hand in my Continental quest. Rustig – a tall, courtly man who always thinks before he speaks – tells me I can go nearly anywhere I want in Russia but that it will be impossible for me to visit Europe. What does he mean by that?

'Well, it's like this, Ken. You see, Europe is not discovered yet. What it will be in 50 years' time no one can tell. To my mind, nationalism is the big danger. We in Russia have a big danger of finding ourselves under a new dictator. This is because we Russians have limited experience of democracy.'

The Rstislavs invite me to stroll a few blocks from the café.

They want to show me an object of controversy: a statue of Yuri Andropov, Putin's old boss at the KGB. Andropov headed the local chapter of the Communist Youth League here in the 1930s, between two towering peaks of barbarity: the famine-producing collectivisation drive of 1932 and the Great Purges later in the decade.

What Rustig wants to show me is not just the statue – whose very existence was criticised as a piece of dreadful nostalgia – but its siting: opposite the KGB headquarters which, he tells me (lowering his voice) is what it remains, albeit with a change of name to the FSB, its successor as the state security arm. I photograph Andropov and, more stealthily, Spook Central, before high-tailing it away.

48 km

You don't have to be black to be on the receiving end of a xenophobic outburst in 'modern' Russia. Fifty metres from my hotel I'm confronted on the footpath by a frenzied man barely taller than myself but carrying a wicked-looking stave which he raises without a word between us, all the while muttering imprecations. Somehow he has sensed his quarry is not Russian. I yell 'Tourist!' (as if this word might elicit respect). But only when a woman appears on the scene, talking rapidly to distract him, can I make my getaway.

53 km

9 May, Victory (*Pobiede*) Day, in a nation where the Great Patriotic War – known to the rest of us as World War II – continues to have an impact far beyond what it has retained in other Allied nations. But while Russians lay wreaths on their granite memorials to the honoured dead of 65 years ago I am preoccupied with a more immediate concern: finding a place to stay tonight.

Kem has the air of a frontier town. Adults don't bid you good day, even in Russian; children scowl; and a policeman asks for my papers, even though we are a long way inland – a sure sign that foreigners in these here parts are as exotic as democracy.

But, in comparison with Belomorsk – that forsaken town down the line I've just come from – it's a home away from home. There tall, eagle-eyed Yuri and his dumpy, perpetually drunk sidekick, Sasha, shadowed me into the only hotel in that overgrown village. In the morning – the hotel's toilet being unreachable – I had to cajole the local 'tourist officer' into opening the adjacent school (closed and locked up for the holidays) so that I could use the facilities there, of which I spare you any description in case this is being read over breakfast.

Then, after I'd bought Yuri and Sasha a couple of farewell beers at the pub opposite the station (Sasha looking crestfallen because vodka is his preferred tipple), my backpack went missing for a crucial minute just as the 'upbound' train was about to depart, and by the time Yuri retrieved it from Sasha's slippery grasp the train had pulled out of the station before I noticed that 660 roubles – about A$33, or a good half dozen vodkas – had disappeared from my wallet. Gasping, I dug further into the rucksack. My fingers 'sighted' my passport before my eyes. Deep relief: things could have been so much worse.

Kem holds no intrinsic attractions for the traveller except that it satisfies an urge to witness the 'real Russia', that vast mass of squalor where dogs run wild and the metropolitan mafia and money merchants are sighted only on TV screens. So why I am here? Because Kem happens to be 10 km or so from the White Sea coast and, if I can establish that the summer boat service to the Solovetsky Islands has resumed, I will be able to fly from Archangelsk to the medieval monastery out there and catch a boat back here, before resuming my rail journey north to Murmansk. Thus endeth Plan A.

After Belomorsk my luck turns. Three students from Moscow Technical University – Pavel, Alexei and Dmitri – who are returning from a river-rafting expedition in the Far North also have Solovetsky in their sights so we all pile into a taxi for the ride out to the coast.

Diss May. The ice has thawed, but this year the first boat will not sail until 1 June, three days after my Russian visa expires. 'Navigation' is given as the reason, though clearly they mean the absence of it.

The official holiday has trapped us in this backwater till tomorrow, but only one hotel has any rooms. The receptionist welcomes my new best friends and registers them at once, but takes one look at my wheelchair and shows me the door. While I refuse to leave the moderate warmth of the foyer for 3 °C or so outside – and now sleet begins lashing down – she makes a show of ringing the owner and tells Pavel he has ordered her to call the police.

This is surreal: my reflex is to cite equality of access under the European Constitution, except there isn't one yet and, even if there were, it wouldn't apply here. So I prepare to bluff my way through with a little spiel along the lines of 'You can't do this: we're in Europe'. But she can, and in the only sense that matters we're not.

At this point Pavel persuades me to leave rather than provoke further unpleasantness. Outside, he assures me he has a plan. I must hide in town until nightfall and then we will all return to the hotel and he will smuggle me in. The plan nearly works. But then we realise that, with their room full, I will still need one of my own. After all, I can hardly sleep on the corridor floor. Fortunately, the night receptionist is a different character – the owner's wife – and, unlike him, she is loath to throw me out.

With Pavel by turns reasoning and translating, we reach an understanding that I can have a room if I leave before nine in the morning (she knows her husband well enough to be sure he will not surface before that hour, and it's no problem for us: the students have an early train going south to Moscow; and I have one going way out east to Archangelsk). What can I do but agree? Operation Barbarossa was doomed to fail: this may be the eleventh hour, but Victory Day has come just in time. *Pobiede*!

58 km

Good riddance to Kem. Quarter to seven this dismal wet morning finds my Muscovite friends and me at the station. After joining forces to hoist me aboard the Archangelsk train, which leaves before theirs, they depart for another platform.

A frisson of anticipation always courses through my veins immediately before my little world and I are jolted into motion. Check my watch: seconds to departure. Suddenly Pavel and Alexei have returned, and – before I can quiz either – Alexei, by far the more impetuous of the pair, has leapt aboard. Now the train is pulling out, Pavel jogs alongside the carriage, shouting, 'Alexei will go with you.' And, even more incredibly, 'He will save you money.'

This sudden change of plan, if that is what it is, fills me with alarm as I sense he has made a terrible error of judgement which – worse still – will place me under some unspecified obligation. This is going to be painful. The unfamiliarity principle has sprung a whopping great surprise with this impromptu acquisition of a travelling companion, and I'm not sure whether the drama we're in for will be a tragedy or a farce.

I have only one word for Alexei, whose English is as halting as, well, a Russian long-distance train, and it's one he happens to know. 'Why?'

'I am top Russian agent,' he begins – I burst out laughing, but he is not to be put off – 'for Swedish company Cricket matches'. He unzips his jacket to reveal a T-shirt proclaiming 'Cricket Matches'.

'You play cricket?' I say, doing my best to simulate an on drive within the confines of a vestibule barely a metre wide. 'No, no,' he says. 'Matches' – and lights an imaginary cigarette. 'Oh!' I say, my incomprehension only slightly abated.

So why, I ask myself while exploring his puppy-like countenance, does a river-rafting student who doubles as a travelling salesman abandon his mates to go 1000 km out of his way with an Australian he can barely hold a conversation with?

One word – and it's a key to the enigma of the 'Russian character' – insinuates itself into my brain: 'impulsiveness'. At least Phileas Fogg could choose his own valet. Intently studying my map of Europe, this Passepartout of the North makes it plain he would be happy to accompany me all the way to Portugal. OK, so farce it is.

'*Sprechen Sie Deutsch*?' I ask him.

'*Nein*,' he replies with no apparent sense of irony.

'*Parlez-vous anglais*?

'*Non*,' he says, confirming it.

'So,' I berate him, 'you see? This is Europe; *Das ist Europa*; *C'est l'Europe*!' For a moment I could swear I'm channelling Basil Fawlty. Alexei – my poor Manuel – is reduced to nodding.

Sometime after midnight, Passepartoutski – having snaffled me a blanket from the indifferent *provodnik* – retreats into the body of the carriage at my insistence, like a faithful dog turned out by its master.

It's 2 am and I'm dozing off when Alexei bursts out of the corridor, breathless, clutching a newspaper with a full-page crossword. 'Kyen,' he pleads. 'Three sisters, English.' He mimes someone writing. What a rare chance to show off in this unlikeliest of settings. 'Brontë,' I tell him. Gleefully he fills in the spaces before disappearing back into the carriage.

To the puzzle of his own presence, though, I haven't a clue. When we reach Archangelsk he will carry my bags into the hotel and stay a night – I feel like a heel, insisting on separate rooms, but after the recent robbery I'm taking no chances – and in the morning he is off. An acquaintance later speculates that Alexei may have thought he could save me money if I weren't travelling solo. But surely they must charge me foreigner's price anyway?

Lacking a Jules Verne to analyse his real motivation, it would only be in the last days of my sojourn in Russia that a credible explanation for Alexei's behaviour offered itself. A Russian drinker at the Red Pub – a revolutionary kitsch bar on the outskirts of Murmansk – inquired, 'Where is your team?' Before I could frame the words 'They're lying twelfth and another wooden spoon is on the cards', I realised he could know nothing of the AFL and that 'team' had to mean 'group', so his query was a variation on the common refrain of, 'Why are you travelling alone?'

At last the kopek dropped. Wolves in waistcoats would be more comprehensible to the average Russian for whom holidays are often collective enterprises; there is even a word for a man who tows the family off to his weekender: *dachnik*.

The Lone Ranger might thrive in Texas; in this physically forbidding terrain, comprising the planet's farthest habitable reaches, individualism was the road to death. In the eyes of a Russian, travelling solo – and, moreover, doing so in a *kaliaska*, the beautiful Russian word for a wheelchair – is the sign of a lost soul.

A couple of hours out of Archangelsk I see a shy, melancholy woman at the carriage window opposite, gazing into the night sky. Then she sees me, and introduces herself: Elena Kokanova, a post-secondary English teacher who has travelled all the way to Norway only to be stood up by a 'friend'. The cost, in money and trust, must be enormous. My heart goes out to her. At other times we would have much to say, Elena and I, but now I sense her preference for silence. Before parting, we exchange email addresses and promise to keep in touch.

Another person with whom I click instantly is Nadezhda

Pestovskaya, the flame-haired receptionist at the Hotel Dvina and the soul of efficiency in getting me a room where I sleep for twelve hours straight. Fiftyish and open-faced, Nadezhda is explicit from the outset that she will look after me, that it is special to have someone come from so far away – and she means it. When possible (the boss is clearly not her best friend), Nadezhda makes the hard road easy. Outside the hotel she is powerless to assist, and when on my third morning at the Dvina I awaken to the sound of jackhammers directly below my room, demolishing the only ramp in town leading up to a first-floor café, I don't know whether to laugh or groan.

Within her domain, though, Nadezhda negotiates 25 per cent off the price of the laundry, wangles a free phone call to Australia, and gives me two cakes of soap as 'a present' – this last gesture such a small thing except that, in a town where a can of shaving cream costs $30, soap has never held such appeal as a substitute lather.

Sometimes, when there's hardly anyone at the bar, Nadezhda – who looks a lot like Janet Frame in *An Angel at My Table* – will wax philosophical.

'Ken, I know you will think me strange,' she says one day, 'but I really miss the Soviet Union.'

'That's not strange,' I say, willing her to explain why.

'Everyone had health care. We had free education. Now I hesitate to give my daughter the best of education because we cannot afford it.'

And then, after a pause to see that I really understand what she has been telling me, Nadezhda produces the most precious gift of all. Scarcely bigger than my thumb, it will rest on my desk as I type these words – a painted icon of St Nadezhda.

'Here, Ken, have this,' says her earthly namesake who leaves tomorrow to take her annual holidays, this year in Egypt. 'She is my angel, and she will look after you on your journey.'

These words are to prove prophetic but just now my rational mind revolts at her patent superstition – even as my eyes, inexplicably, glisten. How odd, I reproach myself, less than two weeks in the country, and already I'm becoming Russian. One face of Russia, Elena had shown me acceptance in response to humiliation; another face of Russia, Nadezhda displayed candour and compassion. Apart from one menacing moment in Petrozavodsk, I hadn't seen the face of Russian racism – that hostility to foreigners supposedly ingrained in the national character. But my journey was still young.

59 km

So here I am in Archangelsk, the port whose resupply by Britain and the US after Hitler struck east in mid-1941 became the stuff of legend. Just over a degree south of the Arctic Circle, it marks the most easterly point of my circuitous route, 41 degrees from Greenwich. I note on my map that this is due north of Saudi Arabia. At journey's end, in western Portugal, I'll be 50 degrees west of here – almost one-seventh of the way around the world. Yes, the journey is indeed young.

Some places enchant you by their names alone. To my ears, Archangelsk is right up there with Zanzibar, Samarkand and Ouagadougou. And in Archangelsk, especially along the riverbank, the sense of spaciousness and unmistakable civic pride cast their own spell, which goes a long way in offsetting my annoyance with the dodgy state of the roads and pavements I clunk along. Occasionally, someone will lurch in my direction and even shout raucously at me (but, thankfully, none carry staves). They must know I'm not Russian by my clothes, I guess. I cycle on, ignoring them and wondering if they take me for an American or a European. Public drunkenness is a national disgrace but, as I will learn soon enough, xenophobia can also be a potent brew.

64 km

Strike Solovetsky from the itinerary. The cost of two flights (Archangelsk–Solovetsky return) followed by one to Murmansk is prohibitive. From here it's 31 hours to Murmansk aboard a train without toilet access. That would take me out of my rather generous comfort zone, so just this once I will have to fly rather than go overland. This one air ticket adds a whopping €191 (A$318) to my budget, but there is no alternative.

67 km

On an embankment overlooking Archangelsk's riverine beach, I find Sobnil, 23, from the Indian state of Madhya Pradesh. On hearing I'm from Australia, his ready smile broadens as he says, 'Ricky Ponting'. He follows cricket as passionately at a distance as many do close up and controversy is still raging over the death of Pakistan's coach, Bob Woolmer.

We exchange theories. 'Heart attack,' pronounces Sobnil with awesome certainty. When I express scepticism, he confides, 'The Paks, they together shoot Woolmer'. He clicks a trigger finger. 'Heart stops.' Sobnil laughs the laugh of one who knows he has told a joke well – but now he turns serious.

'Do you know what happened on this beach last December?'

'A cricket friendly?' I parry.

'No. There was a knife fight.'

'Who was in it?' I ask, assuming he is speaking at second hand.

'The Paks here – I was the only Indian – and the Syrians. All against the Russians. Six of us, one of them.'

'And?' I ask, but really I'm thinking, Why is he telling me this? Now he smiles the smile of revenge – collective, murderous revenge.

'They are always attacking us whenever they find us alone. It had to stop. It stopped.'

71 km

Time to put my feet up and have a good outsider's laugh at the Eurovision song contest. Now Eurovision is a hoot, the epitome of schmaltz – everything it's mocked for being – but it is instructive in its way and by the end of the show I think I understand why Europe is full of Europeans who consider themselves Danes, Swedes, Russians, Spaniards ... anyone but Europeans. Long before the closing credits it is clear that Marija Serifovic, from Serbia, singing 'The Prayer Song', will win – and why. The announcers, democratically spread round Europe's capitals, pop up by live feed to reveal their compatriots' choice.

'Russia gives twelve points to ... Belarus.'

'Croatia gives twelve points to ... Serbia.'

Hey, what's happening here? The Slavs are voting as a bloc – or, to make a broader point, the voters' Euro-vision seems to be myopically limited to their immediate neighbourhood. But wait, there's something new.

'Montenegro gives twelve points to ... Serbia.'

'Estonia gives its twelve points to Russia.'

It's only three years since Montenegro and Serbia were on the brink of armed conflict and a fortnight ago, when I was in Tallinn, the Estonians were fighting pitched battles with 'their' Russian citizens. So what is this tactical voting all about? Could it be that Estonia *gives* Russia twelve points because it wants the Russians to know it will never give them anything else, anything of real worth? Or is this some musical variant of the Stockholm syndrome?

'Sweden gives its twelve points to Finland.'

'Finland gives twelve points to Sweden.'

And now for the real clincher – 'Austria gives its twelve points to Serbia'.

What a pity about the timing. If only Eurovision had been around in 1914, that statement alone might have been enough to avert a world war. And if you think that's flippant, you have no idea how seriously Eurovision is taken here. For three-quarters of an hour after the show – beamed live to 120 million viewers, or one in four of all Europeans – Russia's studio audience earnestly discusses the pros and cons of this year's event, the 52nd in the contest's history, until at 2.15 am it's time to go out partying (or, in the case of this old fogey, to sleep).

While some sneer at Eurovision's vapidity, I think it's been an education. On this model, Europe – far from being a 'union', as it likes to bill itself – is a framework for managing the tensions between neighbours with different temperaments, distinct histories and divergent views of their place in the world. This, at least, is a theory worth testing: before sleep overtakes me I come up with the notion that it might be revealing – as I proceed across the Continent – to ask the Europeans of each nation I pass through what they think of 'the folks next door'.

Postscript. Sure, the voting system will have to change. For the song contest, if not the European Parliament. Only when the phone calls and SMSs are tallied without reference to nation states and ethnic blocs – the Continent's favourite announced with a voice indivisible – will there really be one Europe. But, to quote Buddy Holly, that'll be the day.

76 km

At another café around the corner from the Hotel Dvina – not the one where a ramp had been demolished, but one whose entrance consisted of a few steps so that willing hands had to be found to lift me into the establishment – Elena Kokanova had gathered members of her English class. An engaging group, they possessed one dimension I was eager to explore, their Russian perspective.

My core question to one and all – 'What does Europe have that Russia doesn't?' – was cunningly disguised to see whether any of them would challenge the premise that Europe and Russia were two different places; that Russia was not, at its core, a European country. Here is a selection of their comments:

Grigory: 'I think they are a little bit more tolerant to each other.'

Aliya, a very intense nineteen-year-old: 'Russia is something apart. We don't need anybody else. Our history is very deep, profound. I believe there is nothing in the history of my country which I am ashamed of.' (She needs to learn more history, I muse, but there's nothing wrong with her English.)

Irina: 'In Europe, people take more care of their environment and are more careful of the place where they live.'

Grigory picked up on the environment theme: 'We always think Russia is too big to spoil it all.'

Maria: 'Tolerance, relative stability and common sense in the manner of dealing with things. All people are somehow involved in the running of their country.'

Contrary to what I had imagined, these classmates had first-hand experience of the Europe beyond their national borders. In a January 2008 email Elena, their teacher, would list some of the places they'd been: Finland, Turkey, Spain, Britain, Ukraine, Poland and Sweden.

And then, to flip the coin, I asked, 'What does Russia have that Europe doesn't?'

Anastasia: 'I think they (in Europe) are impatient and they are not afraid of acting against the government. We are more patient.'

Katya (to my silent admiration): 'I don't like to judge people by their nationality because in every nation and in every country there are people ready to help. I don't like stereotypes because they prevent us seeing the good in other people.'

After her charges had their say, Elena was prompted to make her own contribution 'Yes, we are on one planet' – she acknowledged Katya's comment – 'but maybe we Russians have something special: our Russian soul, our Russian spirit'.

Naturally, I asked her to define this will-o'-the-wisp. 'Sometimes it's very difficult to convey. We are friendly on the inside, and we are open on the outside – especially in the North.'

These responses gave me a valuable insight into Russians' national self-image, which is at marked variance with the way outsiders view them. A love of secrecy rather than openness is part of the group portrait I, for one, had of Russians – but then that was partly based on official encounters, a few of them unpleasant, when I was here in Soviet times.

80 km

Day 16, May 16. As I push along the Severnaya Dvina Embankment above the swirling tide, I peer down at my faithful speedometer and read the answer to that question I'm still asking myself 2000 km into the journey, 'What am I doing here in Europe?' There it is on the luminous dial: I'm doing 2.4 km/h. Pathetic.

Sprawling for nearly a block along the embankment is a rusty-roofed edifice, the oldest in Archangelsk and originally a far-flung trading post. Built between 1668 and 1684, Gostiny Dvor has been called the world's first shopping arcade (obviously by someone with a febrile imagination, but you get the idea) although it has long since been converted into a museum. In its barrel-vaulted foyer I meet another intriguing Russian character, Alexander Potapov. What work does he – or indeed anyone here apart from the ticket vendor and gallery attendants – do? Hard to say, but Alexander does have an impressive title: archaeological consultant. And he believes I'm on the right track by beginning my European researches in the North. Alexander confirms my belief that the Vikings' role in the birth of Russia has been understated.

'Yes, the Russians came from the Vikings,' he says matter-of-factly. 'But before then there were "pre-Russians", Varyagi troops, who came here during the period between 4000 and 3000 BC from what is now Germany, near Rostock. They came to Rostov-on-Don – that is the link between Rostock and Rostov, you see? – and later they came to occupy Scandinavia.'

This summary of Viking influence is one I find fascinating, and frankly at odds with some of my book learning. Potapov tells a plausible tale: trouble is, I have no way of knowing how much of his 'history' is backed up by evidence. Seeing that almost all the exhibits are exclusively in Russian leaves me almost clueless. I would love to have known more about a 1720–1721 map of Europe that indicates the land north of here was much more populated then than it is now, with town names jutting out like fish scales either side of the Dvina.

Alexander later introduces me to an icon restorer who (I can confirm from a return visit next day) is almost permanently drunk as a skunk, and who works and lives in a dungeon-like anteroom under the building. Scruffy Pyotr waves an apologetic hand in the direction of a dusty horsehair sofa occupying the corner of his dingy quarters. He often uses it as a bed, he tells me, but the only appearances this Orthodox bohemian seems to care for are those of his icons – and they are meticulous, magnificent.

81 km

A *BBC World News* item informs me that earlier this month Russia summarily closed the land border with Estonia, following the saga of the worker-hero statue. Only now do I realise how lucky I was to get through before such an event put the skids under all my plans.

82 km

Together with a Swede and a German living in this city, I have been invited to address 500 students at the Archangelsk State Technical University today, a rendezvous arranged through Elena Kokanova. (With no lift in sight, I' m hauled upstairs to the fourth-floor auditorium by a human chain gang.) Dr Valentina Golysheva, an administrator who comes across every bit as pompous as her title, Associate Professor of Cross-cultural Communications, introduces us to the assembly. Andreas Edvardsson – polite, self-effacing and Swedish – says he found it 'disturbing' to visit America where people think it a virtue to 'present yourself as better than you may really be'.

'Swedes,' he tells the students, 'put ourselves down low, whatever we may think of ourselves.' Even conceding that we are dealing in generalisations, I can see that such self-abnegation would irk a more open personality, who might associate the reticent Swede with a cold, unemotional visage.

Ludwig Waas, from Munich, who has been teaching German in Archangelsk for two years, selects two 'typically German traits': first, punctuality, 'which I think is a good thing'; and, second, 'being too exacting, too precise, which I think is a bad thing'. Elena's class – who form a small but encouraging cheer squad for the Australian panellist – nod vigorously when I point out that these 'good and bad' characteristics can be seen as two sides of the same coin.

85 km

This menu item in an Archangelsk restaurant – 'hearing under a vegetable's fur coat' – sounds more like a cryptic crossword clue than a fish dish.

Today's flight, over the Arctic Circle from Archangelsk to Murmansk, will cover more than 800 km and deposit me further north than I have ever been.

90 km

The success of the European project – sometimes described as 'ever closer union' – would not be in everybody's interests. Ivan, my taxi driver to the airport, tells a simple story whose poignancy is not lessened by the fact that anyone can see where it's going before he reaches his conclusion.

Ivan's English, you might say, is broken without being utterly beyond repair. Ten years ago a German friend of his, Björn, was living in Archangelsk. 'He and this girl find, how to say, love,' he tells me as we turn on to the airport road. 'He leaves here and promises the girl to return. When he gets back to Germany his girl there, she take him away' – at this point Ivan's hands leave the wheel for one scary moment as he feels words will not be enough to convey the concept of brainwashing – 'and she cleans his head. She says, "You never more go in Archangelsk".'

It is a curious fact that, since the loss of Great Power status – something Putin is determined to reverse – Russia has become one of the only countries in the world with a declining population. The nation's addiction to vodka is often blamed for this. But now, while I await take-off – delayed because someone forgot to put avgas in the engines, an oversight being rectified after we've all boarded – I leaf through this month's edition of Aeroflot's in-flight magazine, *Vlast*, and come across the most remarkable article.

Under the headline LIFE IS SHORTER AND SO ARE WE, it reveals that, according to the latest medical research, the height of the average Russian over the past ten years has shrunk by 1.5 cm. By 2097, we are warned, the stature of the Russian people will be down to 150.5 cm, 'about the average size of today's Pygmies'.

At last, we take to the air. Before the in-flight drinks trolley appears, it is sobering to think that as Russia disappears beneath our wheels so it does – bit by bit – all around me.

The White Sea shimmers under a lemony sun. As we power ever onwards to the far north-west, that cut-crystal line where ice meets water is plainly visible from my starboard window seat. The water is a glorious deep blue, the white blanket of ice fringed light green. Just over the coast of the Kola peninsula you can see the rivers run free – I will later learn that some of the world's most prized Atlantic salmon are caught in them – but the lakes are frozen over.

Out of this wilderness looms a city whose survival 69° north of the Equator gives the locals a justified pride in their self-reliance. Murmansk is neither as compact nor as flat as Archangelsk. It is a harder city to get to know and like, but I will have unforeseen help in that regard. Finding a place to stay will, however, prove a headache.

My first choice, Polyarnye Zori, has been booked out by a convention, they tell me. It bills itself as 'Your Faraway Home', and is a couple of kilometres from downtown – a term to be taken literally here, as Polyarnye Zori sits on the crest of the steepest rise I'll have to scale in the entire journey. Half a kilometre uphill, it takes the worst part of an hour to reach. Way down there on Lenin Prospekt, the Soviet-era Hotel Arktika trades on Polyarnye Zori's 'faraway' location by advertising 'You're in the Very Centre with Us'.

97 km

Over breakfast in the Moryak Café, I see on the television that *Happy Feet* is now screening in Murmansk. Penguins in the Arctic: what next?

105 km

Ekaterina – a twenty-something businesswoman from St Petersburg whom I meet in the Polyarnye Zori's business centre – is frustrated. Anyone would be at the sight of the airhead-in-charge who, asked by her to send a fax to St Petersburg, removes the paper from the machine and holds a single sheet in the air. We look at each other, doubtless thinking the same thought: How does she imagine the fax is going to get sent this way? And then, after Ekaterina admonishes her, she does it again.

Only a couple of days before I leave the Federation it occurs to me that I've found the ideal person to quiz about the 'folks next door'. Six years ago, Ekaterina tells me, she took a car journey to Sweden, Finland and Norway and was hugely impressed. 'For me it's like they are very healthy, easy to connect with, quick-witted and, like, normal people.'

Three years later, she met more Norwegians in a language school, and one of them stayed at her place in St Petersburg. 'I think the most handsome men on the whole planet are Norwegian,' she gushes, looking into my beautiful hazel eyes (but Ekaterina is in full flight so I wordlessly excuse her). And here she turns quite earnest, which strikes me as very Russian, too. 'I think that the Norwegian is a real Viking type, with a strong spirit inside.' (Surely she doesn't mean the urge to rape and pillage, I inwardly respond, while thinking it wiser not to give vent to such an outrageous thought.)

But, I say, when you're in Scandinavia don't you miss the dynamism, the fast pace, of St Petersburg? Ekaterina pauses for just a moment before voicing her impossible dream. 'You know, Ken, my ideal would be for St Petersburg to be located in Norway.'

115 km

Ever since I've been old enough to read histories of World War II it has struck me that the US and the USSR never seemed to absorb the lesson that neither of them without the other's support could have defeated Nazi Germany.

North of the city centre, on the right bank of Kola Inlet, stands the massive monument to Alyosha, the archetypal Soviet defender hero from the Great Patriotic War. Towering over the inlet from a lofty cliff, the city and its docks forming a picturesque sight off to the left, Alyosha stands 100 metres tall in tribute to the defenders of the Soviet motherland. A cairn below the statue, placed there by the regional Government, states that a second monument, 'to the participants of the Allied naval convoys bringing aid to our people during the Second World War ... will be erected in Murmansk'. This shows some recognition, if a tad belated, of the British–North American lifeline offered to the Soviet population – and, incidentally, to 'Uncle Joe' Stalin during their, and his, darkest hour.

But can governments swallow their historic claims of proud self-sufficiency? That day has not yet dawned: 'The memorial will be built by the international non-government fund Eternal Memory to Soldiers.'

Up here, on this sunlit May day, I experience – for the first time on this transcontinental trek – one of those sublime moments I hope readers will not think it pretentious of me to call an epiphany. 'Moment' is a misleading word, who can say how long this happy state will last? It is timeless, immeasurable, indescribable – yet palpably real. On close inspection it evaporates. The onset of this sense of satisfaction is unpredictable, though beautiful scenery is always a component, and often enough it follows an arduous bout of physical exertion or mental agitation. But let's not wax too mystical. Call it being at peace with the world.

I notice something else, an odd pairing of opposites. Elements normally in conflict resolve themselves in harmony. In the middle distance, the hills that surround Murmansk are mantled with a smattering of snow. Immediately in front of my eyes, at the feet of Alyosha – the rock-solid soldier standing steadfast for the millions – burns an Eternal Flame.

Perhaps there is a chemical explanation for all this – the release of endorphins or some such phenomenon – but, as long as an epiphany lasts, my critical faculties abandon their normal function, the quest for explanation.

116 km

On the smooth winding descent from Alyosha's eminence, my wheels roll more freely and I use my hands as brakes less and less. The speedometer now comes into its own, bringing out a daredevil streak in its master. In quick succession I record the three fastest speeds of my four-week-old journey: 20.8 km/h, 20.9 km/h and 22.1 km/h, the last of these attained on a curve. What a buzz. But, strange to say, my joyride is provoking different emotions in the drivers of the oncoming traffic who clearly regard this alien apparition with a mixture of dread and disbelief.

118 km

After two stout patrons had helped me up a few steps, the woman in charge of Murmansk Puppet Theatre motioned me inside free of charge. Later she would refund the payment I insisted on making for a juice she bought for me at interval. Talk about a heart of beaten gold. Once again I have witnessed the big-heartedness of Russians – especially in the North, it has to be said. It's easy to see why this puppet theatre, Russia's oldest (founded in 1933), is also its best loved. Children and parents alike laughed heartily at PC Plod's ineffectual assertion of authority against the little people, the puppets, most of whom appeared to owe their personalities to various vegetables. Pretty Chippolina was called by name and so were others, for all I knew; but to me they will always be Potato Head, Cabbage Head, Marrow Head and their assorted associates from the same patch.

120 km

If a hotel can be a dinosaur, then the Arktika must be *Tyrannosaurus rex*. Forced out of the uptown Moryak by routine maintenance work on the lift, I moved down to the Arktika with great foreboding.

Every day brought a fresh disaster. The first morning I came down to breakfast, the restaurant was off limits. The lifts were 'blocked' from stopping at that level, for reasons never explained, and Olga the receptionist's promise to get the 'block' lifted never looked like being fulfilled. The second day, my laundry was delivered soaking wet inside the bag. By the third morning I'd had enough and headed across the square to the Meridian (probably spelt that way to avoid problems with the Meridien chain, though at these latitudes they should have called it the Parallel Hotel anyway). Upon my mentioning that I'd been staying at the Arktika and – deciding on the candid approach – adding that I'd found it a poor (*plokhoi*) hotel, receptionist Evgenia remarked, 'Everyone knows this'.

Although the Meridian would normally charge 200 roubles (A$10) a night more than the old behemoth across the way, Evgenia managed to undercut the Arktika's tariff and throw in a complimentary breakfast (which I could actually take in the restaurant, much to my delight). It's only taken six days, but at last I'm settled, and this hotel even provides innocent amusement en route to your room. A sign in the lift issues a warning in several languages. In English it says: PLEASE DON'T KEEP THE BUTTONS.

I have made a friend – Osmo Kolu, a 28-year-old Finn who works here as a travel agent. I met him when I went to his office to ask about the bus service to Norway. Later this year he will buy a flat in Murmansk, an act of faith in Russia's future stability that some outside the country would regard as adventurous, to say the least.

Osmo, who obviously loves this city, has educated me on aspects of its history that had escaped my attention. He tells me it was awarded Hero City status on the strength of withstanding the second longest siege of World War II.

And we find time to sample the city's culinary delights – which, as a resident here for two years, he knows far better than I. There have been few occasions when I glimpsed Europe while in Russia. Eating Norwegian salmon soup in Murmansk's Churchill restaurant was undoubtedly one. Another time we ate reindeer meat at the Rvanye Parusa. Just the meat, garnished *à la nouvelle cuisine* with licks of mashed potato. Reindeer? It's a bit stringy – at least mine was – but with enough beer to wash it down (and the Rvanye Parusa brews its own brand, Pilgrim, on the premises) you really don't notice.

At a third restaurant I visited one day for lunch – it served specialities from the Caucasus – something unprecedented in my experience of dining out occurred: the proprietor, seeing how much I had enjoyed my meal, refused to take any money for it.

Granted, there was a bumper crowd in the establishment that day, but still … So overwhelmed was I by this magnanimous act – coming not long after Nadezhda's way-over-the-top generosity at the hotel in Archangelsk and other examples mentioned in this chapter – that I returned to the restaurant with Osmo next day and we paid in full for two more hearty meals.

It was then that he introduced me to the heady delights of snuff, or *snus*, a Scandinavian form of tobacco that is meant to get up your nostrils. Inhale it, and it tingles (they say it also clears) the passages. I must have taken too much on this first occasion (and judging by Osmo's chortling he had known I would) because I felt slightly nauseated. Fortunately, we had finished our meals before taking the narcotic. But this was an education, too. Five minutes sufficed to teach me when enough snuff's enough.

128 km

Sunday morning at St Nicholas Cathedral in the suburbs of Murmansk. Confirming talk of a revival in Russian Orthodoxy, there seems to be a broad cross-section of ages in the incense-wreathed church this morning. It is the Orthodox tradition to stand – pews are not provided – so I'm the only one seated in church today (and I permit myself a quiet chuckle over that). Touchingly, the arthritic babushka on my left places her hand on my wheelchair to steady herself while kneeling for prayer. Only too glad to be of service at the service, which ends with a procession led by the prelate who delivered the sermon.

136 km

And now I'm ready to leave Russia by the back door. Although it is only 6.30 am, the 300 metre trck from my hotel poses a logistical nightmare. I have three bags to get to the bus stop, and the hotel security staff dare not move from their posts even if they wanted to (which – let's be frank about this – they don't).

So Osmo, after only five hours' sleep, has turned up with his best friend, Ilya, in tow. The pair of them are as dependable as a bank but, unlike a bank, refuse money for their services. We wave weary goodbyes in the speckled morning light and, a minute later, as the bus rounds a bridge to the west, I see a road sign: Kirkenes, 213 km.

After four weeks of searching high and low for Europe, I quit Putin's realm without having found a single Russian who thought it was here. Right, then, it must be somewhere over the horizon.

CHAPTER 2

True North (Refilling the Ocean)

NORWAY and NORRLAND (CENTRAL SWEDEN)

Time spent:	19 days
Distance covered:	5063 km
Distance pushed:	53.1 km
Average speed:	2.118 km/h
Journey distance to date:	8165 km

On 6 June 793 the Vikings achieved their first military conquest outside the historical Norse homeland, putting to the torch Lindisfarne monastery, in what is now northern England. Like the Arabs' a century and a half previously, this feat of arms was a landmark event that would change the world.[3] Yet, unlike the Muslim expansion which reached as far as Andalusia in southern Spain, the Viking victory has faded from Western memory.

I have been wondering ever since reading of their conquest whether this date is even remembered by the Vikings' descendants, the Norwegians of today who seem to direct all their sublimated aggression at whales.

Since I shall actually be in the country on 6 June, the 1214th anniversary of that ravaging success, it will be intriguing to see whether the citizens of this prosperous Nordic nation know their own history. Before reading up on the Vikings I believed they'd had scant influence on the development of European societies. The standard historical view is that Europe was built by generations standing on the shoulders of ancient Greece and Rome. The idea that the nation-builders came from the very north of the Continent – indeed the great seahorse-shaped peninsula shared today by Norway and Sweden – was new to me, and I resisted it at first as faddish and improbable. Had you asked me then what we owe to the Scandinavians, I would probably have replied, 'The names of about half our days of the week, and that's about it'.

But the more attention I paid to the countries along the path of my descent through the Continent, the wider my eyes grew: the Norman coast of France was so called because the Normans are the Northmen,[4] and the city of San Sebastián in the Basque Country was founded by Norsemen early in the ninth century. Eric the Red was a Viking famous for exploring Greenland and settling the best farmland there (not a great amount of choice, one suspects). It is now established fact that his son, Leif Ericsson, landed on the coast of North America.

Eric was very modest, I think, not to christen Greenland Redland. And, in one of history's great what-ifs, had he and not Sonny Ericsson kept going west it might have been the old man who ended up being remembered as the Viking who named America (as in I Am Eric, aaaargh!).

It is not as though there was any shortage of land to explore back home. Of all twelve countries I will pass through on this voyage, there is none in which I will do more travelling than Norway. By train, bus and boat I will go more than 4600 km, or 277 km a day, nearly three times the overall average. It is worth spending a few moments to examine why.

A map-gazer might imagine Norway to be bigger than it really is (one-and-a-third Victorias). Here it's not size that matters so much as extent: those long hours between rest stops are due to the Arctic region's remoteness from major population centres – it is nearly as far from north to south as from Melbourne to Brisbane – combined with the profusion of fjords necessitating long roundabout routes rather than direct ones.

It's high time someone came to the defence of those of us who refuse to travel light, who are constantly being urged to go further and do more with less. A pox on the minimalists, I say. My luggage on this odyssey consists of one sportsbag, one suitcase and a large hessian bag full of clothes. Adding my backpack and its contents, that makes about 50 kg of accoutrements.

Some of this bulk is unavoidable. A certain amount of urological gear I must take with me. Some is an indulgence. A dozen books for the road fall into this category. And some of it is there for no better reason than that I am notoriously sloppy when it comes to packing. But, it occurs to me, there is one powerful argument for travelling heavy. If a robber has designs on your belongings, keeping them in a 20 kg bag acts as a powerful deterrent. He can't just lift it and run off.

But how do I cross a continent with so much to weigh me down? The secret is that it's never more than 200 metres between hotel and bus, or railway station locker and platform. That's the theory, anyway. For the most part it works well enough – and when it doesn't I put the sportsbag and suitcase in a locker, if one is available, and carry the rest on my lap. From where I sit, those who pack as little in the way of portable goods for two years abroad as they would for a weekend in the countryside are suffering the severest disability of them all – a lack of imagination. When all is said and done, you only pass this way once. Thus endeth my homily on the unbearable lightness of luggage.

137 km

Just after 10 am (having reset my watch two hours earlier than Moscow time) I arrive in Kirkenes – a neat 'frontier town' even if it is 45 km from the border – just in time to hear that the thrice-weekly 'boat' is about to leave for Mehamn.

North Cape is often touted as the northernmost point of Europe. But look closely and you'll see it's on an island. If you're going to call the tip of an island the north of Europe, the honour should really go to some windswept cape in Franz Josef Land or Spitsbergen. Avoid the tourist hordes with their vain boasts. A quick map consultation reveals your destination as a far lonelier road, a promontory 100 km to the east of North Cape's island. This balloon-shaped land called North Half Island (Nordkyn) is 'tied' to the rest of Europe by the narrowest of isthmuses – just 100 metres across – known as Hopseidet. Here, and nowhere else, you will find True North.

And the town of Mehamn, curled around a fjord at 71° 1' N, is only a few minutes of latitude south of North Cape. Sheer luck has given me half an hour to get to the dock after making a hasty booking with a Mehamn hotel.

'How can I be sure you're coming?' the hotelier asks. 'Because if you don't hear back from me I'm on the boat,' I reply.

The receptionist at the Kirkenes hotel where the bus from Russia dropped me has made her Internet service available, and the town's website confirms that I am not the only person to have seen through the fraudulence of North Cape's pretensions. 'Kinnarodden, northernmost point of European mainland, 71° 8' 2",' it proclaims, with reiteration, for good measure, in Norwegian, *europas nordligste fastland spunkt*.' And right near that point – on the road north of Europe's northernmost town – awaits its northernmost village, Gamvik. That magic box is really rattling now.

138 km

Arrive at the dock after a 1 km taxi ride that cost the equivalent of A$16 (welcome to the world's most expensive economy). There, towering above me, is no mere 'boat' but a towering Hurtigruten coastal steamer, the 16,000 tonne *Trollfjord*. Once on board, sinking into a button-backed leather armchair to starboard, I turn my head to the left for a view of black-and-white sailing photos from a more graceful age, then to the right for a sight of the fjord-cut fringe of land that constitutes the 'brow of the seahorse'.

The sun's lamp on low spreads subdued rays over the gentle swell of the Arctic Ocean, and I'm left alone to ponder the contrast between this morning's rough-and-ready Russian bus ride and this afternoon's life of ease aboard one of the world's most luxurious cruise ships.

On the wall of *Trollfjord*'s disabled toilet is an emergency phone. One of the buttons is marked 'Wake-up call'. As the Americans say, go figure.

About 3 pm we cross 70° N on the placid surface of Varangerfjord.

At 10 pm – I would say 'late at night' but this eternity of daylight empties the phrase of its normal sense – we indulge in a bizarre and, frankly, childish ritual of waving towels in the direction of the passengers aboard the *Kong Harald*, another Hurtigruten steamer, who are waving towels at us as it proceeds on its 'north-east passage'. Per the barman dispenses a free hot toddy which saves me a small fortune and which I down to the strains of Brahms' Hungarian Dance No. 5 being performed by the ship's piano accordionist.

The purser tells me with great amusement that he has had Japanese passengers come up to him in broad daylight – around 1 am – to complain they were misled. 'But where is the *midnight* sun?' they challenge him, apparently convinced this rare article is an additional orb visible only on cruises to the Arctic. Glorious as this one sun is, I can see they'll be wanting their money back.

Back in Australia, as I envisaged that singularly tireless athlete the sun remaining above the horizon almost round the clock, I hadn't been able to get to grips with how it would set in the west (I assumed it did that even up here) and rise again in the east. Would it nip under the horizon and dart back to its starting blocks? No, I now see, its trajectory describes an ellipse so that it sets south-west – and rises south-east – or, now we are in the period it doesn't really set at all but rather skims along the horizon, it keeps circling the horizontal track, running victory laps around it all summer long.

140 km

Mehamn announces itself to the nose before the eyes. Ever after, you will associate it with two smells: fresh wood and rotting fish. In this, one of Europe's most remote corners, it was a clash between the big fish and the little fish that – according to the municipal website – brought 1200 troops racing north to restore order, the only time in the history of 'peaceful Norway' when this had been necessary.

On 2 June 1909 – almost 98 years ago to the day – 'non-local fishermen tore down the whaling factory which had been built by whaler and inventor Sven Foyn and which they blamed for the loss of their fishing income'. So there you have it: mayhem in Mehamn and an anti-whaling protest that Greenpeace would have been proud of. Note that the damage was done by 'non-local fishermen', it's always the out-of-towners to blame. Foyn, in fact, would have earned a prize place on any Greenpeace list of hate figures, having invented the harpoon.

142–145 km

On my second 'night' in Mehamn I learn that there is a youth hostel here. Norway doesn't really have what would be deemed budget accommodation elsewhere, but this place comes close. Except that anything less like a hostel it would be hard to visualise. Picture, rather, a cottage with a balcony jutting over the bank of a fjord. And there, a few hours later, I experience my second epiphany. It is 12.30 am, the sun has disappeared – wait, that isn't supposed to happen at this time of year. What's going on? I roll down the ramp and peer over to where the sun was last seen. And there, as the opening drumbeats of a rain shower hit the roof tiles, the sun has been replaced by a rainbow – or rather the golden shaft of one, bending like a bamboo shoot from heaven, and bathing in a phosphorescent glow the fish-salting-and-drying factory that now stands where the workers' forebears attacked that whaling factory almost a century ago.

146 km

Oot Bjorn, 37, Europe's northernmost postmaster, sorts through 20 kg of envelopes and small packets a day. Oot, who has seen a bit of the wider world, says, 'I have tried to live in the city. I went to southern Sweden, to a place called Falkenberg, to Drummen – a town near Oslo – and then to Tromsø for three months. But I got homesick. The grass was not greener on the other side.' It would be callous to mention that in Mehamn there is no grass to speak of, regardless of colour.

What's so great about life on North Half Island? 'We have much more freedom out here. We have Nature, we have the hunting.' And then – how could you have a conversation in Norway without mentioning fish? – 'There are 800 fishing waters on North Half Island alone.' He seems happy for all this true northerliness to be kept under wraps, saying, 'We want more tourists but I don't want us to be like North Cape'.

True North lies over the hills – ripe with strawberries for just a few days in August – in the village of Gamvik. The headland is pitted with German bunkers. This was a strategic coast for monitoring Allied ships bound for Archangelsk, and it remains strategic today: Nato has laid undersea cables to monitor the movement of Russian submarines. I found that Russians insisted they were a race apart from the Europeans, and now I find the Norwegians – who keep themselves apart from the European Union – are also keen to keep their eastern neighbour at a distance.

At noon on the last day of May, I sit above the wild Arctic surf that beats upon Europe's (and almost certainly the world's) northernmost lighthouse, still tended by its keeper, Ms Rita Bastholm, although these days no one lives inside the obelisk. My mind absorbs the elements' immensity, and the fact that here at 71° 5' 33" N I have reached that part of populated Europe closest to the North Pole (about 2000 nautical miles over yonder as the gull flies).

147 km

Harald Hansen is the principal of Europe's most northerly school. Most of its 21 students have just returned from Poland, which included a visit to Oswiecim, more infamous as Auschwitz. Athina, fifteen years young, was saddened by the barbarous treatment of the Jews there but added 'at the same time I couldn't understand it'. Out of the mouths of babes. And then she said the most surprising thing, 'It could also happen in Norway'. Could such affluent people be barbarous too? I was about to find out.

At Gamvik School I posed my question about AD 793. One student asked whether it marked the introduction of Christianity. A history teacher was the only person I would find in this vast country who guessed the date's significance, saying, 'Was it something to do with a military victory?'

At Gamvik Museum I find a condensed history of life on Nordkyn down the centuries. The pioneering Christians here thought this was *ultima Thule*, the End of the World. Their arrival was certainly the end of the world the inhabitants of this region, now called Finnmark, had known.

In 1621 Lisbet Nilesdatter was found guilty of drowning Abraham Nilsen. Nilesdatter hadn't laid a hand on Abraham but she had cast a spell on him. The witch hunt was on. As the information board has it, 'In brutality and intensity the witch hunt in Finnmark can only be compared to ones in Germany and Scotland. Between 100 and 150 were convicted of sorcery from 1620–1665'.

Lisbet's punishment? To be thrown into the sea, seen as God's holy christening water which would reject the sinful because – as everyone knows – witches don't sink. Thirty witches were thrown in and all floated. But because they were witches they were dragged off to be burned. Suspects who drowned were innocent. Crime, one gathers, wasn't a huge problem in 17th-century Finnmark. In the 21st, of course, the innocent still die, but now we have school trips to Poland, and students such as Athina smart enough to make the connection.

His flowing white beard reminiscent of the Gamvik surf, writer Marius Hage, 57, does a passable imitation of the Old Man of the Sea.

'Why isn't Norway in the European Union?' I ask him.

'Because,' he replies without hesitation, 'as you will see travelling through the country, living standards are so high here that if it joined it would be doing Europe a favour rather than the other way round. The people have spoken twice' – in referendums, the first of them in 1972 – 'and any political party that was pro-Europe would not want to jeopardise its support by raising this matter again.'

Pro-Europe? I think, How can anyone be anti-Europe? Russians have their soul, Norwegians their salmon. At this rate, I wonder, am I going to find that every European has his or her own reason for not 'joining' Europe?

Norwegians, said to have the highest living standard in the world, would appear to be first in the queue for Valhalla. So what have they to worry about? Another Marius – Marius Nilsen, owner of the general store, part-time air traffic controller and candidate for mayor – had to think about this for a few seconds. Mobility is a recent development in a place as remote as this. 'Thirty years ago there would have been no one from here who had been as far as Tromsø,' he tells me. Now that they can leave, many – especially the young – don't come back.

As this is the Continent's furthest outpost of democracy, I ask Marius, 43 – who is running against an entrenched 'conservative' – to let me know how his campaign fares. What are the issues, apart from emigration?

Immigration. Marius says the incumbent is proposing to ship in hundreds of Russians from across the border, for a sinister purpose. 'He'll sign them up to vote for him.' Poles can get €2 an hour picking strawberries, he tells me; in Norway they earn six times that. 'Norwegians didn't want to pick the strawberries here – it's only a few days a year, this work – so they imported strawberry pickers from Poland and Pakistan. Now they are bringing in Chinese.'

Mehamn is the seat of the local council but Gamvik municipality, which lays claim to being Europe's northernmost local government, embraces it and the more northerly Gamvik community. Therefore, Marius will be the Mayor of True North if he wins September's poll. His face lights up at the prospect.

After discussing local politics, we talk Australian. 'Kevin' is a Norwegian name so Marius, a Labour man, takes it as a promising sign that Australians may soon elect their first Norwegian prime minister. Ah yes, the fair hair! Marius breaks off our interview to guide a De Havilland in to land on the airstrip – 'one of 28 short runways in Norway', he informs me – opposite the fish factory.

152–153 km

Today is dreamlike. All day I ride a bus across the gabled roof of Norway, as the most stunning scenery revolves before my gaze. Mountains, streaked with late snow that will be gone by this time next month, rise majestically from the sea. Apart from a few fellow passengers and the occasional weekender on their cottage patio, I am alone beholding the beauty of the world. Make that almost alone: reindeer, solo or in herds, are pronking their way[5] right across Finnmark.

I arrive in the world's northernmost city (Tromsø, 69° 40' N, 19° E) at the exact instant of my 53rd birthday, discounting time zone differences. Of course it feels great to be 23 – as it has done for the past 30 years – so by all means disregard the numerical slip in the previous sentence.

154 km

Hours later I toast the anniversary by raising a glass of akvavit to the one and only midnight sun – and tossing it down my gullet in the approved manner. Replicating the gesture is Odd Magne Johansen, a Norwegian journalist I met over breakfast at the Hotel Dvina in Archangelsk and who there and then invited me to stay at his 'pad' overlooking the fjord in Tromsø. I'm grateful for the company – drinking alone sounds far too Nordic for my liking – but also for the accommodation because, as it turns out, even Tromsø's 'cheaper' hotels are full, booked out, they each claim, by members of the entourage (his own and the media's) surrounding South Africa's Bishop Desmond Tutu, here to deliver a sermon at the Arctic Church on World Environment Day.

Worrying news from home, when I phone later on my birthday. Mum says that Dad, in his 88th year, was diagnosed with a weakened heart last week – an aortic aneurysm, to be precise – and surgeons had inserted a stent in the bloated artery. When I was nine or ten I recall asking our family doctor all about 'aortic aneurysm', an ailment I had just read of in a Sherlock Holmes story.

156 km

In the daily newspaper here I read that Frode Heggelund, eighteen, is the star of a new film, *A Normal Day in a Wheelchair*, directed by his sixteen-year-old brother, Andre, and now on general release. But the cinema in which it is being premiered – one of the oldest in Norway – has no wheelchair access. Ouch.

157 km

Memo. Don't try to 'do' this country on a shoestring: a pair of them cost A$8. At a bar near the Tromsø docks I order a Mack beer for Odd and one for myself. The glasses are 33 cl each: these are not Bavarian jugs. Suddenly I develop a hearing difficulty when the barman says that will be 164 kroner. Quick mental calculation tells me that's €11 (A$18) apiece, $36 the pair. At this price I should have confined myself to the Odd one. What's worse, the Mack brewery is just 200 metres up the road. In all probability I could have cadged a free sample merely by dropping in.

159–161 km

From Tromsø I strike out for the Lofoten Islands. I'm in for 24 hours of what has been billed as one of the world's most memorable voyages – and, for once, the advertising doesn't lie.

The Hurtigruten steamer *Finnmark* is the last word in luxury – one of the latest additions to the fleet. Steaming through lozenge-shaped Trollfjord – a waterway 3 km long but only 100 metres wide – the theme from *Titanic* seems an inappropriate choice of music. But the well-heeled cruiseniks seated for'ard, sipping their gin-and-tonics as they gawp down at snow-sprinkled green banks and then up at the cliffs 1000 metres overhead, seem not to mind. They must be comforted by the thought that in a postmodern summer there are no icebergs at 68° N – so far as anyone yet knows.

What a strange language English can be when used by non-native speakers. When I point out to Andre, the duty receptionist, that there is no link between the computer system that recognises you're back on board as you 'swipe' a shore pass in one section of the ship and the computer system in the purser's office, he tries to voice reassurance by telling me, 'Don't worry, we won't miss you'. Then, realising at once what he has said, he blushes. 'What I mean to say is, "We won't leave you behind."'

Ship's officers Ivar and Mareno regale me with memories from voyages past. At the restaurant's second and final sitting one night, a crew member said to one of the diners, 'I hope you will enjoy your last meal'.

The crew have been known to extract innocent amusement from guileless guests. Mareno says, 'One time we saw a supply ship spouting ballast water into the sea and one passenger – an American – asked, "What's that ship doing?" So my colleague told her. "They are refilling the ocean."'

Later in the 'evening' I am called up to the bridge where Captain Sten Magne Engen – resplendent in his navy blue uniform with enough gold braid piping to have Ivan Baranov seething with envy – is ready to talk about his life spent sailing up and down the Norwegian coast. Remarking that many of those on board are past middle age, and all of them well behaved, I ask whether he has ever had to discipline unruly passengers. The multilingual Capt. Engen, whose most cherished maritime memories include service as first mate on ships that called at Australian ports from Kwinana to Newcastle, admits the occasional buck's party gets out of hand.

'We have a cell downstairs – a brig, as we say – and the deck-hands can be quite useful.' When I inquire whether Capt. Engen has ever played host to any famous shipboard guests, he mentions the Patriarch of the Greek Orthodox Church, who went round 'blessing the water, blessing the ship and blessing the passengers. I was wet all over'.

Unable to afford a cabin but desperate for sleep, I ask whether there is anywhere I could steal a few hours before our 4 am arrival in Bodø. The captain breaks his own ship's rules by letting me kip in the hospital quarters. (Maybe the brig was full. I didn't like to ask.)

169 km

Norway's reputation as an outward-looking country is reinforced by a diverse social mix (although, as we have seen, immigration is a hot item on the political agenda here as elsewhere). In the capital, Oslo, Iraqis constitute the largest non-Nordic community. Here, 1000 km to the north in Bodø, it is an Iraqi who cuts my hair. Sharan, who speaks excellent English, sees the continued occupation of his native land in colonial and oil money terms. Surely he regards Norway as a land of opportunity, a paradise on earth?

'Oh no,' he sets me straight. 'Most of the year it is cold and dark. And Norwegian women are busy and self-opinionated.'

I brace myself to pay the advertised price – equivalent to A$37 – but he insists this one's for free. What unbelievable generosity.

173–175 km

It's almost impossible to find a place to stay in Trondheim, booked out by Goths (Ostro-, Visi- and musical) here for Ozzie Osbourne's tour date. For the second time in a week the visit of a famous person has taken over a town on my itinerary. (And Archbishop emeritus Tutu doesn't even sing!) Must I check the Rolling Stones website to ensure there is no clash? On a hunch I do, only to see that we will be in Hamburg – a week apart. Time is on my side … but only just.

179–181 km

In Adelaide back in April 2007 I met Kolbein Lyng at a disability conference where we were the guest speakers. Upon learning of my impending visit to his country he did not hesitate. 'You must visit me and let me take you fishing.'

And so at Åndalsnes this warm June day he is there to greet me at the station – with his broad smile and booming voice.

Accompanied by his partner, Sue O'Neill – an associate professor from Sydney University newly relocated to Molde, on Norway's central-west coast – he plays host on a sightseeing tour that takes in Trollwall (Trolleveggen in Norwegian), a beetling cliff face famous throughout Scandinavia.

Late in the afternoon we drive 12 km the other side of Molde, to a spot above the boat landing at Fraenafjord. After carefully helping me into his 15 foot runabout, the professor rows me across the pond to the isle of Svansholmen where 45 years ago his father built a cabin.

Spoken Norwegian sounds like snowmelt. The language is babbling, playful, almost fey. And I have already taken to asking Norwegians what they think of their neighbours the Swedes. At this juncture Norwegians cease to be babbling, playful and fey. Even those who acknowledge that as a people they are inclined to be rulebound say that, in general, Swedes are even more so. According to the professor, his people sometimes say of themselves, 'Inside every Norwegian there is a German'. (He doesn't say whether this homunculus is struggling to get out – or to inhabit a Swede.)

We set out after breakfast on Sunday morning. Having again helped me into the rowboat at one end, Kolbein takes up his position at the other. Sue waves us off. I let Kolbein row – pure laziness on my part. We both agree that I should have first go at trying to lure a fish to the rod, even though I have warned him that my uselessness at this task is one of my principal disabilities.

For half an hour the fish of Fraenafjord lie low. Just as I am about to give up there is a tug on the line. Unfortunately you gain no points for reeling in a tenacious tuft of seaweed. Kolbein disentangles the kelp and returns the rod to me. But my heart has gone out of the fight. As I lay down the line, he revs up the outboard. We round a cape of dazzling green and head into the next, wider fjord. There, another twenty minutes on, the miracle takes place. The effects of that second cup of tea I had for breakfast are beginning to make themselves felt in an insistent bladder, so – reaching into my rucksack to fetch my plastic urinal – I announce with all due modesty my intention to use this device and, at the risk of polluting one of Norway's most pristine waterways, to empty its contents into the deep. Before I can finish my explanation, there is a second pull on the line, and after an impressive contest for mastery Kolbein hauls in a respectable-looking fish, perhaps 30 cm long, which he pronounces to be a cod.

Scarcely has it landed, gasping, on deck when there follows a third pull on the line and up comes a *langerfish*. The next ten minutes bring two more catches – both cod, the latter of them the biggest of today's haul.

No conventional angler, I can at least lay claim to being part of a successful fishing expedition. And, although Kolbein brought them aboard, I know it was only my threat to contaminate their freshwater supply that induced these elusive creatures to quit their natural element. My contribution isn't confined to putting the piss back into piscatorial pursuits, it turns out that Kolbein cannot immediately find the gaff he needs to prevent the big fellow from getting away. So I offer the nearest thing to hand, which happens to be my copy of Les Carlyon's masterwork on the battles of the Western Front, which I'm reading in preparation for Belgium and France.

The cod doesn't move again, proving nearly 90 years after the guns fell silent that – just as Les wrote – *The Great War* is still creating casualties.

183–185 km

This is the story of how I fell in with Norway's latter-day Bonnie and Clyde. Per and Tina (not their real names), rather than meeting their deaths in a slow-motion cinematic shootout, have retired from a life of bank robbery to raise a family. Well, that's their story – and they know where I live so I'm sticking with it. Passing strange, then, that we met outside a bank, eh?

I'd come as quickly as my wheels would carry me from Trondheim Central Station, battling the clock all the way. The train drew in at 2.50 pm but first my luggage needed stowing. It must have been spot on 3.15 when I rolled up to the door of my chosen bank. I knew they all closed at three, but this one had been so friendly just the other day, waiving that discouraging 50 kroner (A$6) transaction fee – and it had an equally 'friendly' entrance ramp. Today the tellers glanced up but refused to let me in, citing the late hour. They pointed to the post office opposite, but its only entrance was above a forbidding flight of steps.

So I waited, and waited, my annoyance increasing by the minute. It was then that Per and Tina pitched up. 'Banks are real shits' were Per's first words to me. At that point, I couldn't agree more. Then Per announced he that had an idea. 'What, we should break in?' I joked. No, he said with great earnestness, why didn't I write a sign demanding entrance and pointing out that, as I'd told him, I had only 74 kroner (A$8) of the folding stuff in my possession?

So I penned a heartfelt plea which Per translated into Norwegian and pressed against the windowpane. More than one teller looked up and read it – and looked down and continued tallying.[6]

Per and Tina, whose blue tattooed neck was quite riveting close up, now made the most generous of offers, 'Why don't you stay with us for the night?' After a rapid self-consultation – Well, my locked bags are at the station, safe till tomorrow, so what have I got to lose? – I agreed.

At his car, parked nearby, I was introduced to their rather sullen eight-year-old daughter, and ten minutes later, after a successful raid on Burger King, Per let me into the secret of his hostility towards Norway's banks. My innocent query as to what he did for a living elicited the answer, 'I am a gangster'. And then, amending himself to include his life partner, '*We* are gangsters'.

While I was pondering what exactly I had got myself into, Per gunned the engine and we roared north out of Trondheim, our destination – and this is the hardest part of the story to believe, but a world atlas will confirm it's not made up – a town on the highway and rail line east to Sweden, 30 km from the coast, called Hell.

These days my passport has a visa stamp from Hell – issued by a petrol station, it's one of the only visas you can get in Western Europe these days – and there is even, appropriately enough, a chapter of the Coffin Cheaters' motorbike gang on a hilltop outside the town.

Per and Tina live in a country villa 6 km from Hell. Built in 1876, it is one of a row on the edge of a farmed field. Only upon entering the house did my doubts about their story vanish. There, in the parlour and again in the living room, were more clocks – some of them quite ornate pieces – than one dwelling could ever need. Clearly, they were a serious couple of 'collectors' and all I can say to anyone who doubts that their timepieces were ill-gotten gains is that if you'd spent 24 hours with Per and Tina you'd be as certain as I am that they were stolen goods.

Per – who looked a dead ringer for Angry Andersen – told me he and Tina had both done prison time. She would go in and he would come out; he would go in and she would come out (I started to picture them as a pair of cuckoos) but now they had gone straight because, tattooed Tina told me, 'we don't want our daughter's future to be affected'. Per said he now worked on an oil rig – four weeks on, four weeks off – while Tina was settling down to life as a rural housewife, not exactly living in Hell but only five minutes' drive away.

Keeping my rucksack close by at all times, I used it as a pillow when asleep on their sofa, and on being deposited back at Trondheim Station next day I was relieved, but – whew! – only of my fears.

186–188 km

To Hell and back, then, and from Trondheim back to Hell, and on to Sweden. Outsiders have spoken of the Swedes being reticent, private and humourless. The first two of these I am primed for, but the notion of a humourless people strikes me as most unlikely. At last my European quest has found an object: for the next few days I will turn sleuth, ferreting out the Swedish sense of humour wherever it may lurk.

On my first full day in the country you might say I sniff success. Looking for a glue to put together one of my diaries which is falling apart, I ask at a supermarket in the ski resort of Åre where a helpful sales assistant recommends an iconic Swedish brand, Karlsons Universalkallister ('stronger than Araldite', he informs me) and then adds, mysteriously, 'You will know it because of the red donkey'.

Donkey. Glue. Hmm. Having located it, I see the picture of a braying red ass. Swedish is a difficult language for a foreigner so the assistant translates the writing on the tube. 'The donkey is quoted as saying, "Everyone's using Karlsons Kallister except for me, but that's why I'm a donkey."' Does this tickle the funny bone of a wheelchair user in a Swedish supermarket? Oh no, far better than that. It leaves me rolling in the aisles.

189 km

A Swedish restaurateur from Åre gives me more insight this morning into how the Swedes see themselves, assuring me, 'We Swedish people are mellow'. This must be the other side of the mirror in which Sweden's neighbours – when they look this way – mistake 'mellow' for 'withdrawn' or 'secretive'.

191–196 km

Everyone has heard of Loch Ness, where since 1933 sightings have been reported and a thriving tourist trade has grown up around a certain creature of the deep. But outside Sweden, I dare say, few have heard of Storsjöodjuret, another lacustrine monster whose existence that has been the subject of fierce debate among its human neighbours – and for far longer than Nessie, indeed all the way back to 1635. Forget the Swedish sense of humour, I tell myself: here is a far worthier quest – something of which people claim to have unmistakable evidence. And, who knows but that the monster itself may have a Swedish sense of humour?

The town of Östersund clings to Lake Storsjön (rhyming with 'distortion'). As I head round the lake towards my hostel, I see a park bench with a plaque attached, declaring it to be a 'monster-spotting platform' or, more formally, 'an observation station funded by the European Development Fund'.

On a bridge over the lake I meet Mats Malmqvist, 52, a municipal official and confirmed sceptic. When I ask whether he believes in the monster's existence, he gives me an eloquent thumbs-down.

The Swedish authorities – living up to their nation's reputation for sobriety rather than playfulness – have quite rightly placed the monster under a protection order, and it seems to be working. To date, no reports have been received of anyone injuring or killing a monster in Lake Storsjön (or anywhere else in the country, come to that).

In town, at the Jamtli Museum, I watch a video, *Monstrum Jemtlandia*, in which local residents speak of the devil within. One grizzled veteran, Tomas Gårdvall, delves into the murk of speculation, and surfaces with the observation that some folk regard the monster as a symbol of the collective unconscious (very Swedish, that). Another declares, 'There are tears in the fabric of reality that can suddenly rip open'. How true, I tell myself, but surely someone out there knows how to drop a stitch in time?

Finally, a commentator surmises that the beast is a visitor from the subterranean ocean into which Jules Verne's adventurers sailed a raft after descending through an Icelandic volcano in *Journey to the Centre of the Earth*. Now what did I read at one of those lakeside observation stations? There were fifteen sightings in the 1950s, and 30 in the 1970s, but none at all in the 1960s.

Hang on, wasn't there a spate of Nessie sightings in the Sixties? Eureka! At last the Grand Unified Monster Theory has taken its serpentine shape. Loch Ness and its Swedish cousin are not two monsters, but one. Only its head and tail live 'in' a lake. The extremely long midsection lies under the seabed so that the creature's head surfaces in Loch Ness and its tail roils the waters of Storsjön *except* when the creature gets tired of facing in one direction and slithers past itself in its subterranean tunnel, as must have happened in the Sixties. If more than 99 per cent of Storsjie is under the earth as well as under water, this would explain why it is so rarely sighted. When I revealed this to the curator at Jamtli Museum, he seemed visibly moved – it is hard to tell whether by intellectual excitement or unalloyed pity – that someone who had come so far should have a clearer perspective than locals who had been cudgelling their brains for so long.

Now we beneficiaries of humanity don't expect to be honoured with a special stand at the museum, let alone a Nobel Prize. A small sum of money, sent to Wakefield Press and marked for my attention, will be reward enough.[7]

201 km

Reserved? Mellow? Supposedly not when it comes to sex. But how raunchy the Swedes were I had no idea until I was kept waiting for ten minutes outside the disabled toilet at Sundsvall Railway Station, on the Gulf of Bothnia coast, while a couple in their 30s had sex in the cubicle. I didn't care what they did or where they did it but, with another basic function to carry out and a train to catch, I wasn't in the best of the moods when they emerged dishevelled from their chamber of delight.

The man disappeared as quickly as he could so, adopting a stern mien, I said to the woman, 'You really shouldn't be in there unless you're disabled,' at which a hand flew to her hip and she complained most piteously, 'I have a handicap.' In the circumstances this was totally unbelievable but I must say she carried the deception off with a certain bravura.

CHAPTER 3

Our Bicycles Have Seats

SOUTHERN SWEDEN, OSLO and DENMARK

Time spent:	23 days
Distance covered:	2092 km
Distance pushed:	126.6 km
Average speed:	2.587 km/h
Journey distance to date:	10,257 km

If a Martian arrived on Earth today – or, perhaps more plausibly, an Earthling living in the year 3000 threw the old time machine into reverse – he, she or it might look at 21st-century Europe and be struck by the strangest of paradoxes. One of the most familiar sights from one end of this continent to the other is the Church – Catholic, Protestant or Orthodox. A house of Christian worship appears on euro banknotes, so presumably these edifices tell us something about Europe.

Yet many people in these countries are ignorant of, or awkward about, their own religious history. I say 'their' because the fruits of Western civilisation are sometimes so oddly shaped it is difficult to believe they grew on the same tree. Many form incompatible couples: belief and unbelief; faith and scepticism; commitment and detachment; and so on.

To recognise that Christianity, as adopted and adapted in Europe, has been hugely important in world history is not the same as defending it (you could hardly look at the mass killings associated with the conquistadors of South and Central America and imagine Jesus doing anything but condemning their Spanish – and Portuguese – perpetrators).

Yet, like many a cathedral, Europe is a painstaking work in

progress. Efforts to construct a Constitution acceptable to all 27 EU member states continue to grapple with the question of whether 'Europia' is a Christian project. History prevents millions in Hungary, Poland, Austria, Italy and Spain from looking kindly on Muslims in their midst. The idea of Turkey joining the EU offends many and, even though it is easy to characterise such people as intolerant, they represent a substantial bloc of opinion.

To the extent that Europeans share their ideals – forbearance, charity, democracy, and even the advocacy of global respect for human rights, all that appears to be left of yesteryear's 'civilising mission' – they do come largely from a Judæo-Christian inheritance. Christianity played midwife to socialism, in Sweden but also in Britain. So-called Christians benefited from slavery, yes, but it was Christian ethics that eventually abolished the trade.

I am not saying that Europeans were better than others, but their religion taught them to believe that they had a gift of supreme importance for all humankind. And, being systematic thinkers convinced their belief system was best, it made sense to them to try imposing it on more 'benighted' parts of the globe.

When the Vikings, the Northmen, adopted Christianity – no less than when the Gothic tribes north of the Alps adopted the state religion of the Roman Empire – the North-South fault line that had run through the Continent became of minor importance compared with the East-West rift.

To understand how people think, you must know what they believe. To gain that knowledge, respect for their greatest statements of faith is essential. Their great public buildings – palaces, churches, museums, stadiums – are statements of faith no less than the words they have left us. It would be churlish to come all this way and pass them by.

Whoever finds discomfiting the splendour of cathedrals, or great art on display there and in the Continent's museums, can never discover Europe. Whatever you think of them, these are the products of Europe's brain – as is the European conscience, for better or worse – and the best way to appreciate the thoughts, or beliefs, most commonly held in a population of 700 million is not by performing a partial lobotomy. So, you ask, is religion still an important key to today's Europeans? And I respond, is the Pope a German?

211 km

Behind the altar of Uppsala Cathedral lies the sarcophagus of the warrior king Gustav Vasa, flanked in his eternal sleep by his *first* two wives. Through a translator I ask an old Swedish man about the two royal spouses. He says the king had them sequentially, not simultaneously – and walks away chuckling.

One of Vasa's titles was Duke of Finland, a country he conquered. On one side of the tomb are the ducal arms, showing a polar bear (prowling rather than rampant) clutching a sword. It's hard to avoid the conclusion that this is yet another example of Swedish humour. Now I'm the one chuckling.

Gustav Vasa wasn't well loved by the princes of the Church while he was alive. He is remembered in Sweden for abolishing many of the Church's privileges, and so only merits a marble tomb. Gold is reserved for St Erik (Jedvardsson), who lies a few metres from where a mere 750 years ago he was assassinated – the spot in the church's entrance where I now sit. This church, which took 175 years to build, is named after him and two other saints (Olaf and Lawrence).

In Erik's time the Christian creed, brought here in the ninth century by a wandering missionary, coexisted alongside the popular belief in the old Germanic gods. Gradually the new faith forced out the old, until in 1593 the Uppsala synod threw in its lot with the Protestants, declaring the Church (and this church) Evangelical Lutheran.

Over half a million people a year visit this cavernous creation, which is longer than a soccer pitch and soars 119 metres into the sky. Many are not religious but they know that this is where Sweden's most settled beliefs encounter its long and regal history. And it's a history that, despite Swedes' proud boast they haven't been involved in a war since 1809, is surprisingly bloody. Poor old King St Erik found that out a moment too late, of course.

Diagonally opposite the steepled giant stands Carolina Rediviva, the former library of Scandinavia's oldest university, Uppsala, founded in 1477. Now a museum, it contains a treasure everywhere you turn. This spacc is as hallowed to academia as the cathedral is to believers. A glass case contains manuscripts from all over 'the known world' and all over the millennia, from seventh-century BC cuneiform tablets stolen from Babylonia to 20th-century illuminated texts from Ethiopia. What may just be the biggest book I've ever seen – 1 metre tall by a hearty 2 metres across, with the pages lying open – is from the monastery at Mt Athos high above the Aegean Sea.

How much of Europe's treasures are not Europe's at all, I wonder. Beware the term 'the rule of law' and 'sovereign state' when both have been used to justify grand theft on such a scale. Over here is a map dated 1482, based on Ptolemy's atlas, the *Cosmographia*. So, I wonder, was it rescued from the conflagration that destroyed the ancient library of Alexandria? From this map it seems Ptolemy knew about the existence of the River Ganges – but how? Alexander didn't get that far east. Could Herodotus have? So many questions …

At the far end of the hall is one of two known surviving copies of a 1539 map, printed in Venice and drawn by Olaus Magnus who had travelled in northern Sweden and in Norway (as we know it today). This was the prototype for his *History of Northern Peoples*, printed in Rome in 1555 and thought lost for ever until this copy of the map turned up in Switzerland in 1961.

Between the cathedral and Carolina Rediviva a sculpted specimen of *Homo sapiens* stands, in a class of his own, outside the botanical gardens he made world-famous. We quote the name of a certain Mr Celsius, from Uppsala, more often but Carl Linnaeus, also from Uppsala, could just be the most influential Swede of all time.

In May 1732 Linnaeus mounted his horse and left Uppsala for the North on the trip of his life. But if the genius who invented the plant and animal classification system still in use today wanted to see the world, he was happy most of the time for it to be brought to him. Why travel to India, Linnaeus asked, when there were 'the thickest coral layers imaginable along the [Baltic island of] Gotland coast'? We can only guess at what he would have thought of Queensland.

I am here a month after celebrations of the great taxonomist's 300th birthday. Swedes like to boast, 'God created, Linnaeus classified'.

213 km

This morning, 16 June, at 12.30 am I saw the first star in the 47 days since my journey began. Before I was so far north that the sun didn't set at all; now I am just under 60° north of the Equator.

215–218 km

I first suspected that a splinter of illogicality lay embedded in Sweden's heart when a railway clerk in Östersund told me that on some lines a second-class ticket cost more than a first-class ticket.

For a country so advanced in many ways, I find it enormously irritating that the railways require 72 hours' notice for wheelchair use. Uppsala is one hour by train from Stockholm, and the chief ticket seller there wanted me to believe they needed three days to bring the external ramp from the capital. 'But I was barely in the country, let alone this city, three days ago. Did you expect me to ring all the way from Norrland, introduce myself and say which of the dozen or so daily trains I wanted to take from Uppsala to Stockholm tomorrow?' I asked, arms akimbo. To which she replied, 'Yes, that is what you should have done'.

Borrowing the muscle power of two willing passengers, I got on the train without any help from this hidebound hierarchy. But now the conductor looked apoplectic because there was no assigned place in the corridor. Did I realise that in the event of fire I would be in the way? he wanted to know. I thought of appealing to the Swedish sense of humour by saying that in that case I would throw myself clear of the carriage, even at the risk of ending up in a wheelchair – and then thought again.

Sveriges Järnväg (universally known as SJ) is efficient, I'll grant that. Any desire to assist passengers is bred out of its staff early. But Melissa is new to the service so she greets me from the platform, 'Welcome to Stockholm'. Not to worry, she will probably receive after-hours counselling for this unnatural outburst of friendliness. But she and her more taciturn colleague blanch when I mention that my small mountain of luggage and I are bound for the metro, or *tunnelbana*, whose main station, T-Centralen, is connected by an underground walkway.

Melissa explains that a different operator – Storstockholms Lokaltrafik – runs the *tunnelbana* and SJ employees have no insurance liability if they should have an accident on SL premises. I plead, I beg, I must still get from one platform to the other. Could she not accompany me to the platform where I will (again) ask passengers to get me on board?

As her still silent colleague slinks off, Melissa – clinging to the remnants of this old-fashioned notion that she is there to serve the travelling public – ignores her explicit rules of engagement and escorts me to the urinous lift for my onward journey. During our descent she declares, 'There are way too many rules'. Only last week her 'superior' called her into the office and 'told me off for helping a passenger'.

'What had you done?' I asked, horrified.

'I told a passenger, who had asked me for directions from the train station, how to get to the museum.'

'And what was wrong with that?'

'My supervisor said, "You're here to give assistance for train things, not for other things".'

This episode brings to mind Lyng Kolbein's caution about Swedes' 'Germanic' obedience to rules. Later this evening, at Zinkensdamm hostel – on Södermalm, one of the chain of islands that gives Stockholm so much of its charm – a receptionist who has dared to give me a towel for the shower after I responded coolly to the idea of renting it looks as though the sky may be about to fall in on him.

'No one will be hurt by your act of kindness,' I reassure him.

'I hope not,' he answers without conviction.

220–222 km

In Stockholm you're constantly aware of being surrounded by the silvery sea. Indelible memories of Gamla Stan (Old Town) are stored up. This is a densely touristed quarter but was also a vital port for that great commercial combine of medieval times, the Hanseatic League, where Sweden began its rise to Great Power status.

Outside the imposing Kungliga Slottet (Royal Palace) I see the Changing of the Guard, impressive as these routines always are. You keep looking for someone to put a leg out of line, or miss a beat, but they never do. I am poised to go inside the Nobelmuseet, to explore the history of those famous prizes, when a dull unease grows into a pounding headache, and I realise I'm not up to more sightseeing today. On the way back 'home', in the underground walkway between the train and metro stations, I see the most amazing sight this evening rush hour. In the centre of the broad tunnel a pony-tailed man in a business suit sits in the lotus position, eyes closed. No begging bowl, no placard. His silent statement speaks volumes: you can find peace amid the turmoil.

223 km

For 48 days I have pushed myself to the limits – personal ones, not just the Continent's – two hours a day in all weathers. In seven weeks I've gone almost 5500 km, the equivalent of a return journey across Australia from south to north and back. The speedometer says I've only been doing 2.396 km/h – 2.4 km/h – but my body overrides it and tells me I must slow down the best way it knows: by contracting a fever. My temperature shoots up to 40 °C, and there it will hover for the next five days.

225 km

This afternoon it begins to pour with rain (what else?). Though I'm not to know it, this will be the wettest summer on record in Europe north of the Alps. But my travel plans these days are affected more by my internal temperature than by external ones.

227 km

Hostel crowds and hotel patrons are worlds apart. Zinkensdamm provided a case in point, as my stay there coincided with that of visitors from several countries, in Sweden for Deaf Art Now, a convention of deaf cinematographers. It is a sub-genre of moviemaking I have never given much thought to – though I recall there was a hint of the latent power of deaf cinema in the part played by a member of the groom's party in *Four Weddings and a Funeral* – but I'm keen to learn about these unique artists' philosophies and insights.

My interviewees were a Frenchman and an American, and our conversations were conducted in writing. Jean Cedric Ménard, from the South of France but now domiciled in Réunion (lucky he), laughed at my opening jest that he wanted to bring back 'the silent era'.

'*Non*,' he wrote definitively, 'I am striving to translate the world of sound into something you can see.' Jean Cedric has been deaf since birth so I can scarcely imagine how he envisages 'the world of sound'. When this ambitious 31-year-old was a student at Paris' Ecole de Beaux Arts, he used to watch films in the company of *entendants* (those who could hear) who would interpret for him. But what he aspires to – and by all account achieves with *créations cinématiques* such as *Musique du Silence* – is very simple, moving and profound. He sums it up with a typically French sweeping statement, *'C'est l'art pour moi qui est la liberté d'exprimer'*. ('Art for me is freedom of expression.')

Wayne Betts Jnr, five years younger than Jean Cedric, grew up in Massachusetts and now lives in Hollywood. He first realised he wanted to be in films – behind the camera – when he found that 'instead of following the storyline I watched for the camerawork and editing technique'. His best work so far? 'A short film – *Vital Signs*. It's an experimental work to show that sign language is cinematic.'[8]

229 km

I have just one more destination to visit in Norway – its capital, Oslo – but the raging fever means I will miss most of its 'unmissable' sights. Damn! After an all-night bus journey I embrace the refuge of Haraldsheim hostel 4 km out of the city centre at seven in the morning under a louring sky. I resemble a pharmacy on wheels, feel like death but not so warmed up, and manage to sleep most of the day.

A receptionist at the hostel is proof that Europe attracts those who cannot live without the 'freedom of expression' so dear to Jean Cedric Ménard. Mohammed Abdelmaguid is a 60-year-old Egyptian journalist, clearly an intelligent and cultivated man. In August 1990 he interviewed Nelson Mandela. Today he lives in Oslo, a political refugee since something he wrote (he is coy about telling me what) offended President Hosni Mubarak. Living here lets him pursue his professional life without fear. Mohammed has a radio program, co-owns a bookshop and edits his own Arabic magazine.

Here is a 'European value' for those who doubt that such a thing exists. But does freedom of expression justify insulting someone's most cherished beliefs? The 'Danish cartoons' controversy shows that the right to disagree – as did many in Europe who opposed the decision to publish them – can be an even more revered value.

232 km

So what did I see of Oslo? Far too little. The fever has killed my plans to visit Munchmuseet (to see *The Scream*, of course, restored since being recovered after its infamous theft in 1994); the Kon-Tiki Museum established by Thor Heyerdahl; and, on Bygdøy peninsula, the Viking Ship Museum where I would have pursued my exploration of the Norse impact on Europe. Not to mention thwarted all hope of eating rollmop herring (but there will be compensation for that before this chapter is over).

I did get to wander round downtown and hop on a wonderfully accessible Oslo tram or two, so all was not lost.

On my way to the bus park, and thence to the west coast of Sweden, I remark how impressive Norway and Oslo are (they would be perfect if only this exorbitant nation could get its economy right). But taxi driver Simo, of Macedonian parentage, is no great fan. Echoing the judgement of my Iraqi barber, he dismisses it in a single line, 'Cold country, cold people'. He may be right or wrong about the people but just now he is in factual error about the country. One day last week, Oslo was Europe's hottest capital. Even today the temperature will soar into the low 20s. Now that's a Nordic heatwave.

233 km

At the height of the fever I was delirious, now I'm just confused. What is this here Gothenburg? Why do the English, and we, use the German name for a Swedish city being run by Swedes and which those who live there know as Göteborg? This is not the same as calling Roma Rome, or Moskva Moscow – old-established English names for foreign cities. If the idea is to remind us of the Goths, why not call the place Gotham City? It's not as though New York would object.

234 km

Janne, a lifelong resident of Gotham City, explains what that Norrland restaurateur meant when he called the Swedes mellow. They will go out of their way not to upset, alarm or disturb you, she tells me. But there are regional variations. 'We say, elsewhere in Sweden when you hear a tingle you know it's probably a little old lady on a bicycle. Here it means a 20 tonne train is bearing down on you and you must get off the track.'

Only a self-analytical Swede could lacerate her people in so disarming a manner as Jackie, a waitress in a local café, who tells me, 'We Swedes are known to be boring. Just last week I asked an American who has lived in Sweden for three years, "What were your first impressions after you'd arrived?" and he said, "Charming. Very charming. And then, after about a week, boring."'

236–237 km

The Storsjön monster may have got away from me but here in Gotham I have tracked the seldom sighted Swedish sense of humour to what is surely its last redoubt. Liseberg, which bills itself as 'Scandinavia's largest amusement park' and, even more ominously, 'the most fun in Scandinavia', will make the perfect place to hide. With three million visitors a year, the park obviously has something going for it – but does it leave them laughing?

The first attraction I come to is the Polketten, a circular wooden dance floor on which seniors do-si-do and sashay their way around, watched by a three-piece band, the Sven-Gunnars. Tricked out in traditional garb, the drummer, accordionist and frontman alternating on sax and clarinet play anything from polkas to Swedish folk music. But it's not them you come to see: quite literally, it's the floor show.

Most of the couples appear to be entering their third age or preparing to leave it. It's all too easy to believe that sweethearts who cooed to each other back in the 1930s or Forties 'Save the last dance for me' could be here tonight to fulfil their promise.

One couple are dressed up to the nines, he sporting once jet black, now silver-streaked, hair; she a frock featuring more floral creations than most botanical gardens. Now another couple whirl past. He is in a business suit, she in a black strapless number resembling a muumuu, most unbecoming an octogenarian.

Finally we see a matronly soul clasping her husband close, while his free hand clasps a metre-long tube of Toblerone. He doesn't want to lose her, or the chocolate, and why should he? *Strictly Ballroom* could not hope to emulate this spectacle in a hundred years. OK, I'm laughing – but, I notice, these curious mellow Swedes are not.

Before leaving the park, I stare at the Vertical Death Drop and try to estimate the G-force its squealing riders – clustered around this scary rotating maypole – endure as it accelerates groundwards only to wimp out with a slight bounce near the end of the plunge. Yes, I decide, I would survive that. Congratulating myself on giving the matter such mature consideration, I allow the ride operators to lift me into the Death Drop seat but by now it's too late for third thoughts. Anyway, as shrewd readers may have already guessed, I survive what was, in both senses of the word, a real rush.

243–244 km

On either side of the Kattegat – the body of water that separates Sweden from Denmark – I see a forest of white wind turbines. Symbolic of eco-conscious Europe, the wind turbine is one thing that unites these diverse peoples.

254 km

Skagen, the most northerly point of Denmark, pokes its straggly old finger, or rather its cuticle, between the Kattegat and Scandinavia's North Sea exit, the Skagerrak. With a puff of black smoke from the Sandorman tractor cabin we're off down the stony, sandy track that 2 km from here will bring us to the 'tip of the nail', Denmark's northern extremity, or – as the tourist information officer smugly puts it – 'the beginning of Europe'. She clearly couldn't care less what the barbarians over the northern and eastern horizons might think of that description.

There's something faintly Edwardian about watching a cluster of people gathered on a spit of land, huddling under umbrellas as they watch the two seas collide like sumo wrestlers.

255–262 km

Pushing back from the 'beginning of Europe' – a 7 km slog on a day when I will go a record distance, 12.9 km, under my own steam – I have no cover when the rain starts bucketing down. The further I go, the more I resemble a wet rat. When I get back to town I might take a bath to dry off, I am telling myself, when I run into a gentleman of 75 summers wearing a boater (never was headgear more aptly named).

After he introduces himself as a fellow Australian we lapse into small talk about my hometown (Melbourne) and his – although there is never really any small talk about Sydney. And, while musing on the legendary gulf separating those two fine metropolises, he delivers himself of the Wildean apothegm 'In Melbourne it's who you know; in Sydney it's who you are'.

Leading me, of course, to ask, Who is *he*? I suppose only the famous, or their relatives, can get away with dropping their own name. 'Shand Turnbull,' he answers. 'Malcolm keeps calling me Dad but I tell him we're not family.'

264 km

I've never before been in a country where bicycles have human rights. Today, my second day of train travel in Denmark, I have learnt the hard way what this means. On the Frederikshavn line four people boarded along with me and chained their bikes to the only available seats. Maas, the conductor, seeing I'm new to Denmark, explained before I could put my grievance into words, 'They reserve seats for their bikes, too'.

Nursing my grievance, I thought how odd it was to be a living, breathing, sapient being with my own set of wheels and a ticket yet forced to be a strap-hanger. Maas could read my mind. 'What do you want me to do?' he asked in exasperation. 'Throw them off?' He could decipher my answer by looking at my eyebrows raised in hope. At the risk of provoking him further, I pointed to the signs above the bicycles' seats, which mentioned that they were reserved for the users of prams or wheelchairs – but, significantly, not bikes. Unfazed, Maas had an answer for that, too. 'We can't put all the signs up.'

Another day, on another train, I was lucky enough to get a seat but foolish enough to lose it by popping into the 'disabled WC' for five minutes. When I returned, the proud usurper who had shackled his two-wheeler to my former spot proclaimed, 'In

Denmark our bicycles have seats'. I turned to the bike and muttered, 'I hope you're comfortable'. It seemed more productive to talk to the machine.

This nation is built to Toytown scale, whether you are talking residential streets or commercial precincts. It is, of course, utterly charming. At first glance there are not many differences between Sweden and Denmark – apart from that of scale just mentioned – and before long I begin to think of them almost as one country, call it Swedenmark. But that is not the view from within. The Danes are considered – by themselves and others – to be decidedly unmellow, in fact raucous in public, far more willing to give you their opinion unasked. They don't play their cards close to their chest; they put them all on the table.

274 km

Back in mid-May, somewhere in Russia, I saw on *BBC World News* an item about an initiative being undertaken by PEN, the international author-advocacy group, to create International Cities of Refuge for persecuted writers.

Such a move seemed brave but risky, worth two cheers. Was it going to invite daring assaults on writers who might have been safer out of the limelight? Would PEN provide round-the-clock bodyguards for selected scribes?

The TV report mentioned that one writer – Chinese dissident Jun Feng – had already been afforded this status, in Denmark. I wrote to the secretary of Danish PEN, who had been interviewed in the report, and she put me in touch with him. It seemed to me that one thing Europe stood for – as Jean Cedric Ménard would define it – was 'freedom of expression'. That Jun Feng agreed to meet me (when, let's face it, I could have been hired by his persecutors) demonstrated Europe's openness.

For fifteen years, Jun – a native of Shanghai – has lived in Odense, Denmark's second city. As the bus carrying me from Jutland pulls into the city terminus, there he is waiting for me. Bald-headed and clad in a cotton tunic, Jun – who still looks like the Buddhist monk he once was – cheerfully helps carry my bags. It doesn't take long for me to see that, for a writer who was once persecuted, he has a surprisingly ready laugh. Jun apologises for his English but, as you will see, has little need to do so. In any case, his thoughts are original.

Maybe you heard his name long ago. He opposed Beijing vociferously in a 1987 protest that was dwarfed in importance only by the bloodbath of Tiananmen Square two years later. If I had to pigeonhole Jun by his views, I would call him a libertarian, perhaps an anarchist. 'Beijing used the slogan "Democracy" but didn't know what it was,' he tells me at the terminus café. 'It is not just "majority decide". I think that if my girlfriend and me want to kiss and the majority say no, then fuck the majority.'

How Jun came to live in Denmark – from his house arrest through daring escapades in the east and south of China to his arrest and imprisonment in Laos – is all told with verve in his autobiography.[9]

United Nations intervention led to a demurely worded exile offer, Is it OK for you to go to Denmark? 'At that time I knew about Hans Christian Andersen and that was about it. Oh, and they had a queen. I thought, Such a big country! ... But I was thinking of Greenland, not Denmark.' (Infectious laughter.)

'In that time I thought I was an anti-communist. Now I realise I am an ethical communist. Being so, my first task is to fight against the party because they violate the communist ideals.' How they must wince in Beijing at such blasphemy.

What can he tell me about the Danes? 'They have a very distinctive sense of humour.' (See, there are differences within Swedenmark!) 'But it's always directed against other people. It has a sarcastic point. Danes have a high regard for individualism and personal autonomy. But sometimes I think Danes may be spoiled. They have a big reputation in the world; they forget that can also have a bad side.'

'Are you a European?' He laughs again. 'I'm a Danish Chinese. I don't think it's the same thing. Denmark can be very nationalistic; you don't meet many Europeans here.'

But has living in Europe inspired him to write any poems? Over our cappuccinos Jun replies by handing me a copy of the only verse he has had published in English, but he soon emails me another one written after comparing his old and new lives.

To Live in a Story

The cold air reflects an evening
In Shanghai or Nørrebro.
Broken instants and wisps of rain
An exchange of smiles between two strangers
Waiting for a bus.
I trace back my thought
To a hole
In which I once sat and lit a fire.
Yes, once I was a vagabond
And got help on the way here:
A forged passport, an invented name,
One more name.
The day becomes night.
My nostalgia for a home draws a picture of a journey,
A strange feeling beside the fire.
Barbed-wire fence and soldiers on the lookout.
Once I was an outlaw in a remote forest
And I said I was there to find a flower.
Still cold air
Which I dreamed about in my tropical youth;
Still cold air
In which I dream about my tropical youth.

279 km

I escape the driving rain by visiting the 'house' of Hans Christian Andersen, a museum for the past 99 years. This morning's weather is good for ducklings, ugly and otherwise. The only problem is, he probably didn't live here. His admirers made it all up, a fairytale.

Unafraid of being thought eccentric, Andersen was another Odense writer who was fiercely individualistic. An information board relates that, fearing he would suddenly fall victim to an epidemic, 'as a young man he would sometimes place a note on his bedside table that read, "I am apparently dead."'

One of the great travellers of his age, he was inspired by, and saw most of, Europe, making his 30th and final journey two years before his death. Audio readings are a highlight of any visit here.

One, by Sir John Gielgud, of *The Emperor's New Clothes,* reminds me how wonderfully subversive the fabulist's tales were, able to charm innocent children while packing a powerful satirical punch not lost on their elders.

When this bare-earth abode in the most squalid part of town was later identified as his birthplace, Andersen declared, 'I wasn't born in such a hovel'. Perhaps he had forgotten himself. For eight years earlier he had written in *The Ugly Duckling*, 'It doesn't matter about being born in a duckyard so long as you're hatched from a swan's egg'.

282 km

Hours ago, a distant family member, Steen Thomsen, greeted me at Copenhagen's central station (København H), and we caught buses out to his 'pad' in the suburbs. This evening we took in the music – a swing band – and the fireworks display provided every Saturday night at eleven o'clock in the city's world-famous Tivoli Gardens. A great way to say goodbye to one memorable month and hello to another.

284 km

1 July. 4.56 pm AEST. On Steen's PC I read an email from the True North. Mayoral candidate Marius Nilsen informs he has just been to Oslo with postmaster Oot Bjorn and Oot's two children to attend an Ozzie Osbourne concert. And then he writes,

'For me Oslo is a lot of women and partying. Mehamn is too small for me as coming mayor for these activities.'

Does he realise this stuff could be campaign dynamite if it fell into the wrong hands – his wife's? Apparently not, as he closes with an Arctic weather report.

'Today we have summer, 15 Celsius. Yesterday only 7°.'

285–289 km

Copenhagen is as delightful – or, to quote Danny Kaye, as 'wonderful, wonderful' – as it is said to be. Buskers, alleys, canals, boutiques. This city has all the features of which others have only some – and more. At 800 years of age, Old Square lives up to its name. War against England, from 1807–1814 – in which Denmark backed Napoleon and lost Norway to Sweden – was a turning point in the nation's history. The English bombed Copenhagen in the first year of that campaign, and Steen – full of that nationalism Jun mentioned – speaks with evident passion against the English because of it. Pointing out where a cannonball has been left lodged in a wall as a reminder of perfidious Albion, he says, 'We suffered the first terrorist attack of modern times' as if it happened only yesterday rather than two centuries ago.

Nevertheless he can be refreshingly realistic. Don't waste time going to Frihedsmuseet, a museum in honour of Danish wartime resistance, he cautions, 'There was actually very little resistance to the Nazi occupiers here, but of course they don't want you to know that'.

On our city tour he spies a statue of Admiral Niels Juel – one of his ancestors, he proudly points out, and victor of the Battle of Køge Bay in July 1677. Further along the harbourside I see another statue – this one more familiar than familial. But this one's a copy. Yes, you can visit Copenhagen and see *David* – if not in the marbled flesh, at least looking bronzed.

292–293 km

Johanne, our tour guide to Christiansborg Palace, reminds us that, before the EU came along, royalty did more to promote 'Europeanism' than any other body – if only because most of Europe was governed by members of the same extended royal family. (It didn't stop World War I, but let that pass ...)

'Most of the royal blood of Europe stems from a Dr Struensee who married our Mathilde and introduced reforms in Denmark but who was executed in the public square.' Now Johanne's tour is sounding like a potted history of revolution mixed in with a Hans Christian Andersen fairytale.

Speaking of literature, we pass through a room containing the royal library inherited by Australia's very own gift to Denmark, Tasmanian Princess Mary. Among the 10,000 books on display in the room, I point out to Johanne one whose golden-lettered spine caught my eye: *The Fall of a Throne*. Uneasy lies the head? It needn't: the Danes, along with Australian magazine publishers, adore Mary so she should treat that work as light fiction.

Even a practised speaker like Johanne admits to being awed by royalty. 'When I met the princess it was a Christmas reception and I thought I wouldn't be nervous,' she tells us. 'But suddenly I was number two in a line of four hundred people and somebody said, "You must tell your name and occupation when you meet Frederik and Mary." I gave the princess my hand and my voice disappeared. When I recovered it, all I could say, without thinking, was, "Hi, Mary." She was very gracious about it.' Now that's a Tasmanian upbringing for you.

302–304 km

Christiania, alias 'Freetown', entered the world as a 1970s hippie-style experiment in alternative living. Nearly 40 years on, Denmark's conservative Government has made no secret of the fact that it couldn't care less if the settlement died of natural causes.

In 1971 the 'alternatives' broke into a military barracks and declared it a zone of peace. They, or rather their spiritual (and in some cases biological) descendants, are still there despite a police raid in 2004 that cleared out dozens of drug dealers.

Seated on a step watching her granddaughter is Lene, an 'eternal child' of 60, her hair in golden plaits. She has been a resident here for 30 years, and her daughter Hellene (a.k.a. Liv) is visiting. It is her fifteen-month-old baby, Karl Anton, that Lene watches playing in the grass (no, not smoking it). 'My own mother thought I was mad,' Lene recalls. 'She only became reconciled to it when she came here after a few years and saw it for herself.'

The insistence on separateness can be taken to comical lengths. Leaving Christiania I pass under a sign that reads, 'You are now entering the EU'. Yet, outside the gates, the counter-culturalists have made their own contribution to the land where the bike is king. The Christiania bike is a three-wheeled pedal cart covered by a tarpaulin that protects small children, and groceries of all sizes, from the elements. Three yellow circles form the Christiania 'trademark' and I will encounter these bikes as far south as France. As Steen says with a wicked smile, it would be a great irony if 100 years from now the only relics to have survived the grand experiment of 'Freetown' peace and love were these 'material objects. They would hate that!'

312 km

On my last night in Scandinavia, Steen introduces me to the 'Danish cold table', a culinary ritual with protocol as exacting as the Changing of the Guard. As you might expect, it centres on that noble fish the herring. When our delicious meal was consumed, I asked Steen to email me the recipe. Whether the herring was soused I can't remember but we definitely were. 'The Danish *kold borde* is usually served at lunchtime. As a first course one will in all likelihood eat pickled herring (*marinerede sild*) or another herring dish. The most common herring is marinated either in a clear, sweet, peppery vinegar sauce (white herring) or in a red seasoned vinegar (red herring). It may also come in a variety of sour-cream-based sauces, including a curry sauce which is very popular. The white herring is typically served on buttered black rye bread, topped with white onion rings … and served with hard-boiled eggs and tomato slices … Herring is usually served with ice-cold snaps' – schnapps – 'which according to Danish tradition helps the fish swim down to the stomach. Also the high alcohol content of snaps helps dissolve the fat left in the oral cavity after eating the fish. This allows the lunch participant to more readily taste the different dishes. As a second course one will in all likelihood eat warm foods (*lune retter*) served on rye bread with accompaniments. Some typical warm foods would be: Frikadeller, Danish meatballs, the "national dish"; Danish sausage (*medisterpølse*); pork tenderloin (*mørbradbøf*) with sautéed onions and pickled [*sic*] slices (*surt*). Beer (in particular the Danish brands Tuborg, Carlsberg or Faxe) is the preferred beverage during this meal … It is also quite acceptable to have another shot or two of the akvavit along the way. Finally one is served a variety of cheese along with crackers or white bread. To the cheese there should be added another snaps. If the occasion is more informal and/or in the bosom of the family, there may well be more than two snapses during the lunch. In fact we have a saying, used when the outcome of something was too meagre. "It was like a formal lunch. There was too far between the snapses."'

Ditto the synapses, Steen. And cheers.

CHAPTER 4

The Past is a Foreign Country

COPENHAGEN, NYKØBING and BREMEN

Journey distance to date: 10,895 km

A straight line may or may not be the shortest distance between two points but no physical journey proceeds on straight lines alone. When undertaking a chronological journey – reaching into one's past, one's family's past or even a nation's history – obstructions, some of them mountainous, are bound to impede progress. It was between Denmark and northern Germany that my course across Europe intersected with a route of personal exploration I was always going to take one day. It was only a matter of time …

My mother – Marie Isabel Haley, née Watson – tells me she was born on 18 June 1928 – and, since she is not the sort of person given to lying, I believe her. To tell a family history, one must start with the first generation – not the first chronologically, but the nearest – so that is what I have done. Yet this chapter is not about her.

Marie's mother's name was Ruby Dagmar and her then husband, my mother's father, was Warren Watson, a Melbourne lawyer in the first half of last century. Ruby Dagmar, born into the family Dess – my favourite grandmother, who provided my first conscious memory as she peered over my cot when I must have been all of two – was born in Newtown, Sydney, on 23 November 1899. I will always remember her strong and doting presence. But this is not about her either.

This is a story that forms part of my own journey through Europe while standing as a journey in its own right; a story whose principal characters, Edward and Maud – great-grandparents whom I never knew – could have stepped, fully formed, from a novel. This is a story with the power to shock, and yet it remains a tale for all the family.

If 'the past is a foreign country',[10] the past in one's own land can be just as unfamiliar. But, then, you may have noticed my mother's mother – that loving grandmother who was known to a younger me as Ninny, later as Nin – had two names that would have sounded 'foreign' to those who knew her as a girl a century ago – Dagmar and Dess. Perhaps only her closest friends and some of her brothers and sisters would have known the family's true European origins. In those days it did not do to advertise the 'foreignness' of one's family.

Dagmar is a Danish name. Dess I couldn't place, but for years I assumed it to be Danish too, from the basic knowledge that my mother's mother's father hailed from Denmark. The young man who came to be known in his new country as Edward had been christened Johannes Carl Edvard Ludwig.

Edward marks a setting-off point in my second journey, from the 'known world' of the family hearth into the unknown world of the past over the horizons of time and space. And, although being in Copenhagen brings me closer to *his* first known world, the speed-ometer and diary, map and compass that have served me so well in today's Europe must be set aside for now I truly am entering a foreign country and must do things differently here myself.

How do I know that great-granddad Edward Dess arrived in Australia in 1871? His departure from Copenhagen is recorded in the Danish Emigration Archives, as his arrival is in the Queensland Archive, a statistical compendium of the day. Nin left a small scrap of paper in her belongings, later inserted in a family Bible, stating that in 1871 young Dess sailed on a ship, the *Shakespeare,* out of Copenhagen, bound for Australia.

Even with the light of research shone full on him, he seems much more ghost than man of flesh. It is easier to say what did not induce the move. He does not bring the taint of criminality with him. We have no evidence he ever visited Great Britain but, even if he had done so and run foul of the law there, the use of Australia as a dumping ground for convicts had come to an end in 1868, three years before he set sail.

As I prepared my itinerary for Europe, the prospect of coming to Denmark, land of Edward's birth, spurred me into action. It gave an outlet to my latent curiosity about this relative of whom I knew almost nothing except that he and wife Maud conceived my grandmother, Nin, in 1899, three decades before dying in Melbourne at age 75.

That outlet did not exist solely because I was in the city my great-grandfather had left, never to return to Europe, but because it was the hometown of someone I believed to be a fifth cousin – the admirable Steen.[11]

Steen Thomsen looks nothing like me. He has a glint in his eye and a rough beard. But his personal traits, a wicked sense of humour and an irreverent regard for conventional authority, are not dissimilar to mine. Yet none of this is evident at first sight.

Steen, 58, had devoted countless hours to the history of the Bendixsen clan, which he had explored right back to AD 1225. While I was about to delve into my own piece of European history, he had long since unearthed his own. Proudly he 'introduced' me to Dethlef Thomsen, who had made a fortune in the salmon trade before drowning off the Icelandic coast during a fierce Atlantic storm in 1854, exactly a century before my birth.

At only 21 his son, Hans Theodor August, took over the business and became the most successful merchant in Iceland before his death in 1899, the same year that Ruby Dagmar, Nin, was born half a world away. A grandson of his – Steen's father – was practising as a lawyer in Reykjavik during the 1940s, at precisely the same time Warren Watson, my mother's father, was doing so in Melbourne. Each of them died at the age of 80. These are hardly notable coincidences, but I have included them here in honour of Steen, who – as students of the Danish 'cold table' will already be aware – is a world authority on the red herring.

So what more was there to know about young Edward Dess, the immigrant from Denmark who was the first Australian of his clan? Research by an interested cousin had established that he was born in February 1854, and grew up, in the small Danish city of Nykøbing, across the sea from Germany – that Edward came from a 'broken home' and by the age of six was living in an all-female household with his grandmother, an aunt and his mother, Thora, who would have found a place in any of Dickens's earlier novels.

Further research by Steen reveals that – nine years before she gave birth to my great-grandfather – Thora, along with her parents and siblings, was consigned to a poorhouse, their living quarters shared with more than 30 strangers. This serves as a reminder that for millions at any time the reality of Europe has never yet squared with the ideal of Europia.

By 1855 – a year after Thora gives birth to Edward – she is registered as living in Nykøbing. Edward's father, Carl Eduard, shows no sign of marrying her and, now I learn, is not himself Danish but an immigrant from the German Free State of Bremen, to which he has returned after fathering my half German, half Danish great-grandparent.

This revelation will prove of great significance for my search. But first my imaginative sympathy goes out to poor Edward. At six he doesn't know his own father. *What have they told you? That he is dead*? He is certainly dead to Thora – but still alive across the sea.

In August 1861, *when you were seven, Edward*, in Bremen – 300 km away in a foreign land – Carl Eduard, occupation cigar maker, is registered as the father of baby Elisabeth Henriette Dess by at least the third woman in his life.

Carl Eduard Dess will not be buried in Bremen's cemetery, Walle Friedhof. After 1861 we hear no more of him, but, as we shall see, there are more skeletons in closets than in graveyards.

One of his son's fellow passengers aboard the *Shakespeare* a decade later was Olga, a woman in her mid-20s. They may or may not have had a shipboard romance; at any event, they did marry the following year, 1872. Sometime after the birth of their fourth child, in 1880, it seems Edward up and left. Like father, like son …

Somewhere in Sydney, we cannot know exactly where or when, a new arrival in the Antipodes – Maud Green from central London – caught Edward's roving eye, thus beginning a liaison that would shape the rest of his life and hers. Beginning in 1889, Maud would bear him thirteen (and, if family rumour of an unnamed twin is right, fourteen) children over a 27-year period, the eighth of whom was Ruby, my Nin. Counting the children Maud bore Edward, altogether the man fathered seventeen, and probably eighteen, children by two women.

Another thing we will never know is whether Edward felt any shame at the consequences of his philandering but, three years before his death, he actually married Maud. My genealogically inquisitive cousin was referring to the fact that, at one time a successful tailor, he was eventually declared bankrupt when she said, 'He was a bit of a gambler'. She could equally have been alluding to his love life.

Armed with this new mine of family information, I sit at Steen's computer in suburban Copenhagen and wonder, if Desses still live in Bremen, which is on the next leg of my European trip, whether and how I can bridge the gap between me and my unmet German family. It's time to do some research of my own …

July 2007, Friday the 13th, is an overcast day so typical of this 'wettest summer'. From the stop opposite Bremen Hauptbahnhof (central station) I take the tram out to Walle Friedhof. I am ready to meet the family – the ones, at least, who stayed behind in Europe.

Walle Friedhof (Friedhof literally means 'place of peace') is congested nowadays. Bremen – with half a million living inhabitants – is not such a big city, but it has been renowned throughout Germany since medieval times as a freethinking, independent and prosperous one, qualities that always encouraged people to settle there. Today I find it a pleasant and compact place, as well as a peaceful one – and it is a strange sensation to realise that I feel very much at home here. If this were my hometown, I tell myself, I could imagine not wanting to leave. Several of the family obviously felt the same: their earthly remains are to be found beneath the Friedhof greensward.

Entering the reception area (whose walls are painted a cheerful yellow) I greet the recordkeeper, Sonja Pierach, who is seated between a vellum-bound tome and her computer. Frau Pierach's database lists all the cemetery plots and she looks keen to help but speaks no English. I cannot come all this way and not press my quest so I wait, hoping for someone to turn up who can act as interlocutor.

Not only is the next person through the door an anglophone

but he puts the business that brought him here aside long enough to explain to Frau Pierach that I come from Australia and am descended from the Dess family, several members of which lived and died in Bremen. She pledges to do her best and quickly traces a couple of promising leads from the desk register. A few weeks later, the post brings me fresh tidings. As the haze that had enveloped this part of Europe linked with my people's past begins to lift, I find the Old Country beginning to look less foreign.

Frau Pierach's mini-dossier mentions four family members – a husband and wife, their son and his son. All will survive into old age. Johann Eberhard Dess was born in March 1880 and died, two months after turning 80, in May 1960. His wife, Marie – my mother's name, but surely that's coincidence? – survived him by six years. Their son Eberhard – born on 27 April 1900 – died on 7 August 1973.

As anyone who has investigated family history will know, there comes a point, usually a handful of generations back, when documentation must give way to intelligent guesswork. The period between Carl Eduard's 1851 marriage in Bremen and Johann Eberhard's birth (in 1880) spanned a complete generation. Carl Eduard, he who had abandoned Thora, my great-grandfather's mother, in Denmark, took a second Bremen bride in 1861. There is a real, old-time generation gap here – a missing link in the family chain – and Frau Pierach's researches do not quite cover it. Perhaps, I surmise, Carl Eduard's Bremen wives produced sons whose descendants live in the city today?

Before I leave, Frau Pierach – her words translated by my English-speaking friend – offers a sobering caution against getting my hopes too high. 'When the living stop coming,' she explains, 'it is not long before the plots are recycled.'

If there's one thing more common in these parts than cycling, I have observed, it's recycling. The German love of efficiency and tidiness is legendary – *Ordnung muss sein* (Order must be) – and, when you think about it, there is no reason why such a cold passion should stop this side of the grave.

While still in Copenhagen, aided by Steen, my search for living family in Bremen had made good progress. Today the phone numbers of most people, at least in the West, are a few mouse clicks away, provided you know how to go about it. In the German White Pages, I quickly found a list of eight Desses living within 10 km of the city centre, and began ringing them.

No luck at first. Two of the eight people I phoned spoke English but knew of no family connection with a Carl Eduard. But then I expanded the search to include Desses living within 25 km of town, and immediately scored a bullseye. The first name on my list was Birgit Dess, who took my call, speaks English and wasn't in the least daunted by our being lifelong strangers. Her father, Jürgen, had looked into the family history and she thought, from everything I'd mentioned, that we must be related. But I would have to wait for certainty because he and her mother were on a cruise ship right now. 'Where?' I asked idly. 'Off the coast of Norway.' A few weeks earlier, and we could have passed each other on the deck of a Hurtigruten steamer. My laugh reverberated down the line – and was that a ghostly echo coming back my way?

Next time we speak, Birgit has told them about my call and she has news for me. Yes, indeed, her grandfather Eberhard was the grandson of Carl Eduard, cigar maker of Bremen. Eureka! So Carl Eduard, grandfather to my Nin, Ruby Dagmar, was also the grandfather of Birgit Dess's grandpa Eberhard. Suddenly the sprawling Dess family tree seems more like a stepped pyramid, with Birgit and me on the same level. Collateral cousins, we find ourselves just around the corner.

We arrange to meet in Bremen, near the station, on the evening of 10 July. Steen has accompanied me to Hamburg, where we stay for a few days, but – pleading non-cousinship – returns to Copenhagen while I press on.

Birgit Dess is a young 39 and single by choice. She does not drive a car, and from the very first strikes me as smart, friendly without fawning, fun-loving but also capable of being businesslike. Born at the end of 1967 in Osterholz Scharmbeck, a small community near Bremen, she is amused at my suggestion that she is better settled here than anyone outside Walle Friedhof.

Birgit has a steady job as a secretary to someone in aviation. Very German in her modest manner, she says, 'I never wanted to be a secretary. But I knew English and French. My American friends would say that I didn't have the balls to do something with my degree.' We laugh. She is very forthcoming, an easy person to warm to.

Her early life Birgit dismisses as nothing remarkable but I find one of her first jobs fascinating. Having helped out over the years in her parents' tea shop, she was once employed as an apprentice tea taster. 'You have an inquiry from your customer. He wants to replace last year's order with this year's, not only the quantity but availability and quality. You try to find the right variety or blend from, let us say, the crop of 2000 in a certain area of Assam.

'So you could say I'm a tea connoisseur, just like a professional wine taster.' And does she spend her leisure hours sipping tea? 'Not exactly. I would love my life to be painting, creating things. The father of one of the ladies who married my great-grandfather was like that – a painter.'

This statement is full of insight. Her phrase 'one of the ladies' tells me that the Dess men's aversion to monogamy extended to yet another of Carl Eduard's sons, confirming that this behaviour pattern in the male line is global in more than one sense. Europe and Australia, at least, are not nearly far enough apart to disrupt it.

Birgit has brought along a certificate that belonged to her grandfather. It is not, as I might have expected, his death certificate from 1973, but one issued by the Bremen civic authorities in 1934 – No. 1636 – signed by President Paul von Hindenburg, no less, in the year of his death. Under the capitalised preamble IN THE NAME OF THE FÜHRER AND THE REICH CHANCELLOR, it awards Eberhard Dess an Honourable Cross 'for being a participant in the remembrance of the War' pursuant to the 13 July general decree of that year.

In Germany 1934 was a year of consolidating Nazi power through mass rallies and other public manifestations of enthusiasm for the new regime. So it seems a fair assumption that Herr Eberhard Dess – my cousin's grandfather – was a zealous Hitlerite. But there was an odd exception to his German nationalism. When I ask Birgit why her given name is Danish, rather than the German variant, Birgitta, she smiles. 'He was the one who insisted over my mother's wishes.' Thinking about it later, I conclude that this could have been done in recognition of his own grandfather, Carl Eduard, the German who went to live in Denmark.

Her other grandfather, Birgit tells me, was a submarine commander during World War II. Is she trying to shock me? No, she is telling me how things were. By this time we have trudged so far over the territory of the past that the future seems more enticing. Tell me who you would like to be, I ask Birgit, and she answers, 'I would love to be a wine-drinking nocturnal painter'. Stupidly I ask, 'When would you sleep?' and she replies, 'The days'. Then adds, 'Picasso lived this way; Hemingway lived this way, didn't he?'

Yes, I reply, in 1920s Paris Hemingway was a night owl known to down five or six glasses of red wine at a single sitting.[12] 'But this is a bad example,' comes her rejoinder. 'He had four or five wives and he treated each one of them badly.' (Right on both counts. But she didn't need to go beyond our family to find such examples.)

Afterwards I will examine my feelings at discovering that someone in the extended family was a Nazi military commander – and, while it is briefly unsettling, my attitude is ultimately the same as it is to Edward Dess, my prolific great-grandfather.

Both are members of the family from which I claim descent.

To be so widespread, a tree must have deep roots, intertwining branches and many a shady nook. It may be given to those who come later to know more but that doesn't necessarily make us entitled to judge. For the rest of eternity, Edward, like all those who no longer have to plead their case, has the right to remain silent.

My long journey has now taken me to the centre and the periphery of the Desses' 'known world'. The descending branches of the family tree that sprouted from the union of Edward and Maud are entangled in a thicket of desertion and infidelity, one in which Edward might easily stand condemned. But consider his actions in their context – the stigma of poverty attaching to his mother's family, the lack of a responsible father figure – and his falling for a much younger woman becomes at least comprehensible.

It should not be overlooked that Maud had her own story to tell, and what a tremendous love story that was. Still in her teens, Maud fell for this dapper older man who became her lover and to whom she bore fourteen children. This was a strong and abiding love – for the rest of her long life she presided over this growing brood of theirs, enduring, no doubt, a double alienation: her common-law husband's as an Australian with a recognisably 'foreign' surname –

a German one being an unpopular thing to have after 1914 – and their shared alienation from the standards of conventional morality.

Gaze on her, again, through what historian Manning Clark called 'the eye of pity'. Her looks must have been striking. And, for someone her age, she must have had a steely resolve that she would need to withstand every adversity in the decades ahead. Mum remembers that 'Grandma Maud' spent her last years in a wheelchair – a sidelight I find of more than passing interest – but that even the amputation of a leg didn't stop her getting about. Maud, my mother's mother's mother, died in 1955, when I was just a year old. She was 86 – and only now, for the first time in my life, do I have a clear picture of her.

This journey within a journey – this voyage around my great-grandfather – may have struck you as a gigantic detour, but I did set out to tell you about the people I would meet in Europe and, with so many family secrets now laid bare, it should surprise no one that I've made one last discovery. Part Viking, part Germanic, I am at core a European too.

CHAPTER 5

Fellatio at Eleven

HAMBURG, BREMEN and the NETHERLANDS

Time spent:	28 days
Distance covered:	1929 km
Distance pushed:	231.2 km
Average speed:	2.554 km/h
Journey distance to date:	12,186 km

Soon after my Dutch sister-in-law arrived in Australia, I recall going for a spin down the Mornington peninsula one Sunday afternoon, my brother at the wheel. Els, looking out of the window at bucolic scenes reminiscent of those in her own land, asked nervously, 'Where does it end?' I think we had clocked up as many kilometres on that outing as she would normally have covered on annual holidays back home.

The Dutch are acutely aware of the 'littleness' of their land. As they are wont to say, 'God created the Dutch, and the Dutch created Holland'. This is no blasphemy: *polders* built after the disastrous floods of 1953 extended the man-made segment of the Netherlands into the North Sea.

A personal statistic also illustrates the point. Whereas on this journey across the vast spaces of Russia and Scandinavia I had travelled 32 times as far on public transport as I had pushed my chair, the corresponding ratio in the Netherlands was just 6 km by public transport for every kilometre covered by my modest muscle power.

Not simply land-starved but the most densely packed of peoples, the Dutch have come close to perfecting the art of living together (even though they may have reached the limits of tolerance). They have achieved this not by retreating into private, high-walled worlds like their distant cousins the Afrikaners but by a sometimes confronting openness. One of the most striking sights for a visitor is the clear view afforded into people's living rooms, kitchens and, occasionally, bedrooms. There are exceptions. An old acquaintance, Hans Binnerts of Eindhoven, whom you will meet later in this chapter, waxes indignant on this point, declaring, 'I refuse to live in a showroom'. But he's in a decided minority. Shades and blinds are hung in perhaps 10 per cent of homes. How drapers make a living in this country is beyond my comprehension.

The family quest that took me to Bremen did not consume all my time there. One cannot overlook that city or Hamburg, which lay in my path to the Netherlands. Seeing them both whetted my appetite for more of Germany the following month.

317 km

In the breakfast room at the Hamburg Astoria – a cheap hotel in a seedy, drug-flooded and otherwise colourful quarter of the city – I chat with two Adelaide blokes (Paul and Reno) who are members of a heavy metal band, Raven Black Night. They're in town to play at Headbangers Ballroom, the latest incarnation of the Kaiserkeller, where the Beatles honed their act back in the early Sixties. Raven Black Night have won a $10,000 grant from Canberra (which they had to apply for three times, Paul informed me with a slight trace of hurt in his voice) 'to promote Australian music in Germany'.

I find it amusing that Paul went to bed last night rather than walk around town because 'it looks a bit dodgy'. Perhaps I'm just not used to the concept of a wimpish death-metal artiste.

318–321 km

This morning Steen and I conduct our own city tour, taking in an hour-long cruise along the Elbe, the canals and docklands of Hamburg, which for the past 30 years has boasted of being the world's busiest port. Only a fraction of this city, Steen reminds me, survived Operation Gomorrah, the 1943 Allied firebombing campaign. The first monument we come to – the solitary charred tower of St Nikolai Memorial Church – makes no attempt to disguise the fact. But amid the sombre dedication to the 'Victims of War and Persecution 1933–45' we find the acerbic observation that this church was originally built between 1845 and 1874 'from plans by Sir George Gilbert Scott, London'.

Steen gives me wonderful, but belated, advice as we sip coffees opposite St Michael's Church, where a son of J.S. Bach was music director for half a century and is buried. 'Norwegian is very easy to speak. You just take Danish and pronounce it in Swedish.' I must try to remember …

At the excellent Hamburger Kunsthalle (Hamburg Art Museum), I see the work of German expressionist Max Liebermann for the first time, as well as magnificent altarpieces dating from 1424 in a near-perfect state of preservation. And not only dyslexics will be interested to know whether you can find Dog in church. In one gallery here, I happen upon the works of more than one Dutch master who depicted dogs free to roam inside Reformation churches.

337 km

I see Nadezhda, the hotel receptionist from Archangelsk who gave me her guardian angel icon to watch over my travels, has sent a charming reply to my latest email, in which she says I'm lucky to be able to travel and meet so many nice people – amen to that – before adding, 'What is your next destiny?'

344 km

At Bremen youth hostel, overlooking the River Spree, I meet a history teacher about to take his secondary-school charges to Beck's Brewery for the day. Unfortunately, they lacked time to visit the World Heritage Listed city hall (Rathaus), a 600-year-old wooden structure – but the school is to be congratulated on designing a curriculum that will appeal to students far more.

358–359 km

Back to Hamburg to experience Friday night on the Reeperbahn, Hamburg's famous sex strip. To get there I had to slalom between some of the 20,000 Harley Davidsons parked in St Pauli district for a 'convention'. I settled down to dinner at a pavement café when a street fight exploded on the other side of the square. That didn't put me off my meal – although the waiter's attempt to add €5 to the advertised cost did – but half an hour later, as I wandered down a side street, seeing a busty blonde give a customer a blow job inside a caravan with the door wide open did interfere somewhat with my digestion.

Still, you've got to laugh. A music artist who plays in a bar just off the Reeperbahn bills himself as Jake the Rapper. (Really, you'd think Jake's agent would know how to spell Reeper even if *he* didn't.)

Outside German railway stations it may be hard to avoid being accosted by ageing skinhead beggars with pit bull terriers to support. But inside – by delightful contrast with Sweden and Denmark – service staff have repeatedly shown they need no more than ten minutes' notice of my wish to travel and they will have a ramp at the ready. They even radio ahead to ensure one is waiting at my next destiny.

366 km

Events today go partway to demolishing the myth of German efficiency, which Germans themselves boast of. In the cosmic scale of things, I was due to incur a loss after yesterday's moment of elation on finding that – three days after I had left my sportsbag and suitcase in the left-luggage locker at Hamburg Central Station – my missing passport had indeed slipped inside the case, averting a laborious and costly trip to The Hague for a replacement (not to mention saving my irreplaceable visa stamp from Hell).

Today, five minutes out of Hamburg en route back to Bremen, I rummage in the hood of my rucksack and find key No. 1429 to the left-luggage lockers. Fifteen minutes earlier, unable to find it when necessary, I had forked out €21 as a penalty. Now placing my hope on logic – normally a safe bet in Germany – and buoyed by the statement of the conductor, Oliver ('I think you will get your money back'), it came as a crushing blow when Hamburg's left-luggage office refused to let Bremen's give me the €21 back in return for the key. My argument, that Die Bahn was a national rail network, cut no ice with Herr Timpe at the Bremen service desk, who eventually lost his temper, screaming at me 'Empty!' (which was puzzling, but it turned out he meant 'Enough!') after delivering the official ruling that €21 was actually the cost of turning the master key in the lock. *Ordnung muss sein.*

367–372 km

Further disappointment awaited me in Amsterdam, where the internal staircase warren at Bob's Youth Hostel, at which I had booked, made it impracticable to stay there. Travelling on a budget for several months, I had vowed not to pay more than €40 for a bed, but a major European capital thronged by tourists on a Saturday night in summer made this seem a personal commitment to the impossible.

'High season' is a comic phrase in a city wreathed in cannabis smoke but after six hours of searching I was ready to act on the suggestion of a sympathetic receptionist at Bob's that I head for the outskirts of town. He suggested I take the 357 night bus to Gaasperplas where right opposite the station I would find a hotel, one of a French chain, that might not be too expensive. At nearly 1.30 am I wheeled into the hotel, only to learn that price was no consideration: it was fully booked. Mercifully, the receptionist allowed me to slink into an armchair in front of the soundless TV, until dawn if necessary. About 4 am he tapped me on the shoulder. One of the guests had left early and, since the room was already paid for, I could sleep there – if I didn't mind an unmade bed.

Next day the hotel manager took compassion on the weary traveller, and as my itinerary allowed nearly two weeks for Amsterdam we struck a deal I could afford. It dawned on me that I couldn't have done better had I known what I was doing. Gaasperplas is 22 minutes from Centraal by high-speed suburban train; day and week passes are economical; and it adjoins extensive parkland with attractive lakes so the stresses of the city are balanced by a rustic ... well, I'm not a real-estate salesman but you get the picture.

391–393 km

Haarlem is 17 km from Amsterdam – far enough, by Dutch standards, to warrant an overnight stop. The bus driver drops me 200 metres from the accessible hostel (this time I checked) but the bus has gone by the time I realise that the bus ramp has deposited me on a high-kerbed traffic island – and, now the heavens burst open, it becomes a traffic island surrounded by rising water. Adrenalin kicks in and I leapfrog onto the road. A minute later I am indoors, soaking wet but safe from the wildest weather of the journey to date.

The leaning tower of St Bavo's Great Church has long dominated the town's skyline. From the church noticeboard I see that during World War I more than a million Flemish came to the neutral Netherlands when Belgium was overrun. Better Flemings than lemmings, I suppose.

Call me superstitious but normally I loathe wheeling over graves. Inside St Bavo's, though, with fifteen centuries' worth of inscribed flagstones, the practice is unavoidable. Curiously, there is also a chapel – set aside for 'dog-hitters' – known as *honderslagerskapel*. The dog-hitter was a 17th-century Dutch officer authorised to confiscate and smite any hound found in church. This runs counter to the clear message from those Dutch masters I saw in the Hamburger Kunsthalle that dogs were acceptable here, presumably provided they were house (of God) trained.

400 km

18 July. 1.42 am AEST. A second email from the aspiring Mayor of Gamvik graces my inbox. Keen to know how his campaign fares, my eyes dart across the screen.

'Hi Ken. The sun is shining and everything is Well. I have just arrived home after a weekend in Sweden. Me and two of my friends did drive to a car dragshow in this town. It's 950 km one way … It was lots of fast cars to watch, and lots of drinking. Only one thing was wrong, it was only young girls at about twenty years old at the camping. We are drinking. But is OK, it's not home … Marius.'

You'll have noted that the modern politician has trouble concealing his Viking origins – which is not to rule out a conquest come September's poll.

411 km

21 July. 1.01 am European summer time.

Even before midnight the pavements of Spuistraat, in Amsterdam's bibliophiliac heart, had vanished beneath a long queue stretching from the mouth of Waterstone's bookshop up to Damrak before snaking round to the right and ending halfway round the block. Tonight is Harry Potter's last bookstand – and his Dutch fans are out in force. Three metres above the road stride witches on stilts hired by the bookshop to add authenticity – and a touch of scariness – to the event. 'Go home, muggles,' they scowl at us. Muggles will, eventually – they always do – but not until well past the witching hour.

Twelve-year-old Julia, two streets away, sports a black cape, painted cat's whiskers and a broomstick. 'She's a good witch,' her father assures me as Julia sweeps into a nearby café. Perhaps she's more of a partygoer than a reader. Many in the throng are older – late teens, twentysomethings – soon-to-be ex-kids just mad about Harry.

Down the road the American Book Depot, not to be outdone, has laid in 3000 copies. Selling them all tonight would be the greatest disappearing trick in the history of magic, but they are going to try.

J.K. Rowling has added a dollop of morbid excitement to the occasion by revealing that one of the characters in this series finale perishes. 'Who should die?' I ask the throng corralled outside Waterstone's window. Voldemort, they chorus. How worthy, eliminating the incarnation of evil. But that would be too neat, wouldn't it? What about Dumbledore? I suggest. The mob pounces upon my ignorance. 'Oh my God,' a middle-aged man gasps, as if I had suggested skewering a black cat. 'Don't you know? He died in No. 6.'

At the appointed minute the front door swings open, and Elian, aged eleven – at the head of the queue since early afternoon – receives his prize. He says excitedly, 'I won't sleep tonight. I'm going to read the *Deathly Hallows* right through until whatever time it takes – five or six o'clock tonight.' When you've just read all six of its predecessors in a week, as Elian has, sleep must seem a dreadful waste of time.

419 km

24 July. 19.25 pm AEST. Six weeks before election day, democracy continues to grip the minds of Europe's most northerly inhabitants.

> Hi Ken. We had a great party on Saturday evening, with a good band and lots to drink. Today we had an open day for all at the airport. You were invited to drive firetruck, ambulance and police car. I was testing my car but I had too much speed and almost drived out of the runway. Marius.

421 km

At 26, unemployed and broke, Vincent Van Gogh decided to become an artist, 'to leave humanity a certain souvenir – to express genuine human feeling'. Who could dispute that, in terms of the goal he set himself, Van Gogh was an unqualified success?

In a single decade – his only decade – of artistic activity, he produced 900 paintings, 1100 drawings and 800 letters, many of which are on display at the Amsterdam museum named after him. Van Gogh's well-known tragic life provides a stark counterpoint to the sunny colours he brought to the world from the South of France and a teeming brain. If only he had stayed here in the Netherlands, tulips would now be worth €20 million a bunch, I think, but the world would hardly be raving about the creator of *The Potato Eaters*, a dark study of northern Dutch peasants badly received in its day but now an exemplar of Vincent's worldview 'before he saw the light'.

In 1887, living in Paris, Van Gogh's work 'explodes with light'. To art lovers who worship at his shrine, the *Self-portrait* of that year, with his yellow broad-brimmed hat, is almost iconic. In '88 Vincent moves to Arles in the South and everything changes. In *The Bedroom* he displays his most vivid application of colour yet, in such a homely scene. The work ripples with humour – other paintings of his are hung on the bedroom wall – and with irony (he wanted to denote rest and sleep, and used the most lurid colours imaginable, yet the bed draws you in so that you *can* imagine resting there). Obviously, I am not the only visitor so affected. Even while standing before *Sunflowers* a young American woman utters the memorable line, 'I can't take my eyes off *The Bedroom*'.

Then you see *The Harvest*, also from Arles in '88, so uplifting I can imagine it having the same effect as Tolstoy's championing of harvest-gathering in *War and Peace*. It makes you want to pick up a hoe or rake and get stuck in. And yes, each work is signed, simply, Vincent.

Van Gogh and Paul Gauguin were too headstrong to work together. Gauguin left Arles at the end of 1889, after heated arguments and the famous incident in which Vincent cut off – no, not his ear, you see how a legend grows – part of his left earlobe.

We move towards the end with a sense of sad inevitability.

A painting by Gauguin of Van Gogh painting sunflowers in December 1889 sets me wondering whether it was a row over this that broadened into a more dramatic rupture. Vincent was a stickler for painting from observation, and in France there are no sunflowers in December.

After his move north to Auvers-sur-Oise in 1890, Van Gogh became convinced of his waning artistic powers. 'I feel like a failure,' he wrote. 'I feel as though *this is my fate and that it will no longer change*.' (My emphasis.) It is this last aspect – the feeling that a road of intolerable suffering will have no turning – that can will a potential suicide to active self-destruction.

425 km

Growing up in Macao, Gordon – a man so private he will not tell me his real surname – was 'raised with cats', so when *Poezenboot*, the Cat Boat founded by an Amsterdam woman in 1966, advertised for someone to act as principal minder to a floating population of felines, he applied straightaway. Inside the barge, moored at Singel Canal to circumvent the city laws against keeping multiple moggies, you can find Gordon's Wall of Fame, a photo album comprising his pet loves. The rest of the space is taken up by … the pet loves themselves.

434 km

I could not see the bulk of Rembrandthuis without organising a lifting party that would only have distracted other visitors from the enjoyment of their time here. Never mind, there is much to see in the accessible part. The great painter and etcher lived here from 1639 – when he bought this house on Jodenbreestraat at the height of his fame – until 1658 when it, and everything of value in it, were sold at auction to pay off debts after he had been declared bankrupt. Like his compatriot Van Gogh, Harmensz van Rijn Rembrandt was a textbook case of an artist not appreciated – and hopelessly under-remunerated – in his own lifetime. The estate of his principal creditor, Christoffel Thiesz, dominates his 1651 etching of Haarlem, with St Bavo's Great Church shown at left. It is natural to assume he produced this work in a desperate attempt to propitiate the man.

440 km

Sign at the Happy Inn laundrette on Warmoestraat, 'Yes. The washer starts with a spinning. It's a part of the process. Don't worry.' I love Dutch signs. They make the routine sound like a branch of philosophy. I suppose this even applies to one in black paint on white canvas at Koningsplein, hanging from what looks like a bank converted into a squat. It reads, IK STUDEER KRAAK (I STUDY COCAINE).

443 km

Exactly two weeks after it opened, I visit Openbare Bibliotheek, the grand new national library opposite a floating Chinese restaurant. Featured attractions are free books, free Internet (and unlimited access to it: no one will come round to kick you off even if you spend ten hours at a terminal) and free music. Inside the entrance is a piano for the use of anyone who cares to play it. In the few hours I am there not one child of three is allowed to clunk all over it, not one adult whose playing skills peaked with *Chopsticks* dares to show off his or her talentlessness. On the contrary, we are treated to thoughtful, well-executed pieces from the pop and classical repertoires. Sheer delight.

448 km

Where else could this be but in Amsterdam? Here we are at the Hash, Marijuana and Hemp Museum. They also call it asa, bhang, cañamo, chanure, dagga, ganja, hanf, hemp, hennef, kannabis, konoroli, marijuana, qinnab and ta ma. Take your pick of the crop.

A series of still photos is enticingly titled PLANT SEX. The banner headline seems a trifle sensationalist. *They've been doing it for a long time*, I think, and find immediate confirmation with a quotation from Shen Nang, a Han Dynasty official who opined back in 3727 BC, '*Ta ma* is one of the superior elixirs for health'.

In 1994, we are told, the Netherlands resumed cultivation of industrial hemp and since then 'more than 100 countries have followed suit'. (I find this improbable, but then my critical faculties are still intact, maybe because I haven't done much inhaling lately.) Tolerance has been state policy on 'soft drugs' since 1976. Coffee shops have sprouted across the city. In some of them you can even buy coffee.

Outside a display room of hydroponic plants that are forced to floracate under constant fanning and bright lights, my eye is caught by a newspaper article about Eagle Bill, a Cherokee 'half hippie, half rocker' who moved to Amsterdam in the Seventies and praises the health benefits of a superior bong known as a Vaporiser™. The first time Eagle Bill was busted, poetic justice saved him. The cops apparently succumbed to temptation and from the whole crop not a single lab sample remained, so 'the charges were dropped due to a lack of evidence'. E.B. insists, 'This plant has done so much for me, and I want to do everything for it. It's given me everything in the world that I've ever wanted'. (Has Eagle Bill been having plant sex too? I can't wait to ask him.)

The article proceeds, 'This love and respect for cannabis obviously runs deep. When Eagle Bill leaves this planet' – hey, who said he's going anywhere? – 'he wishes to be cremated and have his ashes distributed in mason jars to friends, so that he can be combined with the earth that nurtures their cannabis gardens.' This is one step short of Keef Richards snorting his old man.

On my way out, I ask the receptionist, 'Could I meet Eagle Bill?'

'No,' she says curtly, eyes averted. 'He passed away two years ago.'

'Oh, what of?' But I sense the answer before she can even utter the words 'Lung cancer'.

452–454 km

The enchanting town of Leiden is famous for De Valk – a gigantic 250-year-old windmill. A couple of hundred metres from the modernistic railway station I pop into Café Eigenzorg, which has been in business since 1850 and run by the same family continuously since the 1930s – even while the Dutch were under Nazi occupation. When I tell the free spirit who serves me where I have come from today, she says, 'I don't like Amsterdam. When I go there, shopkeepers address me in English and say, "Can I help you?" This is my country!'

I sympathise – in English.

In Sweden they want three days' notice of intention to travel; in the Netherlands, three hours. But this still complicates the exercise enormously. Much worse than the three-hour rule is an *Alice in Wonderland* interpretation of just what assistance entails. Instance my departure from Amsterdam.

Nothing is quite as absurd as a post office that won't sell a stamp – yes, I came across one in the outer suburb of Reigersbos the other day – but what gives it a run for my money is a Tickets and Service Bureau operative who thinks he's served you by scrawling a phone number for you to ring – *for service*. This morning, at Centraal Station's 'service bureau', clerk No. 4 said (without feeling), 'Can I help you?' On my pointing out that I was 75 minutes early and would need help carrying my bags to the platform, he responded with a tight smile but said nothing to indicate this would be problematic. The hapless 'assistant' who soon materialised, though, made it clear he *could* not help – why do people say *can't* when they mean *won't*? – because 'it's not my job'.

In a station with no porters or trolleys, whose job is it? Or must I become a one-man shuttle, leaving one bag at a time on the platform while I fetch the rest? They haven't yet hired the service assistant who can – or will – answer this. Almost at the point of saying to No. 4, 'The next time you're conflicted between obeying the rules and helping a customer, which are you going to choose?' I hesitated, having been taught since childhood that you should never ask a question to which you already know the answer.

At this point, a woman in her mid-50s with twinkling eyes – Janne, an Eindhoven doctor – offered to carry my bags to Platform 13A for me, saying, 'Forget those people. It shouldn't be like that. They won't help you. Let me do it'. When we got to 13A, Dr Janne refused to supply any contact details. She had just wanted to help.

Murphy and Parkinson are old hat. Here's a station announcement, call it Haley's Law, honed in numerous bureaucratic battles. People in service bureaux who wish to help won't mind telling you their name; those who are determined not to help will.

When the conductor appeared in my compartment, he took one look at me, declined to inspect my Eurail pass and sighed wearily, 'I know it all'. A Dutch fellow passenger assured me I was only one of many victims of 'this Amsterdam attitude', but the assistance provided at Hollandspoor Station in The Hague was so impressive it was as if, instead of travelling a mere 124 km, I had left one country and entered another. Not only did Muhammad and Savash – no shyness about giving their names, they were only too happy to help – carry my bags to the service point, but after a quick confab they decided to keep on carrying them the entire 600 metres to my hostel, on the basis – surely right – that construction work on the Netherlands' tallest structure which lay between the station and my destination would have made it difficult for me to find my own way there, however well directed.

While on the subject, I should mention that Rotterdam was more Amsterdamned when it came to official unhelpfulness from Tickets and Service staff. One of their number blamed the lack of prior information that I had three bags with me, and a sudden ailment – colloquially known as a bad back – for his inability to help. When I left town, the excuse of the day was, 'We don't have trolleys'. While carrying my second piece of luggage through a tunnel I noticed, lying unused and unattended ... a trolley! Which I commandeered. When the escorting 'customer service officer' saw me, she nearly exploded. 'That is not for you. It is for the cleaning lady!'

I replied with a brief homily on the virtue of self-help, normally so admired by the Dutch. At that, an information officer (yes, some stations still have people dedicated to helping passengers: this one, it turned out, was a Gambian) stepped in and accompanied me to the main hall for my last bag. 'Don't worry about these people,' he told me. 'They can smile on the outside but inside their hearts are so hard. These people don't like their job – and they don't do a very good job.' Hence Haley's Second Law of Railway Service, which goes like this: If you want information, go to the service counter; if you want service, you're better off going to the information desk.

It's long been a pet theory of mine that every country has some innovation we could learn from. The Dutch post office issues householders JA and NEE stickers which they put on their front doors to indicate whether they do, or do not, wish to receive advertising mail. Another good idea, seen in The Hague, is the provision of brief biographies on eponymous street signs. These state when the person the street is named after was alive, and his or her claim to fame.

466–469 km

As Natalie, our tour guide, plied us with facts about the history of the Hague Peace Palace, it occurred to me I'd made a grievous error, confusing this colossus with the far more newsworthy International Criminal Court. A frenzy of note-taking hid my embarrassment, but I couldn't help reproaching myself, *Just as well you weren't sent here by a newspaper to report on the trial of Charles Taylor, and ended up 'filing' instead on the intricacies of the maritime dispute between Romania and Ukraine.* Items seen on the tour included: a tapestry donated by the last Shah of Iran; elephant tusks from the King of Siam (as was); twelve million mosaic squares; a replica of the Paris Opéra staircase; four Ming vases – in the Japanese Room, no less; busts of Edward VII, Schweitzer, Gandhi and Mandela; and a statue of Christ donated by Argentina after a decision on its border dispute with Chile by the International Court of Arbitration, which also sits here. Just as well Argentina didn't gift it *before* the ruling – or there might have been a suspicion of corruption.

Later I went in search of the International Criminal Court, only to discover that The Hague has an abundance of them. Outside one, a security guard said I was too late today but a hearing was coming up on Wednesday (too late for me, alas). The Charles Taylor one? 'No, it's only for the former Yugoslav cases,' he said with an air of disappointment. 'Don't worry,' he brightened up, 'we get confused too.' As we spoke, an employee was leaving the barbed-wire-ringed compound. A couple of minutes later, seeing him at the bus stop, I said, 'You work at the criminal tribunal, don't you?'

'Yes,' said the man, a cook from Ghana.

'So tell me,' I said, with an air of forced levity. 'Did you poison Milosevic?'

A hearty laugh: 'No, it wasn't me.' But then he turned serious. My question had reminded him of something. And now he handed me a journalistic scoop.

'My friend, who is a cook at the Liberian [International Criminal] court, he told me that Charles Taylor asked for his own Liberian home food to be served, or else he would go on hunger strike. How can he demand that? First he kills his own people' – strictly, this begged the question, but I was not disposed to argue the point – 'and then he says, "You must serve me the food I like best."'

'And did they agree to his request?' I asked.

'No.'

So there you have it. LIBERIAN EX-PRESIDENT, 'WAR CRIMINAL', IN FOOD PROTEST, with details supplied by 'sources close to the court'.

471–472 km

Confidently billed as 'the smallest town in the Netherlands', Madurodam – spread over just 18,000 square metres – appears at first blush to be an amusement park but is actually the world's most unusual war memorial, containing some 80,000 bulbs – 30,000 tulip bulbs and 50,000 light bulbs.

Intensive pruning keeps trees that would normally grow 15 metres tall down to a maximum height of 60 cm. The attraction – named after Resistance hero George Maduro, who died in Dachau concentration camp – is a veritable Little Holland.

In all, it contains 185 structures miniaturised to one twenty-fifth of their actual size – from Schiphol Airport to a speedboat called the *Abel Tasman*. As you would expect, it's a magical experience for all visitors, a particular favourite among children and effortlessly educational. For all that, one does tire after two hours of wandering its scaled-down streets. But I will remember Madurodam, above all, as the scene of one of my worst faux pas.

First, my excuses. A day of arduous pushing had dulled my usual alertness – but I also blame the undeniable fact that a thick Dutch accent can lend itself to misunderstanding. For whatever combination of reasons, then, I was amazed when I heard the woman selling me my ticket – and so kindly, too, at half price – urge me to stay on until later in the evening.

'Why?' I asked innocently.

'Well,' I heard her say, 'if you stay some more time we have fellatio at eleven o'clock.'

You say what? For a moment I squinted at her face to see if it looked familiar. Had I seen it recently inside an open caravan on the Reeperbahn, perhaps? No – impossible. The ticket vendor could obviously tell from the disbelief inscribed on my dial that I had misunderstood her. 'Why are you so shocked?' she quizzed me – and this time I was all ears. 'I told you, "We have a laser show at eleven o'clock."'

475–476 km

Along and near Koningskade, one of The Hague's main avenues, you cannot miss an outdoor exhibition of Australian art installations housed in glass cubes. One, a sculpture called *I O U*, consists of three giant letters (you guessed it): I, O and U. A head melting into sand I quite liked, and the next one – a mother and baby motorbike – was ingenious in its way. But nothing (and no one, for that matter) came near *Cow up a Tree*, a boxy Friesian in the cleft of a metallic elm.[13] With a degree of trepidation I approached a sleepy-looking Dutch officer perched in a police van 100 metres from this bovine cultural statement. Testing his intelligence, I inquired, 'Do you know what that is?' He looked up and shook his head. 'No.' 'That's a cow up a tree,' I explained, as though it were nothing remarkable, and certain at any rate that such a sight would pique the interest of any dairy-conscious Dutchman. 'Well, you know,' he shrugged, 'it is art.' Not really looking for an argument, I was happy to leave him to his opinion.

478 km

A rare balmy night brings with it another epiphany. The serenity experienced by the glassy lagoon known as Hofvijver, beneath the soft lights of Binnenhof Palace, continued – despite an outward change of scene – through a perfect dinner at Hardans, a traditional Dutch restaurant in Nobelstraat. Duck breast in apple sauce. Part of the evening's perfection sprang from my ignorance. It was late, nearly 10 pm, and the restaurant I'd had in mind (Puck) was closed, as it is every Monday.

Finding an affordable place to stay in Rotterdam wasn't easy. The Maritime Hotel was worth the search, though. Its more expensive rooms face the River Maas but a selection of unadvertised, small yet clean rooms at the back – normally reserved for sailors on shore leave – suited my budget perfectly at €27 (A$45) a night. The hotel is literally shipshape, and the wavy corridors must induce seasickness in a mariner who's made it back three sheets to the wind.

Over breakfast I got talking with the English expat couple opposite. They operate a *pension* in Picardy, not far from my route through northern France in early October. Spontaneously, they invited me to stay a night free of charge. Naturally, I accepted.

499–500 km

Of Europe's less glittering art showcases, I cannot say I've had a more enjoyable time at any than I did today at Rotterdam's own Boijmans van Beuningen Museum. This must have something to do with repeating my Hermitage luck. Entrance is free on Wednesdays (I didn't know that) and today, 1 August, as luck would have it, is a Wednesday.

I head straight for the room with the three Dalís. Despite being a museum of rank (in terms of acquisitions), it obviously can't afford the best-trained staff. An attendant, asked for directions to one of the Dalí rooms, tells me I'm in it, even though there isn't a Dalí in sight. How surreal can you get?

In my layman's view, Salvador Dalí at his best manifests three qualities – ambiguity, humour and the power to shock. *Le Grand Paranoiäque* (1936) is hard to describe better than the catalogue does: 'a head ... formed by various figures'. Alternatively, the head could be taken for a rock formation – a typical Dalíesque double image. There is also great humour here: *White Aphrodisiac Telephone* (also from 1936) is a phone whose receiver is a plastic rendering of a crab. Humour, too, in *Tête Otorhinologique de Vénus* (1969–1970), a sculpture of the classical goddess with an ear for a nose, and a nose for an ear, both on the left side of her head.

Peter Paul Rubens was just as shocking in his time, of course. On display here is *The Martyrdom of St Livinus* (1633–1635). St Livinus, a seventh-century Irish missionary, preached in Flanders before he was attacked by godless robbers who tore out his tongue and threw it to the dogs – for which God punished them by way of thunderbolt. This work has several centres of action. In one part of the canvas we see horses rearing and angels aiming bolts; in another, St Livinus, in mortal agony, appeals to God; in a third, the transfixing spectacle of an assailant holding a large pair of tongs that clasp a brilliantly delineated human tongue while three hounds vie for the meaty pink morsel.

Perhaps you think I am over-emphasising the fine arts. But, historically, the Dutch have been trendsetters in visual representation. As if to prove the point, a panel on one of the gallery walls states that, in the century after the bourgeoisie took over from the Church as principal patron of the visual arts, 'between five and ten million works of art were produced in the republic'.

Speaking of imagery, they took their Protestantism seriously here. Opposite the museum is the façade of the Remonstrantse Kerk, with all the saints on its entablature defaced.

503 km

A visit to the suburb of Blaak goes a long way to justifying Rotterdam's reputation as the hometown of Europe's most original buildings. It has been named Europe's 2007 City of Architecture but this reputation rests on far more than a single impressive year. It is in Blaak we find studio flats shaped like huge dice in mid-roll – or giant Rubik's Cubes, if you prefer. These 38 Show Cubes, as they are known, are now a quarter of a century old.

I soon see there is no access. They're reachable only by staircase, and even I think it will be a bit confrontational to crawl upstairs and knock on residents' doors. Just then I meet Juliana as she is arriving home from work. She takes my camera up to her apartment, and whizzes off half a dozen photos to show me what an interior (or at least hers) looks like. Illogically, I had assumed everything inside would be at a crazy angle but now I see – as gravity dictates – that the décor is arranged on the good old horizontal and vertical planes. Juliana amazes me with the news that she has lived in her cube for twenty years. Three years, I'd imagined, would be the maximum before you climbed the slanting walls. She says cube houses are ideal for singletons and small families. And how much would one set me back today? 'About €200,000 (A$333,000).'

504 km

The Netherlands is a latecomer to the ranks of Western countries that have banned smoking in restaurants. Its tardiness I attribute to the Dutch championing of tolerance (extended, as previously mentioned, to smokers of a different weed). This morning the Maritime Hotel posts a notice about the ban, which came into force yesterday. 'Dear Guest: As from 1 August 2007 smoking will no longer be allowed in our restaurant. However, you can still smoke in the Maritime Café*, with the exception of the no-smoking area.*'

512–528 km

Late at night I discover that the sound of double basses being wheeled in their cases along a path is almost indistinguishable from rolling thunder. A rumbling wakes me in my room at the Apeldoorn hostel, on the edge of my sister-in-law's hometown. Before I roll over and drift back to sleep, I see the cream-coloured cases gleaming under an electric light. This will bear investigating tomorrow, I tell myself.

And so it does. Over breakfast I get talking with Jurjen Toepoel, in his late 20s, who is tour manager for the Dutch National Youth Orchestra (Nationaal Jeugd Orkest), which at 50 years is much older than anyone in it. The 70-strong orchestra – divided for concert purposes into two ensembles of 35 members apiece – is domiciled at the hostel here for three weeks while on its summer tour. Tonight it will be performing less than an hour away, in Arnhem. Would I like to join the tour bus and hear the concert? Sure thing.

Despite the 'national' in its name, the musicians in it now hail from Poland, Spain and further afield. They are more European than Dutch, more global than European. So is their repertoire. Tonight they present the world premiere of a work commissioned from the Japanese-American composer Ken Ueno especially for them.

I meet Ueno at Arnhem's Muzis Sacrum Concertzaal and, after he makes a startling admission for a classical composer – declaring 'I'm a musician because of Jimi Hendrix' – we just riff.

'I had a different life plan to that of many musicians,' he tells me. 'US West Point military academy.'

'What were you aiming for there?'

'You know – the usual. Maybe general or senator.'

'No higher than that?'

'Well ... then I discovered electric guitar. I think there's a crossover, although I wouldn't exaggerate it. You won't find me inserting death-metal passages into the middle of symphonic movements. What really grabbed me about classical music was when I heard Bartók's string quartets and Stravinsky's *Rite of Spring* and they hit me viscerally, direct. Duke Ellington used to say, "There are only two types of music: good and bad."' And so to *Necropolis*, the piece he wrote for the youth orchestra. Ueno created the work while living in Rome, on a fellowship at the American Academy there. He found inspiration in Etruscan burial sites visited near the Italian capital. 'The city of the living is in ruins, but the Italians are living over the dead,' he explains. So the work plays itself out on parallel plateaux, as it were. It is in three movements, but two are 'submerged' in silence (a touch of John Cage there), so only the second one is audible. Almost unheard of.

529–532 km

Apenheul Primate Park has them all: squirrel monkeys, lemurs of the red-bellied, red-furred and ring-tailed varieties, bonobos, coatis, chimpanzees, marmosets, lion-tailed macaques, woolly monkeys, tamarins, yellow-breasted capuchins, sakis, and everyone's favourite – lowland gorillas. Spokesman Bert Smit is used to fielding questions about the park, founded in 1971, which has become one of the Netherlands' leading tourist attractions, with 500,000 visitors a year, but still draws flak from those who see it as nothing more than a glorified zoo. Striking a tone of reason, Smit ticks off the pluses. 'Some people say if you really want to have zoos this is the way to do it. The animals have all the space they need. There is a lot of safety for them. They have places to hide. We always keep them in social groups. They have the best of veterinary care.' Apenheul's breeding groups supply monkeys of several species to other zoos, and not only in Europe, Smit tells me. 'Some of the gorillas went to Taronga Zoo in Sydney.'

And then it's off to see the park on my own. I read that howler monkeys 'have developed a very energy-efficient *lifestyle*. They move slowly and carefully and spend much of the day resting.' Yes, I know people like that, too – but with them it's pure laziness.

533–534 km

In Australia we are used to bizarre royal antics, but I hadn't expected to find that sort of thing among the sensible Dutch. Near the stables at Het Loo, the Summer Palace here in Apeldoorn, there's a wonderful 1890s photo of Queen Wilhelmina in her carriage. The photo is signed with her name – along with that of her favourite steed, Kordaaz. That's one extremely talented equine…

539 km

You know when you've reached the Take One bar in Maastricht. The wooden floorboards are littered with peanut shells. A taller-than-average man with what would pass for a Marine crewcut on someone 50 years younger is seated on a bar stool. He appears to be waiting for service. The rest of the establishment is dead quiet, just like him.

From the pavement into the bar is one step, of 25 cm – too high for me to negotiate unaided. 'Can you help me get up, please,' I call out. His stare is so even I don't know if he sees me only through an alcoholic haze. He speaks like a fish drawing breath, 'No'. And with that turns back to his drink. I'm miffed but try not to show it. 'OK, I'll just wait.' Thirty seconds later I stop a passer-by who gives me the assistance required. Now the man at the bar stands up, does a passable approximation of a smile, and greets me, 'Welcome, victim'.

So this is the famous surly bar manager, Piet, himself, I see, as he moves behind the bar lined with wall-to-wall coasters. Suddenly animated, he offers me an obscure beer and a pack of peanuts. 'Go on,' he exhorts, 'throw the shells on the floor.' For once, I do as I'm told. 'It feels good, doesn't it?' Although I feel far more liberated than Iraq, I wouldn't have said this was one of life's greatest thrills. But Piet is not a man to be crossed. 'Yeah, it feels great,' I say obediently, and indeed tossing stuff heedlessly onto the floor does feel like a devil-may-care act, now I think of it. 'Now you are *you*,' says Piet, rising to make his point. 'If you do what everyone wants you to do, you are nobody.'

A simple philosophy – and a perfect introduction to a very non-Dutch part of the Netherlands. The man's reputation precedes him. He is said to be rude (I would have chosen 'abrupt'), provocative, abusive, witty in four languages, and popular with customers – many of whom return for more humiliation. Not only does Piet not give a rodent's fundament, he revels in the attention. 'I'm an arsehole, a bastard, an evil person,' he proclaims, pausing for maximum effect before delivering his coda – 'and so are you. But you know the difference between us?' I give an involuntary shake of the head. 'I know who I am – and I can handle it.'

One of the regulars – they file in over the next hour or so – tells me that the other amazing thing about this publican is his encyclopædic knowledge of beers. While handing me a foaming Erdinger wheat beer from Bavaria, he admits to knowing '7000 or 8000' – and by knowing he means that, once he has tasted a beer, he can identify it on any subsequent occasion, almost as if a photographic memory has been transferred from brain to palate.

A Dutchwoman in the bar tells me that the locals consider Maastricht 'not so Dutch'. A receptionist back at the hostel will later confirm this, contrasting the mellowness of southern speech (known as 'ordinary civilised Dutch') with what she deplores as the guttural hawking noises of the north. Other dichotomies exist: the south is more Catholic, enjoying the life of the vine and a well provisioned table – 'the Burgundian lifestyle' – whereas the north is Calvinistic, more austere.

542–545 km

Today is the only one of the entire trip – undertaken in what is turning into Northern Europe's 'wettest summer' – when the temperature exceeds 30 °C. Here in Maastricht it peaks at 33°.

At 2 pm, by prearrangement, I meet old friends from my 2002 visit to Istanbul – Emilie and Hans Binnerts, a Dutch couple who have spent the past few weeks at their holiday house in the south of Spain, and driven across France on *Samedi Noir* – the end of the French summer vacation notorious for kamikaze drivers on the *autoroutes* – to be here before we go our separate ways (they back to Eindhoven, I on to Belgium). We have promised ourselves a river cruise on the Maas and board the *Skiphout* just before 3 pm. (They insist on paying for all of us.) The recorded cruise commentary informs us that waste from the ENCI cement company is deposited on a slagheap in the suburb of Pietersberg that, at 168 metres above ground level, is 'the fourth highest mountain in the Netherlands'. You can't help liking these people.

Today I leave this country whose bespectacled prime minister looks jaded beyond his years and who is despised by a significant swath of public opinion, largely – though not solely – because he sent troops to Iraq in defiance of popular opinion. No, I haven't flown home to Australia, I'm still in the Netherlands of Jan Pieter Balkenende, also known by the nickname 'Harry Potter'. What's the difference between Balkenende and the *real* Harry Potter, a Dutchman asks me. I shake my head. 'Harry Potter can work magic.'

Before crossing the border it's time to check on what the Dutch think of their southern neighbours. Already a young Dutchman from Arnhem had volunteered, 'We (the Dutch) think Belgians are too rich' (meaning 'pretentious') 'and they think we are cheap' (meaning 'cheap').

And what did Jurjen, the national youth orchestra's tour director, think of them? 'Belgium is a very strange country,' he replied, weighing each word, 'very old, industrial, corrupt and depressing.' Corrupt?

'The impression they make is that they are a little shy.' He conceded, 'They are more polite and more proper than the Dutch.

'We make jokes about the Belgians.' You don't say …

CHAPTER 6

Why is there a Belgium?

FLANDERS and WALLONIA

Time spent:	13 days
Distance covered:	939 km
Distance pushed:	90.1 km
Average speed:	2.655 km/h
Journey distance to date:	13,125 km

Why is there a Belgium? This question began as a margin note scribbled in my travel diary – one I initially posed to myself and later proceeded to put to the Belgians (thinking they might know). Now they have taken to asking it of themselves. You'll be among the first to know if they come up with an answer. A government will have been formed that considers breaking up the homeland an unpardonable offence rather than a serviceable weapon in an endless war of words – or the country will have split in two.[14]

For 45 years the East-West focus of the Cold War obscured the Continent's fundamental division between North and South. It was a Dutchman in Rotterdam who told me, 'The map of Europe folds at Belgium – and so does the character of Europe'.

Southerners are supposed to be warm and exuberant, northerners their polar opposite – cold and rational. But reality rarely matches the ideal. Amsterdam and Berlin have hedonists aplenty, and science was not exactly moribund in Renaissance Italy. Belgium's location at the 'European Equator' has always been a strength. Historically, merchants met there (in the diamond trade, centred on Antwerp, they still do). But it is a cultural fault line that is weakening the mini-state and may yet tear it apart.

So how different really are these supposedly incompatible cultures? Over here are the Flemish (*Vlaamisch* in their own language), cousins to the Dutch, who in medieval times had their own independent state, Flanders. Many of these burghers, lovers of the good life, regard themselves as a cut above the snobbish francophones. Over there – in the south – are the Walloons, cousins to the French, who have Napoleon to thank for their capital city not being Paris. Many of those sophisticates, lovers of the good life, regard themselves as a cut above the 'provincial' *Vlamencs*. Each claims a monopoly on the 'Burgundian lifestyle' – and both, as it happens, share a Catholic faith – giving them more in common than many in either camp like to admit.

In the election of 10 June 2007, Christian Democrats (the main Flemish-dominated party) gained a slender advantage over the eight-year-old Socialist-Liberal coalition. The usual post-election jostling soon degenerated into farce and then severe international embarrassment. 'Leaders' on all sides now huffed and puffed, *Why is there a Belgium?* (with the subtext *when there could be Flanders and Wallonia?*). Many wondered if this time they would blow the house down. Another election, in 2010, would leave a Flemish independence party with more seats than any of its opponents, but another indefinite period of uncertainty lay ahead as other parties planned to put together a blocking coalition.

Within the past 200 years the fertile soil of this land has witnessed three military campaigns that shaped Europe. One lasted less than a day; one was all over in four weeks; one rumbled on for four years. Soldiers from many lands spilt blood to preserve the House of Belgium: the French (three times), the Dutch (twice), Prussians, Australians, New Zealanders, the British, Canadians and Americans. Foreign armies no longer fight over Belgium. The Flemish and Walloons are perfectly capable of doing that themselves. Eight months after the poll, Belgium still had no government. Mass marches failed to loosen the grip of populist politicians on the nation's windpipe.

Would it be such a shame if Walloon and Flanders went separate ways? After all, each could probably survive on its own. It would only mean the death of an ideal: that it is possible and better to reach across divides than to put up walls or erect more frontiers; possible and better to cherish all cultures – Flemish, Walloon, and German in the east – within a single welcoming state.

Many supporters of European unity hold that same ideal dear. Until now the tepid Belgians – not flashy look-at-me types – have enjoyed the good life quietly, content for their land which is half Tasmania's size to be just one of the Low Countries. After 180 years of nationhood they cannot go much lower now before it disappears altogether.

547–557 km

Antwerpen in Vlaams, Anvers in French. Must I say everything twice? Must I say everything twice?

Belgium is overcast. But only when it's not raining. Which makes the grander clocks and mirrors in the gilded Royal Café at Antwerp's Centraal Station all the more dazzling. Even under reconstruction as it is now, the terminus's flying buttresses put one in mind of a magnificent church and it comes as no surprise to learn that its nickname is the Railway Cathedral.

And so to the sights. Buffeted by powerful gusts of wind, I ascend the broad ramp to Zuiderterras, overlooking the River Scheldt, just in time to see a mean weather front closing in. A cosy restaurant will be extremely welcome. Just as well the Belgian Government of 1962, when it drew a line across the national map giving preference to Flemish north of the 'linguistic divide' and French south of it, didn't impose culinary no-go zones at the same time. At Façade – which offers French-Belgian cuisine right in the Vlaams 'capital' – I enjoy the crispest, most magnificent example of that famous Parisian dish, spaghetti – washed down with Australian red wine poured by the sommelier, Igor. Flemish art may not be what it was, but great value is still placed on artworks, even of the commercial variety. On the wall in front of me hangs an elegant framed coffee poster from the 1950s. 'For better coffee, de Boekelaar' ... I think that's what it says, I'm a little drunk on the wine by now ... 'with chicory'. Igor tells me it's worth a cool €4000 (nearly A$7000).

560 km

If you liken Centraal Station to a cathedral, then the standard you have in mind must be the city's landmark, Onze Lieve Vrouwkathedraal (the Cathedral of Our Lady). I have seen what I thought were great churches – in Uppsala and Haarlem – but this is the first encounter with ones that are (the word is carefully chosen) glorious. Externally, its sheer scale inspires awe. Sit beneath the ornately chiselled portal and gaze at the steeples rising 123 metres above you – two-thirds the height of Rotterdam's Euromast, one of the 'great towers' of the world – and, moreover, call to mind that this monument took 170 years to build (1350–1520) long before the advent of modern technology, and your sense of wonder must be dead if it isn't stirred by these reflections.

Inside, what leave a lasting impression are the magnificent Flemish artworks, principally by Rubens, Antwerp's most famous son. The most stunning are *The Raising of the Cross* (1609–1610) and *The Descent from the Cross* (1611–1612), from two triptychs commissioned for the cathedral by the Arquebusiers' Guild. Yes, the makers of deadly weapons. Did the Church feel a pang of conscience at accepting money from the arms industry to revere the Prince of Peace? Evidently not. In those days the Church militant wasn't a contradiction in terms.

In a darkened corner of the church is a memorial to several Flemish priests massacred in November 1964 during the first Congolese civil war. My thoughts fly back to the visit I made in 1988 to Zaire – which Congo had been renamed – and Kindu seminary where I stayed a few days. Kindu is the capital of Kivu province, where those murders had taken place. I expect the Belgian priests at that dining table would have known the victims, despite the difference in their years.

567 km

This evening, outside Cartoons cinema, the projectionist and I sit discussing many things over coffee. At one point Hannah waxes lyrical about Antwerp, saying, 'I love my beautiful city by the river'. Then she chides me for giving it only two days of my time, protesting, 'But there is so much to see. And, you know, we are the centre of fashion'. (Dare I breathe the words 'Paris' or 'Milan' in her presence?)

But Antwerpeners (pardon my Flemish) do not take themselves too seriously. Hannah relates the risible history of the city's new Palace of Justice – a building she says I should see. Its construction was a succession of scandals. The cost overrun was vast, the design wholly inappropriate. Its entrance gates are narrower than the police department's vehicles, so detainees – violent criminals among them – cannot be transported to the cells built at great expense to hold them.

569 km

I find the Flemish brand of humour appeals nearly as much as their world-class beers. Soon after the train pulled out of the station-cathedral I was reminded of this – as well as of the helpfulness of Belgian railways staff by stark contrast with certain of their Dutch counterparts.

'Are you comfortable?' the conductor asked me, a question unheard-of in Amsterdam or Rotterdam. 'Yes, thank you.'

'Good. We throw you out in Brugge.'

Bruges is what the French and the English – and, by extension, we Australians – call it; Brugge is what the people who live here call it. But then what would they know? This city is one of the most touristed in Europe, so I am prepared to be repelled. But Brugge's charm captivates *despite* the crowds. Probably the most impressive city hall I've ever seen, and certainly Belgium's oldest, occupies one whole side of Markt, the central square.

571 km

I've hit upon a great lurk. Although I carry a laptop with me, it's often more convenient to check emails at the local library. So in several countries now I have got into the habit of introducing myself at libraries as an Australian travelling through Europe (no word of a lie there) and asking if I could access the Internet for an hour or two. Nowhere had this request failed – until today at Brugge's public library. The librarian wasn't hostile to the idea, it's just that Internet access there is governed by library card recognition. My feet being useless, I was forced to think on my caster wheels. 'How much does it cost to join the library?' I said. 'Five euro,' she replied. 'But that will be far too much for you.' I slapped the required amount down on her desk, countering, 'Not at all'. Within a minute I was a proud member of the Brugge public library. Come to that, I still am. Haven't borrowed any books but six hours at the library's terminals over two days cost me considerably less than an Internet café would have charged.

Tonight completes 100 days of travel. According to my trusty speedometer I have pushed 575.3 km, or five-and-three-quarter kilometres a day. The distance covered by pushing and taking public transport combined comes to 12,392 km, or almost 124 km per day. My daily budget for the 100 days was €62.40; actual spending has been €64.34 – or almost €2 (A$3.33) a day over budget. *Not bad*, I tell myself, *but must do better*. Still, like St Augustine putting off chastity to another day, I decide to reward my near success at fiscal self-control by splashing out.

575 km

So I'm at Lokkedize restaurant enjoying a succulent steak and *frites* – the Belgians claim to have invented chips, and I'm not arguing, just wolfing them down – when the owner discovers I'm Australian. 'Did you know we have an Australian living in this street?' he says. I cringe, not having come all this way to meet compatriots. But when, apparently sensing my lack of enthusiasm, he adds, 'He's a painter', my reluctance melts away. An Australian artist living in Brugge: now that must be an adventurous soul. I don't know the half of it …

Later in the evening the artist, Svein Koningen, drops in and we enjoy a couple of beers. He drives me back to my hostel in the relentless rain, and agrees to pick me up this morning at eleven to visit his house, meet his wife and – not least important – see his art.

Belgium is the perfect domicile for Svein, in whom North meets South. Of Norwegian descent, he happily dubs himself 'the Australian Viking'. The man-of-action tag is no pose. In his time he has stalked Black Panther saboteurs in the Caribbean with firearms. Since 2005 Svein has lived on one of the only Brugge streets not paved with cobblestones, in a two-storey terrace with his studio at the back of a small garden. At 61 he is as fit as a Mallee bull in a non-drought year. Born in Trondheim, Svein was raised by paternal grandparents in Amsterdam. Taught to draw at a young age, he annoyed his primary-school teachers by drawing all over his exercise books.

A high-school dropout, his early jobs embraced light engineering, the aluminium industry and graphic design. Melbourne trams and buses displayed ads he had created. But the Viking in him was never far below the surface. 'After a year in Melbourne I was a young man with a temper' is all he will say about that. His father found a business opportunity on the Caribbean island of Curaçao, about as far from Australia as you can get without leaving the planet. The business supplied insulation for vessels in ports and oil refineries. Svein built it up until 200 laggers were working for him in 'Puerto Rico, Aruba, Curaçao, all over the shop' (it warms the heart to hear that Australian turn of phrase so far from home). But the Black Panthers had just moved in.

'I remember trying to buy a gun and I couldn't; I did get an air rifle, though. People were climbing up on roofs and lighting fires, all sorts of bullshit. One time there was a sound on the roof. I went out expecting to be jumped on – and it was a lizard or something.'

'Dianne' – who has been standing at the kitchen counter making tea and smiling with amusement at the tale of her Viking James Bond – 'is my third wife,' Svein says before going on to tell of how, now back in Australia, he became a stockbroker and financial planner.

His art education began in the mid-Sixties 'when abstract was the mainstream art'. But Svein didn't become a full-time painter until he was 49, 'a pretty late age to take up a profession from which you can't be sure you'll make any money'. His first show, in Brisbane in 1996, flopped. 'You couldn't sell abstract art then.'

For an Aussie male – and a Viking, to boot – Stein appears remarkably in touch with his feelings. Once he attended a spirituality course in Gippsland – 'eight of us lying on the floor, and the lead facilitator says, "Imagine you leave your body and you go on a train and you see eyes. Whose eyes do you see?" And I said, "I see my father's eyes."'

The third time he did that exercise he saw female eyes – Dianne's. 'Six months later I said to her, 'Do you mind if I become an artist?' She must have given the right answer because here they are in Brugge today, with the struggling-artist phase at last behind them. On 11 November Stein is looking forward to exhibiting 40 works in the town of Kapelle op den Bos (Chapel in the Bush) outside Brussels.

Before leaving, I photograph one of his larger canvases, *Gorges de Verdun*, a favourite of Dianne's. She ticks him off, not altogether in jest, for having left it out in the rain. Perhaps, I suggest, it was a deliberate technique, to make the colours run? Svein clearly makes a mental note to use that for his excuse next time.

579 km

For a different artistic inspiration, I visit the Groeningemuseum. Just now it has a temporary exhibition called 'Exotic Primitives', focusing on the way they became the first European artists to incorporate non-Europeans into their artistic visions.

In the 21st century it is more than a bit Eurocentric to see a phrase such as 'the known world' used to explain how much of the world was known – to Europeans – in the 15th century. Australia, after all, was known to the Aboriginal nations, most of South and North America to Amerindians, and Aotearoa to the Maori.

In *Rest During the Flight to Egypt* (1575–1600), Johannes Sadeler ventures into pictorial theology by drawing European churches, gables and a windmill in his backdrop. There are not many of those in the Sinai even today. But, even as Europeans were setting out to conquer what was to them the New World, the odd artist broke the mould. *The Adoration of the Magi* (anonymous master, 1510) depicts one of the Three Wise Men as black. Exotic animals and slaves would soon be counted among the curiosities at the courts of European kings, reminding us that from the vantage point of European supremacists the rest of the world was theirs for the taking.

On 12 April 1994 the Belgian Government, moved by public outrage over the deaths of ten Belgian peacekeepers, withdrew Belgium from Unamir, the United Nations Mission in Rwanda. Unamir's commander, Canadian General Roméo Dallaire, would later write of how he despised the Belgians for this, noting that exactly 50 years earlier his father and father-in-law had been fighting in Belgium to free the country from Fascism.[15]

Let us get this in proportion. Nearly a million 'Rwandan lives' were extinguished in 90 horrifying days, three months of mass slaughter in which there was a death toll the equivalent of a 9/11 every single day. But what is a 'Rwandan life' worth? Like the

Rwandan currency, it is very cheap, taking many thousands to equal one US unit – and there are even more to the euro. In case you were wondering, I put the quotation marks around 'Rwandan lives' because I recognise there is no such thing. Nor are there 'American lives', a term that sometimes appears in media reports as if we ought to care more, or take notice. If we don't hear about 'European lives', it is probably because the sense of a 'common European home' (Gorbachev's phrase) rather than an assemblage of nations is not well developed, even now.

Lives don't have nationalities; people live and die. That they are Americans, Iraqis, or Rwandans, presidents or villagers, businesspeople or paupers, should be of secondary importance – in the eyes of God or from a humanist perspective. We should need no reminding, but heritage runs deep. From the 16th to the 20th centuries, Europeans fanned out across the world, exploiting non-Europeans with little or no compunction, slaughtering many thousands in the Americas and Africa in the name of their so-called higher civilisation, doing things unto others they would never have had done unto them.

And what was the basis of this superiority? That a Christian God ordained it? Some thought so – though not the founder of their religion. That they had the guns? Some said might was right, but in that case we ought to applaud massacres and terrorists everywhere. Two world wars should have put paid to the myth of European moral superiority for all time. But this belief in the comparative insignificance of other people's lives – the Eurocentric conceit – continues to blight our vision much closer to home. When the Government of Australia, in 2008, proposed to apologise to the Stolen Generations, certain newspaper columnists focused on the legal precedent and the issue of compensation. One would have thought an apology was the least that those wrenched from their mothers' arms deserved. But among us still are those of European descent who selectively activate their cerebral powers to argue that there must have been good reason behind such actions. Perhaps they cannot bear the thought that, under the veneer of rational power, Europeans and their descendants, which means most of us, could be just as savage, just as brutal, as any 'primitive' tribesman in the jungles of Africa – or the Simpson Desert.

580–582 km

Today I will be confronted by a farmer with a rifle, and cop my own souvenir of war – not a bullet, as a tour guide gave me at Gallipoli, but a rusty English water bottle. 'Thank you' hardly seems adequate.

Within the space of a few days I shall visit three battlefields – Ypres, Waterloo and the Ardennes – not because I have a particular interest in military history but because you cannot hope to understand Europe without sensing how it has been shaped by war. Still, it seems wise to follow the dictum of Spanish historian Felipe Fernández-Armesto,[16] 'Where received information conflicts with experience, the latter is the more reliable guide'.

For eighteen years Sharon Uyttenhove-Evans, a Queenslander now in her early 40s, has conducted tours to the Ypres battlefields. Her father was in the air force; a great-grandfather in the Queen's 16th Lancers fought in the Boer War and on the Western Front in World War I. So hers is a family drawn to history like a magnet.

They were living in Germany in the *annus mirabilis* of 1989 when Sharon, travelling around Europe, fell in love with Bruges (as she prefers to call it). 'It just had everything I like. Small, safe, cosy, drop-dead gorgeous.' So, I ask, why is there a Belgium? *If anyone knows, Sharon will.* Yet her answer, too, is historical. 'The idea was to make a buffer zone originally, between the Dutch and the defeated French after the Napoleonic wars.' 'Yes I know,' I reply, 'That's why there *was* a Belgium, but surely keeping the Dutch and French apart isn't reason enough any more?' Sharon concedes the point – but before we can explore the matter further it's time to be off.

As she drives us out the 60 or so kilometres to the killing fields of the first Europe-wide war for 100 years – the first since the conflict that led to the creation of the Belgian buffer – our guide gives us a thumbnail sketch of why a war triggered by an assassination on the other side of Europe should have erupted in Belgium first.

'The Germans could have invaded France by the Swiss Alps. But the border had medieval fortresses. Instead they gave the Belgian king, Albert I, an ultimatum, "Let us through or we invade." Belgium was allied by treaty to Britain ...' And Belgium's geography master was just as cruel as its history master, for it lay on the direct route between the two principal foes, Britain and Germany.

The four battles of Ypres have been exhaustively documented, nowhere more vividly than by Les Carlyon in *The Great War*. Suffice it for a visitor to know that the Germans' overriding ambition was to break through to the Channel ports, which would have left them poised to strike at England. And that the Allies' grim resolve was to prevent them.

In the Battle of Passchendaele – now Sharon has parked the minivan on a slight rise in the ribbon of asphalt so we can see for ourselves – on those gentle indentations in the landscape that you would be exaggerating to call valleys, 'for every metre of ground 35 British soldiers died'. Directing our gaze to Passchendaele Ridge off to our right, she points out that the Germans occupied 'the *high ground'*. They could see, and fire down on, Allied troops; they controlled the water sources, and could stem their flow.

Late in the morning we arrive at Tyne Cot just as the sun has won its own battle against intermittent rain. We alight from the van and spend twenty minutes contemplating mass slaughter and individual dissolution where they come together in a sight that can always reduce me to tears – a war cemetery. Under these bright green lawns lie 7000 unidentified remains, 'known unto God'. The uniformity of many inscriptions can leave you unmoved, and then an individual utterance asserting faith in the face of experience – 'Some day we'll understand' – breaks you up. How strange, I reflect, that we cannot hope to take in the statistical enormity of war: 65 million under arms; ten million battle deaths; twenty million irretrievably wounded; two million Belgians fleeing their country in panic. But the impact on the individual – and on their eternally serried ranks – we can.

Sharon's words have the power to make you see beyond the graves. 'For the first ten or twelve years after the war, the Belgians lived like cattle. Nothing grew in these fields. The churches you see in Belgium – apart from the great cathedrals – are 80 years old, maximum.' When she mentions the gas attacks at Second Ypres in 1915 I ask whether it is true the Germans were not the first to use poison gas and she confirms this. 'The French were using gas in February of '15. African lives' – those of Zouaves, Moroccans and Senegalese – 'were the first to be snuffed out by mustard gas, phosgene and "yperite" ' – gases outlawed by Europeans as contrary to civilised (European) norms.

At this point Sharon could see some light relief was needed. She recalled the time when King Albert's son Prince Philippe went on national TV and announced, in all seriousness and bad Flemish, 'My wife is pregnant – and it is from me'.

World War I is still full of danger, still taking lives 90 years after the Armistice. 'Every year there are still three or four casualties from World War I shells,' says Sharon. With half a billion still lying around, not all of them 'live', it will take 60 to 100 years to render the battlefields safe.

Sharon is a regular visitor to the farm we've parked opposite now. With permission I photograph pig-and-vegetable farmer Roger Vanderginste who is holding an 18-pounder cordite shell. And now he's confronting me with a rifle. Sharon says not to worry. 'Last week he tried to throw a hand grenade at me.'

In mid-afternoon we stop a few metres from a roundabout that looks identical to any suburban intersection in your own hometown. Sharon invites us to look along the gutter about 10 metres from the crossroads. 'Seven years ago the remains of six Germans were found right there, in a dugout. Blue clay preserves bodies. The Diggers called this "the hottest spot on earth". Hellfire Corner. At the height of battle there was an explosion there every five seconds.' Not far from here we turn in to a roadside restaurant for afternoon tea – and another break from the gloom of unremitting war. More humorous relief we certainly need, but the last thing I am expecting is a belly laugh.

Sharon and her husband live not far from West Vlieter, the Trappist monastery that brews Leffe, 'the world's best beer'. It must be handy to have the monastery so near, I remark. 'Yes,' she says, 'every two weeks I ring up the monks to place an order.' Mindful of the famous Trappist vow of silence, I'm intrigued how she handles this. Sharon, who can tell what I'm thinking from my furrowed brow, wastes no time in putting me out of my misery. 'They have a telephone answering service.'

Oh? 'Yes, they got a special dispensation from the Vatican.' When I can stop laughing long enough, I ask, 'And what does it say? "I'm sorry, we can't speak at the moment."? ' 'No. It gives delivery hours and asks you to leave a message. When there's no beer left, the voice says, "All our beer is sold out. Please wait for further information. And, if you have empties, here's where you drop the bottles off ..." '

Hill 60. It was one of the few patches of turf fought over in both world wars and, with three shells landing per square metre, one of the most fiercely contested on the Western Front. Its labyrinth of tunnels was so extensive that much of the fighting was underground. In two days the British gained three-and-a-half miles for the loss of 60,000 troops. But again it is the individual gesture that means more. I see where the ashes of John Olliff, who fought in World War II and died in 1987, are interred with his father's from the First War.

And so to Ypres itself. Founded in the ninth century, its prosperity was built on cloth production. At no point did the Germans capture it (not for want of trying: total battle deaths in West Flanders alone for 1914–18 were 450,000) but everything built up over eleven centuries was destroyed. 'By the end of the war,' says Sharon, 'it was said that a man on horseback could see everything in the town.'

And Menin Gate. Just under 55,000 names. Every Armistice Day 55,000 poppy petals descend through the skylights. The highest number of VCs won by any unit were awarded to members of the Royal Australian Military Corps. Sharon wastes no words in summing them up, 'Very brave men'.

The danger posed even now by World War I is still visible a metre under Flanders fields. Late in the afternoon we meet 'The Diggers' (De Diggers). Not Australians, but men and boys of Vlaanderen, volunteers who have given up their leisure time to excavate small patches of farmland with the owners' permission. Sharon speaks with barely controlled emotion. 'They're really concerned with finding men and giving them a decent burial. I don't think it's asking too much – considering that they gave their lives for the freedom of this country – that they get a decent burial instead of being bulldozed.' As of three weeks before my visit, De Diggers had unearthed 214 bodies. The demands of the living – even prospects of wealth – frequently take precedence over respect for the dead.

Construction companies are generally unco-operative towards the Diggers, says Sharon. 'Often the companies will say, "We don't care about that. We will just pour concrete over it." '

Eight to ten of them dig in all weathers. I photograph three of the Diggers with a 40 kg German howitzer shell they found earlier in the day. While one of them, Pol Lefèvre, is talking to me, an exclamation issues from a new trench about 10 metres away. Thibaut Milleville – who turns eighteen today – has found a rusty water bottle. Older heads identify it as English, 1916. It looks worthless. Perhaps that is why he says I can have it. 'No, it's Pol's pot,' I quip, wishing it away. Clearly no museum would want something in this condition but it is still with a sense of jettisoning a historical relic that I quietly dispose of it back at the hostel this evening.

In Ypres Sharon told me the story of an expat in a Bruges boutique looking at a tapestry, who said to the shopkeeper, 'Is this made in Belgium?' whereupon the shopkeeper drew herself up to her full height and retorted, 'No, they are not made in Belgium, they are made in Vlaanderen'.

586 km

This Sunday finds me on a platform at Brugge Station, in the care of two stout Flemish yeomen and station assistants, Jan and Ivan, who wait with the crucial ramp for the arrival of the train that will bear me off to Brussels. A statuesque woman – in her mid-70s, I would judge – approaches Jan, her ticket extended. At first I pay little attention.

'Monsieur,' she asks him in French, 'could you tell me what platform I must wait for my train on?'

Jan's lips actually curl. 'I do not speak French,' he says in English.

Finding this highly unlikely, I ask him, 'Not even a little?'

'No,' he glares at me, diverting his wrath from the francophone woman he has left standing there, amid rising anger all round.

I think she's getting a rough deal but don't want to upset Jan on whom, after all, I depend to get me out of here. So I open conversation with the *grande dame*, explaining that I can speak a little French and asking if I may translate into English for her. She obliges, Jan dismissively indicates the correct platform, and Madame stands transfixed between thanking and reproaching her reluctant informant.

Till now my sympathies have been totally with her but they shift 270 degrees when I ask whether she speaks any Flemish and she proudly answers in the affirmative, explaining, '*Mon père était Vlamenc.*' ('My father was Flemish.')

'Well, then,' I say, striving to keep my voice even, 'since you are in the Flemish part of Belgium, surely you could have asked the gentleman in his own language, which you can speak.' At this notion she sniffs the air, gives a taut double shake of the head – so much more emphatic than the word '*Non*', on a par with '*Jamais*' – and sallies forth to catch her train.

I've heard of many such encounters, but until you see two 'civilised' adults refuse to have a civil conversation in a language they both comprehend (and Jan later confides to me he *does* understand French) you really haven't been to Belgium. Now I have.

Even more amazing than this encounter is one an hour and a half later, at Bruxelles-Midi Station, where I come across that rare bird, the European, which I have sought with scant success over a route that's taken me 13,000 km, halfway across its presumed habitat. Diane – Dutch by birth and breeding – is one of the station's information officers. She spends her working life in a transparent round booth 4 metres in diameter. Does she feel Dutch, or Belgian by adoption? I ask, and, if the latter, Flemish Belgian or Franco-Belgian? 'None of them,' Diane declares on the instant. 'If anything, I am a European.' *Rara avis* indeed. No wonder they have put her under glass.

Brussels' polyglot character – what some mistake for soullessness – is just right for a city at the crossroads. As an official booklet (produced, significantly, by the Commission of the French Community 'to promote the European dimension of Brussels') points out, 'One-sixth of the city's population was born in other European countries, and another one-sixth in countries outside Europe'.

Which gives the clue to the real reason why there is a Belgium. Now it can be revealed. Because to break it up would drive away 'the capital of Europe', in both senses of the phrase. The European Union – 50 years old while I'm passing through, and in self-congratulatory mood – gives this splendid old city an importance in the modern world that Brugge and Antwerp can only envy. It brings in money, too. To lose Brussels would, in soccer parlance, be to score several own goals in rapid succession.[17]

This excellent booklet also describes a city landmark with such wit that I can only guess whether it was intentional. 'Egmont Palace,' it itemises. 'Begun in 1534, this Italian Classical palace was home to the great and the good before it became part of the Belgian Ministry of Foreign Affairs.'[18] So there you have it: the Belgian Ministry of Foreign Affairs is not great, and no good.

590 km

Another campaign dispatch has arrived from True North.

> 13 August. 1.03 am AEST.
> Hi Ken,
> It's less than one month to election day. How it will go is hard to say, but I have good hopes.
> It looks like young against old in this election. It's still summer here but we have no more midnight sun, it stopped at 31 of July. The sun was shining red and beautiful just over the sea. But I had no one to share this moment with.
> Marius.

Long live Viking democracy. The loneliness of high office appears to be getting to Marius already – and he hasn't even been elected yet.

591–598 km

A bus timetable on a shelter in Brussels North displays refreshing candour but has me scratching my head. '*Départ Théorique*', it announces. 'Theoretical Departure'.

Late today in the stately central square, Grand Place, I meet an 86-year-old man and his 54-year-old wife. He is bursting with civic pride. '*Voici le plus grand place du monde*,' he exclaims. 'This is the greatest square in the world.' To mention rivals in Beijing or Budapest would be churlish, and anyway I must defer to age. Looking around me, though, I concede to myself that he may just have a point.

The Maison de Brasseries, one of the famous guildhalls that used to surround the square, sparkles in the evening sunlight. Most of the buildings around us now were built in a spirit of angry defiance within seven years of Louis XIV's order to bombard Brussels back in 1695. The one building that was Louis' real target – the Hotel de Ville, which according to my elderly informant dates back to the 14th century – escaped the bombardment intact.

The more I see of it, the more of a slur it seems to say that Brussels is charmless. Especially evocative are the pavement restaurants on the Rue des Bouchers near the Galeries St Hubert shopping arcade; the cathedral, magnificently illuminated by night; and a neon-lit office tower on the Place Rogier. For romantic revolutionaries there is the Place de Barricades, just up the road from the hostel where I stay in Brussels North. Victor Hugo lived here in 1830 – when Belgium was newly minted, and no one was devising ways to make it smaller still.

At 722 members the European Parliament must be nearly the most 'populous' in the world, second only to China's National People's Congress. Near the Schuman roundabout stands the Charlemagne Building, named after a notable European. But, by the Continental breadth of their military reach, Napoleon and Hitler were Europeans of the first order, too.

604–607 km

Electronic noticeboards at Bruxelles-Midi advertise services to Waterloo. For a moment I think it will be easier to reach the famous battlefield by train than by bus – until I realise this Waterloo is the one in London, over 300 km away, named after the scene of Wellington's greatest victory. It seems grimly fitting to visit the scene of the agony that led to the birth of Belgium while 18 km to the north – far less dramatically – signs begin to appear that may be portents of its death throes.

Waterloo, the work of a single day, still resonates nearly 200 years on. With 12,000 dead, far fewer than at Ypres or in the Ardennes, it was the most decisive campaign of them all. Consider. It took more than Ypres to turn the tide against the Kaiser, more than the loss of a Belgian forest to defeat Hitler.

As I am hoisted up into a Bedford truck – the passenger seats in the open-backed tray being inaccessible – our Moroccan tour driver, Aziz, tries to evince interest but he has clearly met his Waterloo a few too many times ... Our recorded commentary – in French, English and German – begins. (Aziz knows when to push the buttons.)

It is Sunday 18 June 1815. Napoleon has shocked the diplomats of Europe, gathered in Vienna, by escaping from the prison island of Elba and retaking Paris. The 'Continental powers' – Britain, Prussia and the Dutch-Flemish fighting as one under the 23-year-old Prince of Orange – are arrayed against his troops. These 300,000 men massed on the field of battle are gambling for the future of Europe. At stake is whether the Continent is to be a French Empire as mighty as ancient Rome, winner takes all. The commanders spring to life. Behind that 3 km defensive ridge – the one we are now driving towards – Napoleon's 72,000 troops slightly outnumber Wellington's 68,000. Yesterday evening the French placed 80 cannon on this ridge: but it rained all night, their emplacements have sunk into the mire and they will be largely ineffective today.

Battle is joined at 11.30 am. The future of Europe will be decided, right here, in less than ten hours. The battle advantage will see-saw all day, until, after the capture in early evening of La Haie Sainte farm, which puts victory within his grasp, Napoleon loses it all on one final fling against the forces of Prussia's 73-year-old Marshal Blücher.

The battlefields of those days are the sugar-beet fields of these. This is said to be the richest farmland in Europe. Is it irreverent to suggest that all that blood and bone fertilising the soil made it so? After June 1815 these fertile acres also entered the vocabulary as a byword for irreversible defeat. It was all about the 'civilisation' of destruction, and the destruction of civilisation. As even the victors agreed, it was all about Napoleon.

Before pushing off to catch the bus back to Brussels I take one last look at Lion's Mound, the great pyramid built to commemorate this famous victory, this cataclysmic loss. Every bit as impressive as Giza's Great Pyramid, its existence stems from the same delusional pharaoh complex, the immortal dream of vain men that they might be all-powerful.

608–610 km

The most gorgeous chocolate shop I've ever seen, right next to the clichéd *Mannekin Pis* statue, is called Chocopolis. Great sadomasochistic pleasure is to be derived from watching the molten liquid billow from a mechanical fountain that gives it a good whipping as it flows. And you get a free sample. Yum. The shop is now run by Chinese, but everyone likes chocolate and, since this sublime creation actually comes from Central America, associating it with Belgium – or Switzerland, for that matter – is about as authentic as a cup of 'English tea' grown in Darjeeling. Who cares? If it takes chocolate to hold Belgium together, so be it.

From what Belgians themselves tell me, Brussels drivers set a pretty poor standard. They are certainly not the only ones ever to have made or received mobile calls in their cars, but tonight I look on in horror as a motorist sends a text message while his car sails over a road crossing, almost running into another vehicle that hurtles round the corner, nearly skittling a small cluster of pedestrians on the crossing. Cacophony erupts. Plentiful use of the horn, of course, not so much of the brain.

For my farewell to the capital of Belgium, I raise a glass of something that should truly unite this divided land, a lambic (fruit) beer known as Kriek. Want the secret of a recipe for putting Belgium's woes out of your mind? This one takes the cherry.

612–614 km

In Rochefort, deep in the heart of Wallonia, I stay at a friendly *gite d'étape* (family-run guesthouse) whose owners at first appear nonplussed by my habit of hauling myself up the grand staircase like a self-trained walrus. (But this is the *easy* way to reach my room, and there are none on the ground floor, so needs must.)

On Rochefort's main street I see a sign – quite a brilliant shaming tactic, the like of which I have not seen before but one that should really be imitated elsewhere. Above a disabled-parking bay next to the town's tourist information bureau, it reads, 'You want my place? Take my handicap as well'.

627 km

This evening in picturesque Namur, I submit to the random kindness of Belgians when a bus passenger pays my fare before I can do so myself. Now this could happen anywhere, I agree, but the fact is it *has* happened here in Belgium. I like this country, more than some of the people living here like it. The only question is whether my benefactor would have considered herself a Belgian. Too late to ask …

Epiphany visits when least expected. It's Friday evening and I sit, Leffe beer in hand, on the porch of Namur's *auberge de jeunesse* overlooking the Parc à la Plante and the brooding River Meuse. Perfection.

628–633 km

In the south-eastern corner of Belgium, close to the Luxembourg border, I hike 3 km into the countryside beyond Bastogne to the site of my third battlefield in a week, where another gamble by another would-be master of Europe came to grief.

The offensive was launched on 16 December 1944, six months after D-Day. Hitler was playing his last card. His objectives were to split the Americans from the British and give himself enough time to develop, deploy and dispatch his new weapons of mass destruction – the V1 and V2 rockets. If the Führer's gamble failed, the road to Berlin would be wide open. Game over.

I wheel up the green slopes of a hill – the Colline du Mardasson – crowned by a star-shaped American memorial and a museum of the traditional type surely preferred by GIs well into their pensionable age. Ardennes – the Battle of the Bulge, as the Americans call it – was measured in weeks rather than Waterloo's hours or Ypres' years.

As you enter the dark rotunda housing the exhibits, your eyes are drawn to a lifelike diorama of three American generals – Patton, Eisenhower and Bradley – conferring at Bastogne barracks on 3 January 1945. Hitler's battle plan relied on inexperienced *Volksgrenadiers* – every male between 17 and 45 he could conscript – to break through the Allied lines, race across Belgium and capture

Antwerp. In three days they had reached the Meuse; in another three, the Germans issued Bastogne with the ultimatum 'Surrender or be destroyed', to which General McAuliffe delivered his immortal riposte, 'Nuts!' The enemy had no idea what he meant. The translator upon meeting the German messenger explained, 'It's a definite no. If you don't understand the phrase, it means "Go to hell".' To the French it was faithfully translated *'Allez au diable!'*

On Christmas night the Luftwaffe, subjecting Allied troops to the campaign's most intensive bombing, destroyed US headquarters along with much of the town. Many GIs later confessed they were thinking, This is the end. But next day Patton's troops broke through the encirclement and forged 100 km across icy and snowbound terrain to save the beleaguered town. 'Bastogne breathes again,' Patton cabled Eisenhower. When the Germans retreated on 8 January they had lost 110,000 men; 80,000 Americans had been killed, injured or taken prisoner. Churchill called Ardennes 'the greatest American victory of all time', with justice. They'd been outnumbered three to one from the outset.

In the museum shop, handkerchiefs emblazoned with the Stars and Stripes are on sale at €5 apiece. I'm surprised no one has succeeded in having them removed from sale. If burning the flag is shameful, why would blowing your nose on it be acceptable?

On my descent from the war memorial I set two new speed records: 23.6 km/h and then 24.1 km/h. It's tempting to exceed 25 km/h but a speed record's not all I might break.

Tomorrow I head back into Germany, so it's time to ask, What do the Belgians think of their powerful eastern neighbours? They trade with them – obviously – but, considering their history over the past 100 years, I duck the challenge and opt for a quiet night.

Ivan – 'I am happy to remain a peasant' – Baranov, doorman at the Nevsky Palace Hotel, St Petersburg.

When you're exposed to the open air for 20 hours in the vestibule of an old Russian train heading into Arctic latitudes (because the corridor is too narrow for your wheelchair to fit), protection from the elements tends to be as basic as it is essential.

The English class of '07, from Archangelsk Technical University, interviewed at Café Polyarny. Their teacher, Elena Kokanova, is third from right (partly obscured). The students were intelligently critical of their society and government, although one was a 'My country can do no wrong' patriot. None identified Russia with Europe.

Marius Nilsen, the mayor on top of Europe: the general store manager and assistant airport traffic controller won the election running on a fear campaign about his opponent, the incumbent, who he said was planning to bring in thousands of young Russian women.

The author tries to keep his balance while transferring from his wheelchair into a rowboat at Fraenafjord.
Photo: Sue O'Neill

My bogan hosts:
Tina and Per, self-described as Norway's Bonnie and Clyde.

Up I go. At Östersund – easy does it, with none of the restrictive rules about booking 72 hours before travelling that awaited me in southern Sweden.
Photo: Ben Weidemann

Om is where the hearth is. This impeccably dressed lotus eater was an oasis of calm during the evening rush hour at Stockholm Central metro station.

Distant cousin Birgit Dess, 40, retired apprentice tea taster and company director's PA, fills me in on family history at a café near Bremen central station.

Ghosts on stairs.
(Permission granted by Mode Museum, Antwerp, and the artist Bernard Willhelm, creator of its *Het Totaal Rappel* [Total Recall] exhibition.)

Munich's Marienplatz metro station.

At Nuremberg, today's funfair blots out the Nazi Colosseum, built 70 years ago.

Gardien de la Paix. Vincent Jacquot, chief of the 11th *arrondissement* prefectural police, on the job trying to find a pathetic Aussie straggler a hotel room – which he succeeded in doing on the Rue Servan.

The strain shows: long-serving conservative mayor Hubert Lelieur in a priceless moment of togetherness with Victor, the five-year-old son of his communist opponent in March's elections. This may well have been a photo neither of them wanted, but Victor's dad, Christophe, was mightily amused.

Country and Eastern, a rest from square dancing at the Ostbahnhof, Berlin's main eastern railway terminus.

The beautiful Alabaster Coast at Etretat, and the chapel I couldn't reach.

Histrionics lesson. A woman in Monaco throws herself across a tow truck in a frantic bid to stop her beloved (and illegally parked) car from being taken away. The parking officer and observers in formal wear look on bemused.

Gilles, my personal casino attendant at Monte Carlo who helped me bet my bottom dollar.

Fish fight. A sudden row between market vendors threatens to turn physical over the placement of one stall a few centimetres the wrong side of an imaginary line. Note a restraining hand on the aggrieved vendor's waist.

Pepe the Málagan troubadour sings his heart out to a less than impressed audience at an outdoor café.

Feel like an interview? Just roll up. The author being interviewed by Radio SER's Montse Buil. The recorded interview went to air after it was translated into Catalan. Photo: Mexi Meritxell

Show us your legs: hams hanging from a shop ceiling, a common sight in Spanish and Portuguese shops alike. These ones were on sale in Salamanca.

Grand Old Man About Town: the 90-year-old dapper gentleman seen emerging from a Braga pharmacy.

This is bliss: the author rapt to have completed his 25,000-km trek across the Continent. Photo: Mario Anagua

CHAPTER 7

Close to Civilisation

GERMANY

Time spent:	34 days
Distance covered:	3079 km
Distance pushed:	248.7 km
Average speed:	2.829 km/h
Journey distance to date:	16,204 km

Other nations have culture, Germany has *Kultur.* The capital seems important, but then German Capitalises Many Words. You Won't See That Sort of Thing Here.

Kultur is the key that unlocks the heartland of Europe, but the land of the heart? That's France. Germany idolises logic, aspires to efficiency. The heartland of Europe rewards those who use their head. Who has ever made more mathematical, cerebral music than Johann Sebastian Bach? Yet this is also the land of Beethoven and Wagner, those grand stirrers of emotion.

It is the land of Goethe, Classicist *par excellence* (sorry, I mean *über alles*). But it is also home to flights of fancy (so long as they have clearance from the tower and are capable of landing safely after a controlled descent). Formalistic Goethe was at ease with lyrical Schiller.

Here, on their Olympus, I can hope to meet some of Europe's cultural gods – Beethoven, Bach, Goethe and Schiller – and to see with my one-sixteenth-German eye how German hearts sing, German brains tick, and German people see the world from Europe's greatest position of strength.

The consequences of being the strongest kid on the European block have not vanished, but after bitter experience Germany has adapted to the fact that its weight of numbers (82 million at last count, but falling) can intimidate the neighbours; and has learnt to tread, if not lightly, with agility.

Outsiders often think of Germans as intense, earnest folk. Those who come here soon know better. Mediterraneans (Greeks, Italians, Spaniards) are said to know how to enjoy life but you may have noticed that Santorini has never hosted the Oktoberfest. That Europe's chosen anthem is *Ode to Joy* tells us something about the whole Continent, but let's not forget where the melody came from.

Germany is now at the head of a peaceful, orderly, life-loving Europe but Germans have spent most of their history as members of fragmentary mini-states. Creating a unified nation, glorying in its strength, provided a purpose worth fighting for. The Germans are a purposeful folk, inclined to be dogmatic. Who else could have produced Karl Marx? And does anyone here still believe in him, insist on his correctness? If they do, I am sure to meet them somewhere here.

The German perfectionist admires things in their classical form but passion is never absent, just held in check. To a German, the love of order, or an abhorrence of chaos, may often see the greatest virtue of all. *Ordnung muss sein*. But even perfectionists aren't perfect. Like me, they love to go a-wandering …

638–643 km

By train from Liège to Köln (in German the ö de Cologne is pronounced as in 'colonel'). I needn't have worried that Cologne Cathedral (Kölner Dom) would be hard to find. Step outside the *Hauptbahnhof* and it's there on your left, its twin towers soaring 157 metres into the sky – that's 30 metres taller than Our Lady of Antwerp. Charcoal-black, slender-steepled, how could this Gothic pile have withstood the firestorm bombing of World War II, I wonder. If I can't miss it, how could they? The body of the cathedral was raised in seventeen years, nothing short of a gallop by church construction standards. But the hulking edifice we see today was not completed until Kaiser Wilhelm I placed the finial atop the lofty south tower (the emperor must have been unafraid of heights) in 1880, a leisurely six centuries after the foundation stone had been laid.

Visit Cologne Cathedral and you start to measure time in centuries. Here is the oldest monumental crucifix in the West, donated by Archbishop Gero in AD 976. Light on this storm-threatening day streams into the Chapel of St Stephen through the Newer Biblical Window, a mere stripling at 727 years of age.

The pilgrimage to Cologne was one of the largest of the Middle Ages, after the bones of the Three Magi (still claimed to be here) were transferred from Milan. By this stage the Three Wise Men had been travelling westwards for more than 1000 years after Jesus' earthly ministry. I suppose you have to stop sometime. And even the oldest part of the cathedral is recent compared with the side entrance to the ancient city's Roman north gate, dated *circa* AD 50, which stands in front of the Dom.

Inside the cathedral I see the appalling sight of a tourist video-taping parishioners in a side chapel lighting candles – in memory of their dear departed. On reflection I think the solution, in a famous church such as this, is to set apart certain hours for tourism and others for devotion. The two activities mix like oil and water – crude oil and holy water.

This evening I'm off to the jazz pub Papa Joe's Klimperkasten. A Cologne institution, Papa Joe's has been around since the early Seventies. Two working pianolas endow the joint with period atmosphere but, work as hard as they might, they cannot upstage another pair, a singing accordionist and a trombonist who have merely to raise their eyebrows, wink or leer to raise a laugh. You can even criticise their clothes sense without hurting their feelings. They don't care all that much, but then neither would you if you were made of wood.

646–651 km

The challenge of finding an affordable hotel in Bonn looked likely to drag on for hours, but then I had a lucky break. Upon asking at a three-star establishment that would normally have been too expensive for a long-distance traveller, I waited while the receptionist went to see the owner. She returned with good news. Not only could I stay, but he had insisted I be given 'the nicest room in the house'.

This was an owner I had to meet. Leading me into his office, the receptionist introduced me to Herbert Böttger, a 60-year-old who beamed at me broadly from his wheelchair. Herr Böttger wasted no time on pleasantries. 'I got my injury in Australia,' he told me. He had lived there in the early Seventies and broken his spine on a return visit, in a car accident near Carnarvon, two years before the suicide attempt that left me a paraplegic. From time to time he returns to Australia, where his adult son still lives.

A leaflet on Bonn obtained from reception makes this city sound distinctly unsafe. At least five times in its 2000-year history all or most of it has been razed to the ground. Our friends the Norsemen burned it down in 811, and again eleven years later, just to make sure.

The most popular town boss was Elector Clemens August (1723–1761) who, we are told, 'danced himself to death'. (No explanation is provided, but his sad fate can surely serve as a lesson to us all.)

Ludwig van Beethoven was born here in December 1770. On the street outside Beethovenhaus, which has been a museum since 1885, I gaze up at the first-floor room, hoping against hope that he might be in. Not a sound. The ticket seller on the ground floor – seeing that I wouldn't take no or 'His spirit is all around you' for an answer – says the upstairs apartments are inaccessible to wheelchairs but, not to worry, the great man is always in the backyard. In a way she is right: there, in the garden, is the bronze bust of a shaggy-haired composer.

It is five o'clock now and it would be inexcusable if I left and just missed him. So, rather than idle, I go a-wandering into the parlour. Strange to say, it is full of empty seats arrayed in rows, as if in readiness for a concert, all facing the front of the room where a pianoforte stands with its lid auspiciously raised. Suddenly, music sweeps across the room, raising the hairs on the back of my neck a double octave, as it appears to be emanating from the piano. Now I'm no expert on classical music but that's Beethoven, make no mistake.

When the last chord has announced its departure, I follow suit. True, my last glimpse is of a CD player behind the window curtain, but the music has left me in no mood to quibble. By six I am back on the pavement, a completely satisfied – and not a little spooked – audience of one.

659 km

Koblenz is a meeting place. Here, people from all over Germany meet to admire a statue of Kaiser Wilhelm I on horseback and here, at Deutsches Eck (German Corner), the fast-flowing, coffee-coloured Rhine meets the slow-flowing and (Homer had the word for it) wine-dark Moselle.

663–664 km

'Typical German,' spat Hans, who owns the hotel where I'm staying in Koblenz, when a guest pushed past us this morning and occupied the hotel lift I'd been waiting for. I don't think Hans said it to placate my wounded feelings, but rather because he finds his compatriots are often single-mindedly selfish.

But at lunchtime, seated at a mahogany table in one of the hotel's bay window alcoves, I met a German of the opposite type: Johannes Weikamp, 81, a priest from Schönstatt, about 10 km out of Koblenz. Patre Weikamp, who did missionary work in South Africa for two decades and last year notched up 55 years as a priest, told me, 'I have Parkinson's. It is a very strange change'. And in his tremulous voice I thought I detected a dread of the future, of the wolf lying in wait along his path through the forest.

667–671 km

So fierce is the rivalry between Düsseldorf and Köln that it puts the odd divergence of view between Sydney and Melbourne in the shade. The rupture can occur over a beer. In Köln they drink Kölsch, in Düsseldorf Alt. Or at Karneval time, when in Köln they shout 'Alaaf!' but in Düsseldorf the cry is 'Helau!' Since both seem untranslatable into English, they must mean pretty much the same thing. Unless you hail from Düsseldorf or Köln …

Apparently the only thing that unites these cities is the Rhine. I will spend today, the midpoint of my journey across Europe, aboard a KD Line ship, after carting my luggage piece by piece 600 metres from the hotel down to the jetty. KD, in case you hadn't guessed, stands for Köln-Düsseldorfer. Our ship, the *Stolzenfels*, was named after one of the many castles, or *Schlösser*, we will see today. This one, its turrets rising like periscopes out of dark green woods, was built as a customs fortress in 1250, destroyed in the 17th-century

Palatinate War of Succession (the rights and wrongs of which I still have no fixed opinion on) and rebuilt in the 19th century.

Where I board at Koblenz, the Rhine is 200 metres wide. The number of kilometres upstream from the Swiss border, where the river enters Germany just north of Basel, is written on riverside markers spaced at kilometre intervals.

One of those happy coincidences that can occur to the long-distance traveller arises this morning. As the *Stolzenfels* skims grandly along, prompting me to wonder what aspect of this experience I could possibly enjoy more, I read these words penned by Rabelais,[19] 'The trees on the banks appear to be moving. Yet it is not they that move but we, with the movement of the boat.' He was a very sharp observer, old Rabelais – and his impression rings just as true in Mitteleuropa as it ever did in France.

The cruise is a delight. An offshore breeze is blowing and the temperature on this sunny day, in the low 20s, is unseasonally warm for this wet, wet year. What is more, at one point I have the boat almost to myself. In the shadow of St Goarshausen, the largest castle ruin on the Rhine, the hamlet of St Goar is the most picturesque sight I've seen since Norway; and there have been more than a few of them. About 2.30 pm we come to fabled Lorelei, all appreciation of which is tarnished by the woman in front of me – and a German, no less – speaking aloud into her mobile phone. It is all I can do to resist leaning forward, detaching the instrument forcibly from her left ear and tossing it triumphantly into the swirling waters below.

Kilometre 541 places us at 50° 2' 32" N, according to a GPS unit consulted by Horst Sfering, a technologically fixated tourist from Münster. Minutes later, Horst's GPS registers that we have crossed the 50th parallel of latitude and are now at 49° 59.9986' N. Perhaps it's my newfound heritage stirring, but I find myself sharing this German love of precision. A little calculation shows we are – or then were – 3 metres, less than a second's sailing time, south of the invisible line.

Just after 7 pm we tie up at Wiesbaden and, truth to tell, I'm apprehensive now. There is no taxi rank at the quay, and it's several kilometres to the other side of town. This time the 'successful traveller' would have been stranded if not for a remarkable stroke of luck in the person of Peter Jaeger, a veteran journalist who has spent 46 years writing for *Stars & Stripes*, the newspaper of the US forces based here. At the pier to meet a friend who failed to show up, he offers me a lift to Wiesbaden's hostel, or *jugendherberge*, about ten minutes away by the direct route.

But that is not the route we take. Peter is passionate about Wiesbaden's architecture, particularly its neo-Classical heritage, most of which is original (bombs destroyed 40 per cent of the Aldstadt, or Old Town, in World War II, he tells me, but nothing outside the city ring-road). It is after eight when at last we reach the obscurely located hostel, and Peter slopes off to check that reception is still open. The car windows had been wound down to give me a better camera shot from a hill overlooking the city, and now the dark clouds unleash a full-scale *Sturm und Drang* performance. I scrabble in vain to find the right switch and when he returns, ten minutes later, Peter finds the ashtrays full of water and me well on the way to being drenched.

677–682 km

Fresh off the InterCity Express from Mainz, it doesn't take me long to decide that Freiburg, like Bremen, is one of my favourite towns in all of Europe. The relaxed atmosphere of this modern city, which has made the transition from medieval university town without losing any of its character, wins me over immediately. Of course, part of Freiburg's appeal stems from its proximity to mystical Schwarzwald, the Black Forest.

683–685 km

Saw a swastika worn in public this morning. An astounding sight, at least in the more enlightened west of the country, given that the symbol is banned in Germany. It was cunningly done, though, the top half of the symbol obscured by a one-finger 'salute', an emblem on the arm of a youth's jacket, and he looking the neo-Nazi part, it must be said. But the whole design could be taken (as I'm sure he would have explained to the police if stopped and questioned) as giving Nazism the finger. On the other hand it might be construed as 'I'm a neo-Nazi, fuck you'. I didn't linger to ask which message *he* meant by it.

Augustinermuseum. It sounds less like a place worth seeing than a diary note on how I've been spending my time lately. August in a museum. But it is well worth the visit. A recent lift-out published by the local newspaper justly headlined this must-see attraction with its many treasures *Das Wunder (*The Marvel*) von Freiburg.*

Housed in a former Augustinian monastery are a stunning collection of medieval artworks that would have touched the heart of Midas – among them reliquaries and orbs of gold, and a golden platter with two gold egg cups standing on it. Seeing such treasures stored up 'where moth and rust corrupt' naturally arouses a strong distaste when the wealth they represent could have done much to alleviate poverty. But we who gaze in awe at these marvellous things have the Augustinians to thank for both their aesthetic taste and their acquisitiveness.

687–690 km

Time to go a-wandering off into the Black Forest. I've booked ahead to a log cabin in Hebelhof with its own mountain-viewing terrace. Having discovered from experience that I can often stay in seemingly unsuitable premises – the only adaptation necessary being to the mindset of the hotelkeeper or guesthouse proprietor in question – I omitted to mention the small matter of my wheelchair.

The man who greeted me on arrival, Thomas, was taken aback. His first response, rather than an outright no, was amusing in retro spect, translated by his daughter as 'I'll have to talk to the owner'. It turned out Thomas *was* the owner.

And a fascinating character he proved. His bar-restaurant walls were blanketed with trophies – about 200 in all, everything from silver steins and ornamental cups to a huge deer with formidable antlers. But my assumption that the man-made trophies were for hunting turned out not to be the case. Thomas was a champion skier from the mid-Seventies onwards and his daughter has followed in his tracks. The trophy collection belongs to them both.

A plaque near the chairlift at nearby Feldberghof hints at the grandeur of this Alpine range. The Erstreckung spans 360 km from Germany's highest peak, Zugspitze, at one end to Europe's second highest peak, Mont Blanc, at the other. At the chairlift terminus on the lower slopes of Mount Feldberg, we are 1450 metres above sea level. Forty metres above us is the top of a tower that affords stunning views of the Erstreckung range.

Assisted up five steps by other visitors' willing hands, I make it to the viewing deck from where it is impossible to tell which part of the thin blue line of mountains is in France, Switzerland or Germany. Up here nations are subordinate to Nature, what you might call a healthy perspective.

26 August, 3.52 pm. Definitely my last speed record, I promise myself. The casters have developed a wobble at anything over 20 km/h. But the spiralling asphalt strip that curves down from Feldberghof to the main road is freewheeling paradise. I hit 25.4 km/h and, if not for that wheel wobble, feel certain 30 km/h would be attainable. Better not to think about it; best not to try.

695 km

From northern Sweden to southern Germany these days you stumble across Australian restaurants and bars in the unlikeliest places. This afternoon I spot one in a Freiburg outdoor shopping court. If we are going to take over the world, this is surely the way to do it. Subtly infiltrate a non-Australian space and always, but always, go for the throat.

698–699 km

My first train journey of the day delivered me from Schwarzwald to Karlsruhe, where I had to do a quick-change routine between platforms to catch an eastbound connection to Munich. On the first train I shared a private compartment with two other passengers – a mother, Jutta, and her son Silas. Jutta's English was not very good but she managed to convey the purpose of her journey, and a sad one it was. Two months ago her father, a cabinetmaker, died in Göppingen, a town near Ulm, and today she was going there to see a notary.

On the Munich service this afternoon, everything seemed to be running with celebrated German efficiency, which is more than you could say for this morning's Karlsruhe transfer, until the eight minutes came when it actually had to be done. Service officer Cornelia had hurried to the platform on receiving a phone call from the conductor five minutes before the train pulled in. She greeted me by handing up the paperwork that had failed to inform her of my arrival, let alone of my need for a baggage trolley, but responded admirably to the counter-argument that *Ich bin hier* (on Platform 3) and 'Look, my train is over there' (on Platform 8).

Rising to the challenge, she performed the eight-minute transfer in seven-and-a-half minutes and, even now, as I roll into Munich, a full-scale internal investigation is proceeding at Karlsruhe to discover the error in Cornelia's impression that between 11.58 this morning and 12.06 this afternoon I was on her patch, despite the documentary evidence that I wasn't.

On the Munich leg of the day's travels came the announcement, 'We will be arriving in Augsburg at 2.46 pm. For local connections the train to [one place name] will be leaving at 2.43, to [another] at 2.47 and to [a third destination] at 2.49'. Somehow precision had leapt the tracks and slammed into absurdity.

As we drew into Göppingen, Jutta and Silas sought me out to say goodbye. In sympathy for them, but stuck for appropriate words of farewell and condolence, I wished them 'a meaningful day'. When they had descended from the carriage, the passenger next to me, Ben, inquired why I had used those words. When I explained my difficulty, he said there was a German phrase that would have overcome the awkwardness of the moment, '*Ich hoffe, dein Tag vergeht nicht zu langsam*'. As he translated it, I found it quite moving. 'May your day not go too slowly.'

Opposite Munich *Hauptbahnhof*, in an effort to get my bearings, I ask a dapper little man in a business suit and hat where Senefelderstrasse, the street of my chosen hostel, is. He babbles something unintelligible before turning on his heel and strutting off. When I ask a bystander, who has heard it all and is standing with his mouth agape, what the rude man said, he quotes him, 'If you don't know where you're going, you should stay home'. Welcome to Munich.

I find my way despite him. In the lift of the wonderfully named Wombat Hostel is a joke for the marsupially challenged. 'FACT: Wombat eats, roots and leaves.' Well, isn't it just my luck on being shown my shared dormitory – at four in the afternoon – to find a

German couple in a bed at the far end of the room smack bang between feeding time and checkout?

Wherever I go in Europe, people's knee-jerk reaction on discovering I come from Australia is to exclaim, 'Oh, so far away!' To which I now reply, 'Not really. You spend 22 hours on a plane, disembark and you're right there'. Some are still not convinced: maybe they don't like to admit they're irked by the cost – these people who would think nothing of splashing out on a holiday in New York or South America – so instead they bemoan the loss of a day out of their busy lives. From the way they talk, you'd think they're making the journey in box kites, not jetliners. The point to impress upon the next reluctant European you hear decrying the tyranny of Australia's distance from Earth Central is that we have excellent sleeping facilities for overtired globetrotters. If they doubt this, just clinch the argument by saying, Why do you think koalas choose to live there?

703–707 km

Today I meet Mike Holland, my old friend and journalistic colleague from Oman and Fleet Street days who has rearranged a few commitments so that we can meet up in Bavaria and see something of Munich and Altötting, where his partner Regina's mother lives, before heading south to the Austrian border.

In the hostel corridor scouring my backpack for a lost glove, I look up to see a familiar figure stooped over, peering at a room number. 'Mike!' I call out, and that's how we are reunited after eleven years.

Genial as ever, moustachioed Mike has remained that rare creature, a friend at a distance but often in my thoughts. His father served in the British Army of the Rhine, so he has been familiar with Germany since childhood. A former comment-pages editor for *The Observer* in London, Mike – who bears a striking resemblance to Einstein in hairy late middle age – has lately been forced by ill health to take things a little easier.

But he has not opted out of professional life altogether. Indeed he may be the only sub-editor in the history of *The Tablet*, a liberal Catholic journal in Britain, to have written an article titled 'Why

I am an Atheist'. This comes as something of a surprise when you recall that he was schooled by Jesuits.

Now Mike is as knowledgeable about technology as I am ignorant of it, but that doesn't mean I'm uninterested. Together this morning we stroll the few hundred metres from downtown Munich to the Deutsches Museum. Apart from the Smithsonian Institution in Washington, DC, and the British Museum in London, the Deutsches Museum has no rival as a compendium of Man's state of knowledge about 'the known world' of science and its practical technological applications.

The museum was founded a century ago by Oskar von Miller, whose passion for the new technology of his day was matched only by his contribution to it. He had carried out the first two major trials of long-distance power transmission in 1882 and supervised construction of the first hydroelectric scheme in the Alps. Herr Miller's house of knowledge contains a proud collection of firsts. Here you will see, complete with its tepee-like scaffolding, the telescope with which German-born astronomer Wilhelm Herschel discovered the planet Uranus, and the apparatus used to discover cosmic background radiation in 1965.

Behold: the bench on which Otto Hahn's team of lab scientists discovered the principle of splitting the atom; the original vacuum tubes with which Conrad Röntgen discovered X-rays; and an array of Robert Wilhelm Bunsen's burners, donated by his estate.

The aeronautics hall gives us the giddying sense of being suspended in mid-air ourselves, like the exhibits. Overhead are replicas of the standard-wing and double-wing gliders created by Otto Lilienthal, who in 1891 just outside Berlin became the first human to fly;[20] together with the first helicopter ever developed beyond the experimental stage, the Focke-Wulf F 61 of 1936.

The 'air space' is shared with a Junkers F 13, which in 1919 became the world's first successful commercial plane, and the Heinkel He 178, which just before the outbreak of war in 1939 became the first aircraft propelled by jet engines. But the incontestable star of the show is a Lockheed Starfighter, the combat craft capable of reaching twice the speed of sound which was supplied to the luckless Luftwaffe in the 1950s and 1960s. As Mike points out, 'an awful lot crashed' – 269, to be exact, in which 110 pilots perished, or, as the German inscription has it, '*dabei fanden 110 Piloten den Tod*' ('found their deaths').

Months later, I speak to a German man with contacts in the aviation world who recalls a joke from that time.

'What's the best way to get your own Starfighter?'

'Buy a block of land and just wait.'

On to the astronautics display, and while Mike inspects other exhibits I peer closely at a piece of moon rock sitting inertly (as they tend to do) in a reinforced-glass cube. This rock, we are told, was given 'to the people of West Germany by the American people ... in the hope ... of a world at peace'. A gift from Richard Nixon in 1973.

There are few faults to find with the Deutsches Museum. In the museum guidebook, just occasionally, the obvious bleeds all over the page. There are no prizes for guessing what Homer Simpson would say on reading 'The sun is the central object of our solar system' or 'The basic tool used in computer science is the computer itself'.

Mike and I are enjoying a stein or two (that weighty contribution to beer-drinking pleasure) at Munich's Augustiner Keller when I read in a leaflet picked up at the hostel that Bavaria's 1516 Purity Law mandating barley, hops and water as the sole ingredients in beer – a measure the rest of Germany adopted after unification in 1871 – has been overruled by European law, provoking a public outcry and calls to leave the Union. German brewers still pride themselves on sticking to the simple formula, and on this one I'm with them. *Prost*!

721–723 km

'There's a lot of ol' tat in Altötting,' Mike remarks as we glance at a window full of religious trinkets on the edge of this Bavarian town's main square. But the Chapel of Our Lady (Marienkappel), in the centre of the square, is anything but trivial. Munich would dispute it, of course, but Altötting is 'the heart of Bavaria', which is to say rural, intensely conservative, unswervingly Catholic.

In Altötting a tourist trail has opened, called the Benediktweg (Benedict Path). In 1489 the Virgin Mary is credited with having performed two miracles in this town that dates back to at least the eighth century. In the past five centuries 50,000 votive tablets have been placed at Marienkappel, of which 1845 are on display today.

Called 'miracle boards', they express thanks to Mary for cures and other tidings of joy attributed to her intercession.

It's best I lay my cards on the table at this point. I will not presume to analyse whether 'miracles', supernatural events which repel my rational mind, actually occurred. I cannot decide and would not dissuade. But I do recognise how important it is to many people's faith to believe in their existence.

In we file. The interior is a study in light and shade. A series of silver ornaments illuminate the altar beneath a sign that says, *Bei der Mutter Sind wir zu Hause*! (We are at home with the Mother!) The sight of one old woman in a headscarf looking quietly grief-stricken will stay with me as long as memory functions. They come here to pray for deliverance from grievous illness or distress of all kinds.

In a foreword to the *Altötting City Guide* written in January 2005, Joseph Aloysius Ratzinger waxes lyrical about the nearest big town when he was growing up, describing it as '... a place of festive liturgy ... a place of hospitality, a place where you can spoil your body'. I'm thinking that when the pontiff-in-waiting recommends you go somewhere to 'spoil your body' it's time for a new system of papal election, or at least a new translator.

Grüß Gott! – it means Praise be to God! or *Allah o-Akbar*, according to your linguistic preference – is a common Bavarian exclamation. Not long after Joseph Cardinal Ratzinger became Pope Benedict XVI, it was used with more reverence than usual when the former Archbishop of Munich flew over Altötting. While waiting for the flight, a TV commentator, padding out as they do, told viewers 'the pilot has seven children, all by the same woman'. Bavarians apparently understood this as a typical piece of north German Protestant irreverence, but it may just have been that the announcer borrowed his one-liners from Prince Philippe of Belgium.

Joseph Ratzinger would later cite his having been baptised on Easter Saturday as a sign of Providence's favour. His parents' names were Maria and Joseph – which for a Christian could be claimed as an even greater sign of God's favour – but perhaps the Pope felt that to have pointed this out would have been big-noting himself. Other roads may lead to Rome but the Benediktweg logically brings you to the double-storey white-stone building, neither poor nor pretentious, in which he was born. It had long since passed out of the Ratzinger family when on 19 April 2005 Joseph Aloysius became the first German Pope in 950 years.

Mike says 'the local Catholics wanted to buy it from this lady who owned it and she didn't want to sell it. People didn't like her for not selling it because they thought it was her duty. The story went around that she was holding out for more money. I don't think she was, but eventually so much money was offered that she gave it up.'

I am agog to see how the museum will deal with the Pope's time in the Hitler Youth. An information plaque is candid enough (obviously the decision has been taken that to conceal this part of his curriculum vitae would have been dishonest). There is even a photo of him in his Hitler Youth uniform in the booklet on sale from reception[21] where under the heading 'Stages in Life' it simply states, '1943–45 War Service (flak [manning anti-aircraft guns, *Flakhelfer*] in Munich, work duty and infantry barracks in Traunstein) and imprisonment in Bad Aibling and Ulm'.

Mike explains how the German Pope differs most from his Polish predecessor. 'John Paul II was a global priest who believed in the emotionalism of religion. Ratzinger believes his primary mission is to restore Christianity in the heartland of Europe, where he sees secularism and modernity as the greatest threats to faith.'

There is considerable evidence that Europe has turned away from religion. The Catholic Church itself is concerned by how few candidates there are for the priesthood.

Another Benedict, the fifth-century founder of Western monasticism, aimed at bringing Europeans back to God. Benedict XVI, who visited his birthplace on 11 September a year ago, is unashamedly Eurocentric and still fighting that battle fifteen centuries later.

Mike drives back to Altötting and Regina's mother's house, which is large, comfortable and inviting. We dine in the garden, and afterwards I slump in front of the TV. On this journey in which, for all its excitement, I am cast as the eternal transient it is rare to enjoy home cooking and unfeigned hospitality. Mike and Regina – a cell biology researcher at University College, London, who often returns home to be with her ailing mother – have made this the most contented time of my whole trip, and I am grateful for it.

723–724 km

We proceed southwards, Mike again at the wheel, through the impressive medieval town of Tittmoning, towards the Austrian border. Our destination is Berchtesgaden, where the Eagle's Nest (Martin Bormann's 50th-birthday present of a log cabin to Hitler) was built. Since the Führer didn't get much leisure time after 1938, he didn't really enjoy the use of it – and in any case it no longer exists – but visitors flock here today for a bird's-eye view, of history and the Alps.

On this first day of September we are escorted to the border by drizzle that, once we are there, intensifies into heavy showers. Before ascending Mt Kehlstein, site of Hitler's cabin and today's reconstruction, we stop in the village of Obersalzberg-Hintereck, the Third Reich's alternative power centre, and in the museum there exercise our imaginations as we explore underground tunnels and barrel-vaulted bunkers built for leading party officials in the event of *Götterdämmerung*. Which duly came to them, but in Berlin.

Outside the museum we board a bus that takes us, by corkscrew turns, to the summit of Mount Kehlstein, at 1837 metres above sea level or about the same height at Mount Bogong in the Australian Alps. A gold-plated lift rises 124 metres through solid rock. Up above, they say you can see the Austrian city of Salzburg on a clear day. Today the view is of heavy fog rolling down one slope, light mist billowing up the other, and on a green slope in the middle distance – unbelievably – pools of sunlight. The following day I ring Dad and mention the rather unsettling fact that on our visit the Eagle's Nest lift operator had a pencil moustache. Quick as a shot for all his 87 years, Dad asks, 'Did you happen to notice if he had a lock of hair hanging over one eye?'

724–728 km

Mike sees me off at Altötting Station. He's staying on for one more day before flying back to England; I will take the opportunity to see more of Munich's sights.

A plaque inside the Jesuits' church, Michaelskirche, reminds me that in the First World War the Germans, too, thought God was on their side: 9000 officers and more than 2000 junior officers and privates prayed here at the church before trooping off to '*dabei fanden den Tod*'.

734–737 km

Near the great gate of Karlstor, three classical-music buskers are busted by city police in what seems, to my naive mind, a heavy-handed action. The violinist tells me afterwards that the fine is €250 but they got off with a warning this time. The trio say they will seriously consider applying for a licence. And how much would that cost? Fifteen euro.

Table for five, please, at one of Munich's great gorging experiences, the Augustiner Bräuhaus. The party consists of 'Kaiser Tom' from the Wombat Hostel's reception desk, a colleague of his, their girlfriends and myself. I have the pork knuckle, get horribly under the weather and manage to sleep it off, dead (if not to the world, at least) to the party raging downstairs at the hostel bar.

743–748 km

Kaiser Tom tells me that Munich's 417 hectare Englischer Garten is Europe's biggest public park and not to be missed. Ambling through it from north to south takes up half the afternoon but it's time well spent amid green fields and burbling brooks, a world apart from what is otherwise a gritty urban environment.

At the park's southern edge a violent thunderstorm overtakes me. Somewhere nearby, where waves gush into the park from a subterranean stream, young men in wetsuits regularly ride the rapids. Hundreds of kilometres from the nearest surf beach, this was always going to be worth seeing but now, surely, no one else would be outdoors in such vile weather? Wrong. There they are, under the bridge, six super-fit lunatics, boogie boards in tow, being cheered on by a clutch of spectators huddled under umbrellas.

750–752 km

In Nuremberg I am lucky enough to find a hostel just metres from the medieval town wall. This summer of showers continues but it's worth braving them long enough to buy a steaming *Bratwurstl* (grilled-sausage) roll, just to discover why Nuremberg's *wurst* is Germany's best.

Late into the night, a talented guitarist and fellow guest all the way from Dortmund – Markus Hartkopf, lead singer of the John Porno Band – keeps us mesmerised with an impromptu concert that is all the more agreeable for being washed down with a delectable moselle.

756–759 km

By coincidence, I am in town at the same time of year as the Nuremberg rallies were held from 1933 until 1939. In a former SS barracks out at Luitpoldhain, a museum with the rather off-putting title of Dokumentationzentrum shows how the Nazis employed a mixture of thuggery and flattery to take over Nuremberg years before they became the masters of Germany.

Nuremberg in the Twenties was a Bremen of the south, a stronghold of the liberals and Social Democrats. The first Nazi rally was held here in 1927, and violence by Hitler's stormtroopers during a 1929 rally led to a ban on the party holding any more. So, if their thuggery was no secret, why was Nazism so popular among Germans in the 1930s? That's where the flattery came in. Hitler tapped the yearning for lost greatness by harking back to a medieval myth that had never corresponded with reality. That was the point of orchestrating torchlight processions before hundreds of thousands at Nuremberg.

By 1933, with the progressive forces ousted from power, Nazi Mayor Liebl declared Nuremberg 'the most German of all German cities'. Later, Hitler would designate five Führer cities: Nuremberg, Munich, Hamburg, Berlin and Linz, in his native Austria. The comparison with Soviet Hero Cities is inescapable. Since when did telling the voters they are the best in the world ever do a politician any harm?

Inspecting the captions on a wall full of photos, I shake my head. Can it be? Yes, Hitler was in Nuremberg exactly 70 years ago today. There he is, reviewing Wehrmacht troops in front of the opera house about 50 metres from my bedroom, directly over the town wall, on 6 September 1937, the Day of Welcome. In the evening he returned to attend a performance of *Die Meistersinger von Nürnberg* (Wagner, but of course).

This part of town used to be leisure grounds. They were destroyed by the Nazis but, with beautiful symmetry, the Park-Café Wanner was re-established in 2006. And now, outside the documentation centre, I stand in the vault of the 50,000-seat open-air Congress Hall, the largest example of National Socialist architecture still standing. As I peer up at the Führer's stand, and imagine him accepting the plaudits of the ecstatic crowd, my ears pick up melodic strains from the traditional German repertoire.

I wheel through the entrance arch, follow the lakeside path round, and in front of me is a fairground. Where seven decades ago 'fascination and terror' were created on the grandest of scales, today's children laugh heedlessly, and the only screams of fear come from those oppressed by gravity on the Roll Over ride. The Nürnberger Volksfest fun park is nearing the end of its annual two-week carnival. All the fun of the fair from coconut-shies to shooting galleries is here, but the image of bliss that will remain with me long afterwards is of a young mother dancing with her baby, both swaying to the rhythm of *(I've Had) The Time of My Life* ('No, I never felt like this before').

763–768 km

As the express train sped north-east from Nuremberg to Dresden, I longed, just this once, to escape the orbit of cities. Once arrived in Dresden, my plan was to take a spur-line train and 'hop off' at a small Saxon town or village, it mattered not which one.

The station assistant, Caroline, suggested Kurort Rathen. I liked the sound of the name without having a clue in what direction it lay. Ramps were available only at the bigger stations, Caroline warned me. Never mind, I told her, I would ask one of the other passengers to help me down to the platform. There were only two passengers on this 'train to nowhere' but the driver left his cabin to help one of them get me down. Before resuming his journey he pointed vaguely into the darkness towards a murky stretch of water, and I obediently headed downhill. A floating pontoon crossed the waterway, and its operator somehow managed to communicate that we were on the River Elbe near the Czech frontier. I wasn't the first person to think this was 'nowhere'. As I later learnt, in communist times this area was called *Tal der Ahnungslosen*, or the Valley of the Clueless, because it was the only part of East Germany unable to receive TV transmissions from the West.

On the far shore, now, I could see this was a river resort, little more than a hamlet, whose few hotels were A-frame lodges unlikely to be accessible even if affordable. With little confidence I pushed into the one hotel whose entrance I could negotiate. The receptionist looked as though she'd seen a ghost and warned that the last available room was on the first floor but, after I demonstrated that bumming my way up a few stairs was a mere trifle, she relented.

768–772 km

Come daylight it's a dim light, still drizzling and determined to persist all day. But it's light enough to see that the hotel I've fetched up in resembles a Swiss chalet. That is surely intentional, since this village of Kurort Rathen is situated in the Sächsische Schweiz (Swiss Saxon) national park.

Dismal as the outlook is, I decide not to waste this chance to enjoy the German countryside and set off down a path that runs by a rivulet. Before long, coming from the opposite direction, a hiking party of Germans stops for a chat. They speak English, and I a bare smattering of German, but that's no excuse for the verbal brick I'm about to drop. Asked my favourite places in Germany, I get so carried away with memories of Monday's pig-out (the word could not be more apt) that I blurt out, 'Next time you're in München you really should go to the Augustiner Bräuhaus, they do a fantastic *Schweine-sachsen*'. Open-mouthed at my blunder, they correct me in unison, 'Schweins-haxen'.

When I query them on the difference, they explain. What I meant to say was 'knuckle of pork', what I actually said was 'Saxon pigs'. Keen to put this gaffe behind me, I ask what part of Germany they come from. 'Saxony.'

Further into the Rathewalde I go, stopping to chat with two young Berlin women who are hiking on the same trail (except this time I make a mental note to stick strictly to English). We've just bought refreshments at a kiosk when a short white-haired man who is serving pushes my resting elbows off the counter where I was occupying a corner – apparently to create space for custom, of which there is none (apart from us). Taking offence on my behalf, one of the young women dismisses him with a phrase I last heard used by that hotelkeeper in Koblenz. 'Typical German.'

774–779 km

On Saturday evening I was strolling on the path above the water, a couple of minutes beyond the resort, when a boat tied up at the jetty. On heading down a concrete ramp I discovered from the small gathering there that a paddle-steamer service leaves Kurort Rathen, every morning, bound for Dresden.

This morning at 10.30 sharp the ship's bells of the *PD Pillnitz* chime decorously, as befits her age, and she commences to move downstream with an air of stateliness. The dowager reserves her harshest utterance, a hoot of the klaxon, for cautioning smaller fry and potential trespassers, 'We have right of way'.

This fleet, which is about to celebrate 125 years of continuous operation, claims to be the world's oldest set of working paddle steamers. I suppose such a claim could buy the odd argument with a proud steamboat operator on either the Murray or the Mississippi but this vessel is a veteran in her own right.

Newly settled in a polished walnut deck seat whose elegance is only slightly spoilt by a Formica tabletop, I watch the river flow past and then, as we approach the town of Pirna, out comes the sun for the first time in nearly a fortnight. The first mate comes over and bids me welcome, as if it genuinely matters to him. On this cruise I am reminded that when Germans themselves say people from the east are friendlier they are speaking from experience.

Opposite the community of Blasewitz we pass under the Blue Wonder Bridge, so called because of an unforeseen oxidising effect of the paints used in its construction, which created a blue tinge. Dresden, visible at first as a smudge on the horizon, gradually resolves itself into a dreamworld of domes and spires as we wend our way downriver.

I come ashore beneath the grand terrace that overlooks the river, and push my way up a broad road alongside it. Across the way is a new synagogue and, to judge by their dress, a Liberal congregation. But what are they doing here on a Sunday, I wonder. Fortuitously, the second Sunday of September is the one day when, in an ecumenical gesture, Dresden's Christians visit the synagogue, or Jews go to their churches. This year the synagogue is playing host to the Christians.

Diagonally opposite is a bleak memorial where the old synagogue stood until Kristallnacht. German history is marked by three 9/11s: 9 November 1918, when the German empire collapsed and the Red Flag first flew over Berlin; 9 November 1938, when the Nazis destroyed synagogues and Jewish businesses across the length and breadth of Germany; and 9 November 1989, when the Berlin Wall was brought down.

From 1900 until 1938 the Jewish population of Dresden hovered around 6000. During the German Democratic Republic (GDR), there was a remnant of 60 Jews in Dresden, who performed their observances at home. The city's current Jewish population is 700, most of them ex-Russians belonging to the Reform congregation.

More than 60 years after the firebombing of Dresden the old city governor's mansion, the Courland Palais, still lies in ruins. Rebuilt after an 18th-century fire, it was the King of Saxony's residence from 1806. In an irony that strains credulity, its occupant at the time of the February 1945 bombing was the Association for the Protection of the Saxon Homeland and Culture.

The Icing Sugar Cake is the nickname Dresdeners give their beloved Frauenkirche, a towering church also reduced to rubble in 1945 and whose reconstruction was keenly monitored nationwide right through to its triumphant rededication in 2006. The restoration is magnificent, and Frauenkirche continues to be to Dresden what the Brandenburg Gate is to Berlin, an instantly recognised symbol of the city.

Dresden today may be a replica but it is a convincing one. No city yet seen on my European journey has an architectural ensemble as striking as this one. The Allied (mostly British, some American) destruction that rained from the sky on 13 February 1945 has left a bitterness in many German hearts towards people they regard as war criminals, the unrepentant 'Bomber Harris' above all, which decades of peace have not been able to erase.

I had assumed that the 'sooty' appearance of many building façades was due to that firebombing or centuries of encrusted grime.

One Dresdener tells me, and others confirm, that the buildings look so old because they are artificially patinated to 'age' more rapidly than would occur naturally. At first I recoiled from this as a type of deceit but later came to the view that it was understandable. Dresdeners wanted their glittering jewel restored to them without having to wait hundreds of years, and no one should blame them for that. The result is one of the world's most resplendent cities, right up there with Istanbul and St Petersburg. Wandering around the Aldstadt, I see a piece of blasted earth the size of a large plaza and, behind cyclone wire in one corner of it, what look like Roman ruins. But a noticeboard there, and a Dresden woman who speaks broken English, agree it's from the 17th century. So what is the plan after the archaeologists have done their work? To turn the site into a multi-storey car park. What the Allies didn't destroy, the Germans will.

784–797 km

When I told Germans I was going to Bautzen they asked me what crime I had committed. Bautzen is best known as a 'prison town' where the GDR sent political dissidents. But what draws me to this most easterly point of my itinerary since leaving Stockholm is curiosity, not crime. For 1500 years now Bautzen has been home to a Slavic people known as the Venns, or Wends, who have struggled to keep their culture afloat upon a German sea.

Wheeling north towards the fairytale backdrop of spires and bastions that dot the skyline, the first thing I notice is that the street signs here are in two languages, German and Wend – even on Karl Marx Strasse (and, yes, that the civic authorities have left that name unchanged nearly twenty years after the demise of state socialism says something, too).

Founded in AD 1002, Bautzen oozes medieval charm but it has been more ruthless with the architectural heritage from its recent past.

Ulrike Reicke, a city librarian, says about 10 per cent of Bautzen's 40,000 residents are Wends but adds that they prefer to call themselves Sorbs or Sorbians. This is so much the 'politically correct' term, she says, that in the GDR era some members of the community could be heard to say, 'I'm not Venn, I'm *Sorbisch*'. She says they're the oldest minority in Germany, badly treated in Hitler's day (as, of course, was every minority) but the Balkan wars of the 1990s failed to engage their sympathies, proof of how 1500 years of separation from the mother lode of heritage can dilute one's sense of common identity.

The Sorbian Museum's director, Tomasz Nawka, is a bright and breezy man of about 50, proud of the militantly assertive tradition of Sorbian leaders without which he is sure they would have been assimilated out of existence. In Sir Walter Scott's great novel *Ivanhoe*, I have read reference to worship of the god Chernibor by what he calls 'the Wends' on Black Mountain, about 10 km from Bautzen, and am wondering whether that creed has survived the impress of Christian beliefs. From his defensive reaction – 'The mountain has no tradition; it's not very important' – I can only suspect it has.

On the desk in Tomasz's office is a toy koala holding two flags, German and Australian. He tells me it is a gift from a Melburnian Sorb, Benno Gotsky, who died only last week. Despite the solemnity of the moment, I decide the best course is to ask him straight out, 'Are you German?'

'No,' comes the confident reply, 'I am Sorb, and the state I live in is Sorb.'

Isn't it hard to keep up this illusion when the reality of the German state is all around him? Tomasz remains calm. 'It's not very hard because it's how I feel inside. I don't care what other people think about it.'

In 1937 the Nazis banned the Sorbian cultural society, Domowina, and began a program of forced deportations, starting with priests and teachers. 'My grandfather, for example, was relocated to Chemnitz in '37.' In 1949 the newly founded GDR said the Sorbs could have their own state as a separate nationality, but this never came to fruition. As the booklet speaks of a nation, then, is statehood the Sorbs' aim? 'We have our own schools, newsletter, theatre, museum,' Tomasz points out. 'It's not that we want our own state. Many small states cannot survive on their own.'

Anyway, efforts to strengthen cultural awareness, beginning with language, must take priority. Tomasz estimates that 3000 members of what he calls 'the smallest Slavonic nation', a paltry 5 per cent of the population, speak their mother tongue.

From the viewpoint of wheelchair accessibility, my sleeping quarters in Weimar seem most inhospitable. But Hababusch is a hostel with a difference, run by student volunteers who have their own rooms on top and rent out the middle floor. A narrow spiral staircase in this 19th-century ivied tower brings me to room level and, once they see I am not going to be put off by such trifles as a two-minute haul upstairs, whoever is on desk duty reunites me with my personal transport. Oh, and at €11 (A$18) a night, this is the cheapest bed of the journey so far.

798–802 km

Weimar is a beacon of German culture. The hometown of Friedrich Schiller and Johann Wolfgang von Goethe, it was also the laboratory of Germany's fledgling democratic culture after World War I. But the name of Weimar is still associated with the rampant inflation and a national Government so fragile that it crumbled to dust before the Nazi onslaught.

In the heart of Weimar stands the bronze double statue of Goethe and his protégé Schiller, and it is a rare visitor who leaves town without being photographed next to it. After nearly missing Beethoven in Bonn, I am relieved to know just where to find these two cultural colossi ... directly in front of the German National Theatre, where Goethe himself was the director from 1791–1817 and composer Franz Liszt conducted the orchestra during the 1840s.

It is hard to think of a building of such wide-ranging significance as this theatre. The Weimar Republic's Constitution was drafted there in 1919. And from 1936 to 1944 the Nazis turned *Kultur* on its head, housing their 'cultural police' inside and converting the theatre into an armoury.

Five minutes away is Schillerhaus, where the poet – who died at just 45 – spent the last three years of his life. But the period furnishings there only 'represent the taste of his times'. Across town, by contrast, everything in Goethe's house is 'proved to have belonged to the Prince of Poets'. As Germans rightly boast, Goethe was a polymath. His voracious appetite for knowledge embraced the fine arts, science and politics. Indeed, he went one step further than Plato, governing Weimar according to his own political precepts. Germany's greatest writer lived for 50 years in this palatial mansion, where he died in

March 1832 aged 83. Much of the interior is wheelchair-hostile but this time the latest technology came to my assistance. The audioguide you are given at so many museums these days is, in this case, a videoguide as well, so I was able to park myself at one end of the reception counter and 'visit' the entire house in the palm of my hand.

Even though his 7000-volume library had to be disassembled in World War II for the books' protection, they have been put back exactly where they were. How do we know? Because paper markers Goethe thoughtfully placed on the bookshelves were preserved.

The rebellious youth became a classic conservative, or rather a conservative Classicist, in old age, railing against what he regarded as the saccharine sentimentality of the burgeoning Romantic movement. But, then, if he hadn't insisted on the architectural form of what came to be known as Weimar Classicism, we might not have had such an integrated heritage to view as we roam around his hometown today.

Kai, who is on duty this evening at Hababusch, tells me that shortly after war's end in 1945 the US occupation authorities substituted all German place names honouring Adolf Hitler with the word 'Peace'. So wherever you see Friedenplatz or Friedenstrasse today you can be sure the place used to be named after the Führer. This seems to me a stroke of genius.

803–805 km

When planning my journey to Europe I did not think I necessarily owed it to myself to visit a concentration camp. Not because of any thought that 'If you've seen one you've seen them all' (which happens not to be true). If there was one thought I had carried away from my visit to Auschwitz in 2003 it was that one must never stop remembering.

No, my intention of visiting one was formed in response to the most unexpected of remarks made by Melbourne film-maker Bob Weis who, for family reasons, would never stop remembering. When I told him I would be going to Weimar, and might take in Buchenwald as well, he said, 'You really should. Buchenwald is different from the other camps. It's in a beautiful setting in the forest, so close to civilisation.'

Of all the Nazi death camps Buchenwald was the biggest.

Quarter of a million people from 30 European nations were brought here to suffer and in January 1945, three months before its liberation, the camp housed 110,000 inmates.

The entrance gate, with its lofty watchtower, is familiar from innumerable photographs. The camp was under the control of the SS Death's Head Regiment (*SS-Totenkopfverbände*) whose role – and here is a key difference – was to use Buchenwald as a training base in how to run the 'ideal' concentration camp. As the official English guidebook relates, 'Five concentration camp commanders and many of those who continued their career in the extermination camps and death squads emerged from the SS guard units of Buchenwald Concentration Camp'.[22] This explains the heavy concentration of SS men stationed here: 1617 in 1938, and double that number at the outbreak of war.

As you pass under that watchtower, nothing prepares you for the wasteland on the other side, a rough square whose sides each measure half a kilometre, sloping down the Ettersberg plateau to the treeline of the beautiful forest. Where are the barracks? All you can see, apart from a few structures off to the left and right, is a desolate surface dotted with scree and a few foundation markers where buildings once stood.

You roll downhill, slowed by the rocks. Not until you near the foot of the slope, and get close to the forest, are your eyes opened to what went on here. See that infirmary over on the left. Every camp had one, so what? Debilitated by gruelling labour that would send thousands to their deaths – 56,000 are estimated to have expired at Buchenwald – many ended up inside the infirmary. As a former inmate chillingly explained in the 1960s, Soviet POWs who entered the old horse stables were told to stand against a height-measuring scale behind which stood an SS officer, who shot his victim in the back of the neck without ever having to look him in the eye. More than 8000 were murdered in this cold-blooded way.

It was impossible to know if rescue or death awaited one in this 'hospital'. The first camp commandant, the sadist Carl Koch – himself shot by the SS, for corruption, within the camp early in 1945 – had derided the notion of healing the sick, saying, 'In this camp there are only healthy persons or dead persons.' SS officers strangled more than 1000 in the morgue.

One incredible peculiarity of Buchenwald was that Commandant Koch established a private zoo there 'to provide diversion and entertainment for the men' (his SS men) although he warned them against 'loutish acts' such as filing deer's antlers, and threatened to have them punished 'for cruelty to animals'.

Buchenwald could claim another distinction, a Resistance cell formed by the prisoners, which grew to include captives from more than ten nations. Block Eight, today only a rectangle where the building used to stand, was reserved for children and adolescents many of whose lives were saved after Resistance activists persuaded a reluctant SS that youngsters could be productive members of work details. For once, *Arbeit Macht Frei* was more than a cruel jest.

The composition of this community of death, forged of Sinti and Roma Gypsies, homosexuals, Jews and communists, is far too familiar to tell us anything we didn't already know; their fate – gold teeth extracted, commodities made from their flayed skin – too infamous to make us retch. What is the terrible secret of Buchenwald, then?

That, alone of the concentration camps, its horrors didn't cease in 1945? That, after a four-week respite, it reopened under new management? Nazi Buchenwald's life was prolonged by six years when it became Soviet Special Camp No. 2. Another 7113 inmates died there, according to files that became public after the collapse of the USSR.

No, not even that. The thing you must come to Buchenwald to see for yourself is how culture and bestiality are as close as the tongue and the teeth. Only a short distance, 30 metres, separates the statue of Goethe and Schiller in front of the German National Theatre from the space behind it where from 1937 onwards, from morning to midnight, buses departed full of victims bound for the Ettersberg.

After the war, when it was thought all the horrors of Buchenwald were known, mass graves were found under the green forest floor.

Only with your own eyes can you see how close this ugliness was to Bob Weis's 'beautiful setting'. How near at hand was life in the City of Culture to death outside the limits. How handy Buchenwald was for Obersturmführer Fritz Sauckel, the regional Nazi chief who selected the Ettersberg site because he wanted a large contingent of SS troops stationed close to Weimar.

So close to civilisation.

Another act of extraordinary kindness made today's travel easier. A marketing manager from Halle saw that Weimar was too small a station to provide a boarding ramp and assuming, correctly, that Wittenberg wouldn't be any better equipped, rang ahead on his mobile from the train and, to my amazement, his friend Stephan, along with Diana – both from the Lutherstadt-Wittenberg Tourist Office – were waiting at the station to give me a lift into town.

806–809 km

Every year nigh on half a million people visit the city that gives half its name to its most famous son, Martin Luther. Every June, to the cheers of the local populace, one actor dressed as Luther 'weds' another dressed as his sweetheart, Katharina von Bora.

But don't get Luther wrong. As Stephan explains, he was a Protestant but no Puritan. 'Religion was of ultimate importance to Luther, but he had a bit of fun in his life too.' His 'table talk' evenings with students in Wittenberg wouldn't have been complete without the liberal imbibing of locally brewed ales.

It was Luther, after all, who wrote,

> He who drinks much beer sleeps well.
> He who sleeps does not sin.
> And he who does not sin goes to heaven.

To which Stephan has added his own jot of wisdom:

> But in heaven there is no beer,
> And so we drink it here!

Another quotation from his table talk, observations gathered by his students, goes, 'He who loves not wine, women and song remains a fool his whole life long'.[23]

Luther's keen sense of humour is further demonstrated by a statement he uttered at the first Evangelical (Protestant) service ever held, when he said of his wedding to Katharina, 'That a former monk should marry an absconded nun is a rare event'. Quite so. It is not exactly an everyday one even now.

The tourist information bureau sells many Luther-related items. My favourite is the pair of socks monogrammed with Luther's statement defying Rome, 'I stand here: I can do no other.'

The hostel I am staying in is next to the church where legend has it that he nailed his famous 95 theses against corruption in the Catholic Church. Luther is said to have written in a note dated 31 October 1517, 'I posted my theses about indulgences on the doorway of the Castle Church'. The bronze door we see there today was installed in 1858, a century after Luther's wooden door[24] was destroyed by fire in the Seven Years War bombardment. A plaque on the youth hostel wall records that the building I am sleeping in was struck by that bombardment on 13 October 1760. From 1885–1892 the church was redesigned in neo-Gothic style as the Memorial Church of the Reformation, and in 1996 it was designated part of the World Heritage.

While transfixed by the Castle Church dome, a 19th-century structural addition, many tourists are liable to miss the tasty, if not tasteful, offering in the window of the New York Bagels eatery directly across the street. The Elvis Sandwich is on special. And what is this historical delicacy, which stands a bit apart from the thematic unity of the town, filled with? Why, peanut butter and banana, of course, at least one of which can be blamed for the heart attack that carried the King away in his early 40s. Just €2.20 buys you a real-life – or perhaps a real-death – experience, without the need to go all the way to Graceland.

A visit to Luther House is *de rigueur*, if only to see how every century Luther has been reinterpreted in a new light. By 1817, the 300th anniversary of the Reformation, he was viewed as rational and disputatious, a German national archetype. By 1917 he was a nationalist symbol who had 'consecrated Germany's sword', a useful adjunct to the war effort. By 1967 East Germany was calling him 'a bourgeois revolutionary' while West Germans were embarrassed by his stridency.

Back at St Mary's, I watch as the faithful kindle candles from ones already lit. If the Great Schisms are ever healed, I can confidently predict candle lighting will be as central to the unified faith as it is to Catholic, Orthodox and many Protestant Christians today and millions of subscribers to other beliefs, such as Judaism and Hinduism.

811–813 km

Since the 1920s Berlin has been synonymous throughout the world with a sharp-witted, acerbic, intellectually challenging, irreverent take on life. You can take power away from Berlin but somehow it recharges itself. It is Germany's New York and Washington rolled into one. When I mentioned to a friend, journalist Mark Bowling, that I was going there, he sent warmly nostalgic emails about the city in the late 1980s when he lived there, and especially about Kreuzberg – a then fashionable, now rather seedy but still edgy southern suburb near the old Cold War front line.

My first night in Berlin, after finding my way to Kreuzberg and tracking down my chosen hostel – reachable only via the sort of darkened courtyard where you don't see the shiv until it's thrust between your shoulder blades – the lift I'm told to get into as the only way up to hostel reception gets stuck. I spend the next fifteen minutes warding off panic at the thought that, because the staff double as bartenders and cannot hear me above the din of their Friday night rave party, I might well be spending the whole night in this unventilated goods lift.

At five minutes past midnight my rapping on the lift's steel doors rouses the curiosity of two young drunks in the courtyard – there for what reason I don't know, but it can't have been legal – who prise the doors open and win my liberation.

813–819 km

Rested by a night's sleep in a bed rather than a goods lift, I am keen to get out and see Kreuzberg on this rare sunny day. It doesn't take long to find a typical Berlin pub, a *Kneipe*, as Mark had alerted me to look for: the All-Berliner Bierlokal on Lausitzerplatz.

Girls on in-line skates take their puppies for a roll, living up to Berlin's avant-garde reputation. From what I have seen of it, Kreuzberg is a mishmash of florists' stalls and Mideastern eateries: the Baghdad Café brings a smile to my lips.

As I push past the rail flyover at Schlesische Tor, off to my right is a blown-up photo of soccer star Ronaldo, eight storeys tall, pointing the way to East Berlin. Following Ronaldo's directions I come to Oberbaumbrücke, a bridge over the River Spree and one of eight inner-city checkpoints that became chokepoints overnight in 1961. My eyes involuntarily brim with tears as I visualise how wrenching it must have been to see the buildings across that bridge every day, in sight but out of reach. Westerners with persistence, clout or bribery money could go east for a limited time but easterners were choked off from their city for 28 years. Man's inhumanity to man …

At the end of the bridge I turn sharp left to see a preserved section of Berlin Wall, now known as the East Side Gallery. The oldest graffiti here date from 2005, mostly puerile, but such is its fame graffitists come from all over the world to have their spray.

Triumphal declaration from the True North

> 15 September 6.21 am AEST
> Subject. And the winner is
> Hi Ken,
> The winner of the local election is me!!!
> The Labour Party got 60 per cent of the vote so we won with great margins.
> I will writhe later because there is a lot to do just now. I hope your journey is going well.
> Marius.

Berlin's new Jewish Museum is the most comprehensive imaginable presentation of Jews' role in European history, from the First Crusade in 1095 down to the present day. However familiar the headlines, the full import of their story and what it says about Europe resides in the details, and the personal biographies, set out here.

The persecution unleashed by Christian euphoria at the declaration of war against the Muslims hit the European, or Ashkenazi, Jews hard. Along the established trade routes – principally in Mainz, Worms and the Rhineland – they became victims of 'violence against "the infidels"' even though they were the original People of the Book. After the Plague swept across Europe in 1347, Jews were accused of poisoning wells. Several thousand, in more than 300 cities and towns across the Continent, were killed.

In the Middle Ages, Jews in Europe were barred from many professions and, not being subject to Christian laws on charging interest (usury), many became moneylenders, which put them on the same social level as debt collectors and profiteers. How things have changed, I reflect. Would any Christian these days subscribe to a prohibition on charging interest?

In 1871, with the founding of Germany, Jews were given equal rights in theory that were often withheld in practice. Many Jews helped to shape Berlin's golden age, including Alfred Kerr, the most influential German theatre critic of his day, whose books were later burned, and the tenor Richard Tauber. But, when the economy collapsed, Germany as a whole began seeking out scapegoats. Anti-Semitism fuelled the rise of Zionism, yet as late as 1933 most Jews felt evidently themselves to be part of Germany.

As usual, the little things move you most. Such as home movies, from the late 1920s, of a Jewish family, the Aschers. We don't know what became of them but can be sure that, if they lived, they did so under the threat or actual experience of persecution.

There's a particularly sad display, a grand piano bought in Berlin in 1930 and donated to the museum in 2004 by the daughter of Helga Bassel, the purchaser. The Nazis expelled her from the Reich Music Chamber in 1936, whereupon she emigrated to South Africa. Her daughter Tessa only found out her mother was Jewish long after Helga's death in 1969.

The museum insists that Jews in Germany did not passively accept their treatment, citing the 276,000 who emigrated with the help of their community from 1933 to 1941. In February 1940 came the first deportations of Jews to Poland. The following year brought the yellow star and the year after that the Wannsee Conference which called for the mass extermination of eleven million European Jews. In January 1943 Goebbels declared Berlin 'Jew-free'. By the end of war in Europe on 8 May 1945 some six million Jews had been murdered, of whom about 200,000 were German. President Richard von Weizsäcker's 'famous speech of collective shame' delivered on the 40th anniversary of war's end in Europe is there for all who can read German to see. Sadly, it's not in English as well.

824–838 km

Today I spend a few hours in East Berlin, not just to look at an odd fragment of the Wall but to discover whether life in the city's east 'feels' different. On Alexanderplatz I get talking to Ingo. In his late 40s, he recently returned to his hometown after eight years in Paris, where he worked for a time 'as a messenger' for a radio station.

Here he is unemployed. He tells me, 'I've spent the day begging' and adds, 'not very successfully'. I remark that his bag seems to be weighing him down. Slinging it off his shoulder, Ingo takes out – well, I'll be – a copy *of Das Kapital*, the *Finnegans Wake* of communism. So is Ingo a communist, I ask. 'It depends what you mean …' he parries. Well, does he support Marx's propositions? On this point he is unequivocal. 'Yes. It is an excellent analysis of capitalism. This remains true, whatever has happened, and will always remain true.'

Nothing against Kreuzberg, and I'm sure Mark will understand, but most of Berlin's attractions are in the district they now call Mitte, so I move to a hostel in Johannisstrasse, just over the bridge near Friedrichstrasse Station.

On a visit to Pankow this afternoon, to see what the city's east looks like beyond the swank city shopping districts, I see on the station platform a sticker, *Gegen Nazis*! (No to Nazis!), bearing a diagram of a fist smashing a swastika. Old battles are still being fought over here.

840–843 km

My overriding impression of Berlin is succinctly summed up by a young American woman I overhear on the footpath in Friedrichstrasse, who says to her companion, 'You're in a world city here'. The rate of construction is the fastest of any European city, and third in the world, trailing only Shanghai and Dubai. This city has more parks than any in Europe. And its nightlife, if not quite as racy as in the legendary Twenties, is still electric (sorry if that sounded quaint: photovoltaic).

I am in the Deutsche Bank branch on Unter den Linden (which, incidentally, must be one of the most descriptively beautiful street names in all the world) when I meet a tall, reserved gentleman whose accent, even after decades living here, instantly identifies him as a product of the English upper middle class. Having established that we're heading in the same direction, he offers to put into context the two buildings I will see at the end of the street. And, despite his English diffidence, it emerges that he used to be in charge of one of them.

The first building, one of the most famous in Berlin, has been demolished, though not without a fight. The Palace of the Republic, itself built on the wreckage of a magnificent *Schloss* East German supremo Walter Ulbricht ordered to be destroyed, had great sentimental appeal for many East Berliners, according to my informant, Derek. There were several reasons why this was so. Plenty of GDR citizens had attended concerts or conferences there; and it was the backdrop to many a wedding photograph.

In there, between the exposed girders and concrete rubble, you can make out what must have been a grand interior before the wrecking ball struck. Outside the 'construction site', on Puschkinallee, is a hoarding that trumpets a thoroughgoing lie. 'Palace of the Republic – A Project of Prestige', it says. 'East Germany Asserts Its Legitimacy.' The decision to act *against* what easterners wanted, preservation of the 'people's palace', had to be justified as the will of the people. It was ever thus. 'The building is progressing in response to public opinion', continues the message. ('This is pure doublethink: 'in reaction to', 'in spite of' or 'in the teeth of' would be closer to the mark.)

Opposite it stands a smart two-storey building with an imposing balcony, a survivor because it has found a post-communist use. Formerly the *Staatsratgebäude* (State Council Building), Derek tells me, it was the only place where East Berliners could ever hope to see their leaders in the flesh. In the late Fifties and early Sixties Ulbricht, general secretary of the German communist party, and his acolyte, Erich Honecker, would appear on the balcony after Politburo meetings. Since the fall of communism, the building has been converted into the European School of Management and Technology, churning out today's and tomorrow's capitalist managers. My informant is Derek Abell, the school's professor emeritus. As he says, 'The one thing that would have had them (the old communist leaders) rolling in their graves was to know that an Englishman was running the building where they held their meetings'.

850–855 km

Rain is pouring down this morning and, as I make my way out to Zoo Garden where the tour is to begin, I am thinking what a waste of time this is. Surely it will be cancelled. But, come 10 am, we fifteen or so people, a tightly packed group, set off in spite of the foul weather.

We're on the Berlin 'Walking Tour'. On hearing of its existence I immediately thought, *That's just the tour for me. As a wheelchair user I don't go on many walking tours.* How much of it will be accessible? All of it. Yes, inequality of a sort remains. But, out of deference to the others, I do sometimes slow down so they can catch up.

Luckily, our tour guide is someone who combines an outsider's detachment – he happens to be English – with a genuine commitment to the city. Jason Andrews introduces himself by telling us he came to Berlin six years ago, and fell for a German girl who later moved to Bonn, urging him to join her. He adds, with undisguised wistfulness, 'I would have to say that Berlin is my first love'.

When we get to Friedrichstrasse, he divulges one of Berlin's great in-jokes. Near the top of the Fernsehturm, the TV tower that dominates the skyline and was built as evidence of socialism's superiority, two shafts of light in the form of a crucifix appear on its silver sphere whenever the sun shines (which it won't be doing today). Berliners, who love to nickname their buildings, call this one The Pope's Revenge. Religious symbols were banned under communism, and crosses removed from every church, so in the last years of the GDR the only crucifix you were likely to see in the east was the one on the building the communists had raised above all others.

Reaching Mitte by train, we soon wade our way across to Bebelplatz. In this square on 10 May 1933, just three months into the Thousand Year Reich, the Nazis held their first book-burning. The siting, right opposite Humboldt University, was no accident. Its library was handy for ransacking; and the more 'intellectual' the books on the bonfire, the better for their purpose. Through a Perspex 'skylight' in the centre of the square we peer down to empty library shelves. Nearby is inscribed a chilling prophecy uttered by Heinrich Heine in 1820, which would be fulfilled in the following century not only in Nazi Germany but in Maoist China. The English translation reads, 'When one starts by burning books, one ends by burning people'.

Jason, who has a cheeky English turn of phrase, explains that Friedrichstrasse is where Roaring Twenties Berlin began, with its bars, clubs and cabarets the haunt of playwrights by day, prostitutes by night. 'The Nazis didn't really like women in skimpy skirts doing the can-can,' he says, 'so in 1933 they closed down 250 commercial establishments in the heart of Berlin, bringing that era to a close.'

A few hundred metres south on Friedrichstrasse we wheel right and find ourselves opposite Checkpoint Charlie, the most famous of Cold War flashpoints. Shouting over the storm, Jason tells us a few things we may not have known about the Berlin Wall. It was built after the GDR lost 2.7 million citizens to the West between 1953 and 1961. 'On the morning of 14 August 1961, after a night of feverish construction, 40,000 troops stood here and declared the border closed,' he states. In its 28 years of existence, more than 1000 people were killed trying to breach the 'Anti-Fascist Protective Barrier'.

Jason has a knack for bringing history alive. He particularly likes the story of a ten-year-old boy who lived in the western sector and whose school was in the east. One day he came home in mid-morning and said a border guard had stopped him from getting anywhere near the schoolyard. 'Next day he got a US tank escort to school.' Jason's eyes light up. 'It turned out later he was lying.'

One of the tour group asks how the GDR could afford to build the Wall. That one's easy. 'Extorting money from the West. They sold their own people, you might put it, although I'm not supposed to say so.' (I can't imagine who would stop him: it's a free country now, isn't it?)

Two blocks after we've inspected Göring's Air Ministry building, Jason calls a halt to announce with a flourish, 'And now for Germany's best-kept secret. Directly below your feet, 10 metres down, is where Adolf Hitler's bunker was. Berliners have no idea where this is.' We are at a street intersection with ordinary-looking kerbs, on the edge of a car park, and nothing to indicate that below us is the Führerbunker, the pit.

'After the Wall came down, it emerged that Churchill and Truman seriously considered flushing Hitler's ashes into the sewers, and were only deterred by the thought that they really wouldn't like the idea of his ashes riding through the rivers of Europe.' It sounds improbable but makes a good story nonetheless. 'They were going to open up the bunker to the public and people said, "Don't do it." They obviously didn't want to attract neo-Nazis. So it was decided to seal it off for 50 years and review the decision then.'

The tour finishes at the Brandenburg Gate. The ace up Jason's sleeve is a powerful account of the East German trade minister's press conference on 9 November 1989 when his bosses had failed to briefed him on how soon the travel restrictions were supposed to be lifted, and he blurted out the fateful words, 'As of now'. 'Watching on TV, in Berlin and around the world, people gasped,' Jason concludes. 'And a three-day party ensued.'

860–870 km

It's a long story, how drowning my camera in Berlin led to a personally guided tour of Versailles. It began just on midnight after an arduous day of tooling round the German capital. I was taking off my shirt in the bathroom at the hostel, prior to taking a shower, when – my mind a blank – I momentarily forgot that the camera I'd taken 1000-plus photos with was in the shirt's pocket.

Well, it wasn't now. Before I knew it, the digital had done a swan-dive into the toilet bowl without touching the porcelain. The water was clean, but I knew there would be consequences. The device was fished out of the bowl quick and lively enough but no amount of button-pressing would induce the lens to project itself in the approved manner.

Apart from this morning's Reichstag tour, I cleared the decks of all commitments for the day, and after the tour I headed to the Hotel Adlon. If there's one thing you can be sure of, it is that the chief concierge in a five-star hotel will know whom to approach in an emergency. I felt a bloody fool explaining my plight, and at a severe disadvantage when requesting help, given that I wasn't even a guest of the hotel. After listening with amused tolerance to my tale, Raffaele Sorrentino, the Neapolitan 'customer service manager' at Berlin's most elegant address, said no camera shop these days would do on-site repairs, they would only send it away for a couple of days.

But I would not be put off, and my obstinacy was soon rewarded as Raffaele patiently phoned a number in Schöneberg, a southern suburb of Berlin, and then announced I must see Klaus Borosch, whose address he gave me. An hour and a half later I had located my man, but there was the tiny problem of a staircase standing between me and the first-floor buzzer. After knocking on the wall failed to alert anyone inside to my presence, I used the only other weapon at my disposal, and hollered, 'Herr Borosch! Herr Borosch! Herr Borosch!'

Herr Borosch could not hear me, but retired Bundeswehr lieutenant-colonel Siegfried Karbe, a neighbour who had been trying to relax on his balcony, did. 'Can I help you?' he called out. I turned round, replied yes, and made an instant friend. Siegfried was on the scene within a minute, and proceeded to summon Klaus. Explaining my predicament, he handed over my digital cot case.

Siegfried and I – soon joined by his wife, Ingrid – adjourned over the road for a coffee while Klaus went off to inspect the damage. The tiny compartment containing the memory card looked dry enough but I didn't dare get my hopes up. About an hour later Klaus appeared, with good news and bad. The camera was unsalvageable but the memory card was intact. He refused to take any money for his services – I *did* press him – and recommended a shop in the next suburb where Siegfried was good enough to drive me, even insisting on taking me back to my hostel in the evening.

To join a tour of the Reichstag, you need to apply in writing. My permission came through weeks ago and I was not going to miss it for anything. It was just a damned pity I couldn't take a picture of it. Our tour guide, Nina, says parliamentary standards here are 'relatively disciplined'. Asked what the word 'relatively' means in this context, she equivocates, 'On the one hand we're in Germany; on the other, we're in a parliament like any other.'

After initial hesitation, architect Norman Foster's dome design has become a hit with Berliners. Nina says they like its transparency, in both senses of the word. Lord Foster's original preference was for all the deputies' seats to be grey, until Helmut Kohl put his weighty foot down. Now they sit amid a sea of copyright-protected violet known as 'Reichstag blue'. Nina says blue, associated with conservatives in Britain and liberals in America, is 'politically neutral' on the Continent. 'People look at blue and think of the sky,' she tells us. *Not this summer they don't, Nina. You need to get out more.*

'The Reichstag is the most visited parliament in the world,' she glows, 'with two million visitors a year.' But then she spoils the effect by saying, 'It remains a bit of a mystery why visitors come here'.

In what looks like a locker room full of post-office boxes, everyone who has been democratically elected to the Reichstag at any time since 1919 has his or her own archive, indicated by a small rectangle. Adolf Hitler, who was also democratically elected, is represented by a black box with no name. The decision to include him at all was made only after much heartache.

We go up to the dome by lift. Arrayed around the viewing platform are historical snapshots. One memorable image by photojournalist Erich Salomon (1886 Berlin–1944 Auschwitz) shows Nazi members gathered at table in the Reichstag restaurant wearing their Brownshirt uniforms. Another Salomon photo shows the visitors' gallery on 4 June 1930. Among those present, paying keen attention, is a bow-tied Albert Einstein, his black hair just starting to grey.

The tour over, we disperse, many of us to enjoy the spectacular city views. Forswearing any more speed record attempts, I still find a descent from just under the dome to the start of the spiral ramp irresistible. My time of one minute 27 seconds I consider creditable in the circumstances. Had more people got out of my way in time, who knows? A minute, even, might have been within my grasp.

873–875 km

Today Siegfried meets me by prearrangement at Berlin's famous Pergamonmuseum. He says it is absolutely unthinkable I should leave the city without seeing it. Built from 1909–1930 largely to hold finds by Germany's Middle and Near East archaeologists, it features the Throne Room of Babylon, with its still scintillating glazed and coloured bricks from the 2600-year-old reign of Nebuchadnezzar.

The museum's crowning glory is the Ishtar Gate, named after a Babylonian goddess. Decorated with representations of bulls and 'dragons', it sports one creature with the head and body of a snake, the forelegs of a lion, the hind legs of a bird and a scorpion's sting in the tail. Awesome, not to say fearsome. Again I'm struck by how much history is generally unknown. Who of us have heard of the ancient nation of Hatti, which until its collapse *circa* 1200 BC was a great power in the ancient world?

Tonight Sieger and Ingrid are my guests at a *Kartoffelhaus* (potato restaurant) near the old Red Town Hall in East Berlin, and still they insist on paying. German kindness is not always random and spontaneous, I have found: sometimes it can be quite premeditated.

876–883 km

Today, my last full day in Germany, I take the train from Berlin to Frankfurt, completing a rather large loop since my first European landfall here five months ago. What do the Germans think of the French? If Charlotte, a 28-year-old passenger on the train to Frankfurt, is typical, not much. 'Paris is fantastic, of course, but the people there are unfriendly to outsiders,' she says. I wonder whether the fact she speaks no French – and I have just enough to get by – will make a difference. Should know soon enough.

And so to the bus station, on my 40th day in Germany, for the overnight coach to Paris. This country has energised me. I note that I've done 7.6 km per day, nearly twice as much as I was averaging in Russia. And my overall average speed has risen to 2.57 km/h. Is it possible I am going too fast? The more I see, the more I miss. Oh for the days when there was time to reflect and compare new impressions, when the journey was young. Memo for the future: always try to take Europe at 2.4 km/h.

Our Eurolines bus isn't even doing that. Far from coasting into France, we are stopped at the old frontier. There may be no more border controls in the 'new Europe' but there is a police check in these security-obsessed times. *Ordnung muss sein* to the nth degree. On this score, I'm sure, the French are every bit as German as the rest of us.

CHAPTER 8

French Impressions

THE NORTH OF FRANCE

Time spent:	30 days
Distance covered:	1513 km
Distance pushed:	229.4 km
Average speed:	2.665 km/h
Journey distance to date:	17,717 km

Champagne and champignons. The Seine and Eiffel Tower. French kisses, letters, polish, fried potatoes. *Bon voyage. Bon appétit.* Sorbonne, to a degree. Putting on the Ritz. *Bonne idée. Idée fixe.* Gare de Lyon. Gare d'Austerlitz. *Merci beaucoup* d'état. One revolution gone too far? Tumbrils à la carte but not for Joan of – Arc. De Triomphe posthumous. Parc De Tuileries. Foreign Legion. *Fleur-de-lys.* Laissez-faire the Sun King. Quai d'Orsay. And *musée* too. Verdun. Versailles. Marseilles. Lycées. Rousseau. Marceau. Marcel. Proust. Lumière (the brothers). Encore for the Enlightenment: Voltaire and all the others. *Candide.* The best of all possible glosses. The Panthéon. The Somme. The worst of all possible losses. Descartes: I think, *donc je suis Rodin. The Thinker.* Charles de Gaulle. *Je vous ai compris.* François Mitterrand. *Cohabitation. Le rugby. Le foot. Voilà* Balzac or Jacques Chirac. Marianne. *Mariage.* Go figure! O *Le Figaro*! *Libération. Le Monde. Liberté. Egalité. Sécurité* for Mobutu and Baby Doc. Lavender in bloom. *Chanel No. 5.* TV Cinq. Petanque warfare. Normandy. The D-Day dead. Cheese-eating surrender monkeys also succumb to beef bourguignon, *cassoulet*, ratatouille, bouillabaisse, bouillon, crêpes bretonnes, quiche lorraine, and the Maid of Orléans. *Bicyclettes.* Tour de France. The metric system. Christian Dior. *Elégance. La belle*

France. Left Bank. Right Bank. *Vive la différence.* The Palais des Papes at Avignon where *Sur le pont l'on y danse.* The belles of France at the Palais de Danse. Latin Quarter. City of Lights and *bateaux mouches. Les Misérables.* Hugo and Huguenots. Monsieur Hulot. Brigitte Bardot. Madame Tussaud. Can-can. Cannes. The Côte d'Azur. Claude Debussy. Pilgrims at Lourdes. Vichy. Vichyssoise. *Jeu d'esprit. Joie de vivre.* Legerdemain. *Légion d'honneur.* Champs-Elysées. Gay Paree. André Gide. Antoine de Saint-Exupéry. *The Little Prince.* Rimbaud. Grand Prix. Prix Goncourt. Jean-Paul Sartre and de Beauvoir. Existentialism, applied to Camus, though he's an Outsider, Sarkozy too. Chateaux. Bureaux. Roland Garros. Faubourg St Antoine. Juan les Pins. Le Pen. Le Bic. *Le flic. Film noir.* And then Gérard Depardieu. Catherine Deneuve. *Agent provocateur. Chansons d'amour.* Aznavour. Toulouse-Lautrec. *J'accuse.* So does Zola, But, to amuse, I prefer Rabelais and Molière. Tartuffe. And to awe: Saint-Säens. Cézanne. Bizet. Renoir. Gauguin. Van Gogh. Go for a burn with Renault (*deux chevaux*), Peugeot or Citroën. Marie-Antoinette. 'Let them eat cake.' *Mais non. Baguettes, Marie*! Curie. Roquefort and Brie. *Mais oui*? Why, certainly! *Gruyère. Camembert.* Goat cheese with Beaujolais. Don't say cheese, say *belle fromage. Par excellence.* Pasteur. Piaf. *Je ne regrette … C'est la vie. La Vie en Rose.* Pigalle. Les Halles. Mademoiselle. Maupassant. Croissants. Soupçon. *Soup du jour. Croque monsieur.* Bovary? *Oui, madame.* Nôtre-Dame. Sainte-Chapelle. St Louis. Folies Bergère. Gustave Flaubert. Belloc (Hilaire). Evian. Escritoire. The Louvre. The Loire. Ooh la la. Languedoc. Hilaire (Belloc). Pont du Gard and Gare du Nord. The Very Fast Train (but not from there) to Bordeaux *au bord de la mer. Tout va bien. Manet. Monet.* Down with the Bastille on the fête of *14 juillet.* All stand to sing La Marseillaise. (*Alons, enfants de la patrie, le jour de gloire est arrivé.*) So has death. To Père Lachaise. Oscar Wilde. Tomb defiled. Princess Diana … Paris.

France is a world that lives in the imagination of millions who have never set foot there. The associations of a lifetime are enough to create an ambience in which they come spilling out of the subconscious at the lightest touch. Everyone has a hidden stock, not just *moi.* Try it for yourself. French impressionism is a game anyone can play.

In 845 the Vikings sailed up the Seine to Paris,[25] another historical fact I decided it best not to rub in the faces of patriots hereabouts. Wherever I have been so far in Europe, the Vikings were there long before me: it's worth recalling, as you see the great overhang of Scandinavia on any map of Europe, that the same cannot be said even of the Romans or the Goths. You have to go back to the Celts to encounter a race so widely dispersed.

The sheer brute strength of Europe's true conquerors is something that those who want Europe to be seen as a peaceful and civilised archipelago have airbrushed out of history. But anyone who looks at Europe over the past five centuries rather than the past five decades should think twice before sneering at the strife-torn 'savages' of Africa. If it was the Europeans who invented the mirror, maybe they had more need of it.

876–883 km

The bus from Frankfurt released from that police border check, as if from a slingshot, at one in the morning barrels through the cold starlit night, westward via Metz to Paris.

Having thought it best to book a hostel, I opted for the Blue Planet near the Gare de Lyon. The night porter looked as if I had come from another solar system rather than Germany. I realised at once that I would not be staying there. A spiral staircase wound its way up to the residential section; there were no bedrooms on the ground floor. Starved of sleep, I put my head down for a kip on a table in the lounge room, waiting for the day manager to arrive at seven. Who turned out to be the proverbial Parisian: his instant animosity towards me was palpable. But I exercised abnormal control over my tongue. What could be lost by aggravating him was the willingness – of his subordinates – to look after my belongings while I scoured Paris for suitable digs. Patience paid off when a friendly receptionist who took over at nine spirited them to the storage room.

A foreigner who has lived in France for ten years, and whom I would soon meet, paid his hosts a memorable backhanded compliment. 'Don't forget. When a Frenchman is rude to you, he's not being rude, he's just being himself.'

The City of Lights is not easy to navigate. But after a few days I descried something almost geodesic in Baron Haussmann's design of road arteries meeting at obtuse angles on great roundabout hubs which kept suburbs within reasonable distance of their neighbours, like spokes on a bicycle. By the time I was ready to leave, having pushed more than 13 km a day on the first three days of October, I knew the old capital better than most users of the *Métro*, sadly off limits to me owing to the scarcity of lifts from street level. Most buses, including those with 'disabled' signs, could only be boarded with the greatest difficulty and at the risk of infuriating their drivers.

My quest for lodgings will span several days and make that one exasperating night in Amsterdam seem a cakewalk in comparison. On this first day of 'trudging the streets', I eventually reach the biggest hostel in France, the 439-bed d'Artagnan, only to find it full up for a week ahead.

Unavailability is the first hurdle. It is still officially summer, this is a weekend, and my arrival has coincided with the World Cup of rugby, to which France is playing host. Before long, my ears ring with the constant repetition of '*Complet*' ('Full'). Price is the second hurdle. My €40 (A$67) ceiling is being tested in a capital city not really attuned to budget travellers' needs. Accessibility will be a third, although that is not an issue today.

I find an accessible hotel, with only one step to negotiate en route to a ground-floor *chambre*. Hotel Lux is a definite misnomer, but fussiness would be out of order and I am grateful for the room. Even then, the offer is limited to two nights. A grudging manager has told the welcoming receptionist that the room is booked for Monday, and even though my intuition tells me differently there is nothing to be gained from calling anyone a liar. My €70 (A$117) has rented a room for 48 hours, and bought time to keep looking.

898-902 km

Marcel Marceau died today. Had I been sub-editing when that story came in, I would have submitted the headline 'More than a Moment's Silence, Please', or perhaps a wordless space like this:

where the headline usually goes, which would doubtless have been rejected as too arty by half.

This afternoon, on my way up to Boulevard Diderot, I am greeted by a kindly-looking man with Coke-bottle glasses on the bridge of his nose and a red-wine glass at the end of it. Drinking alfresco, he invites me to sample a *pichet* of *grappa*. Meet Nunzio, an Italian 30 years resident in Paris and owner of the *trattoria* in front of which I find him. This is a fortunate meeting for me, how fortunate I cannot yet know …

After a couple of hours' rest I venture across the boulevard to explore the quarter I am in, the 12th *arrondissement*. It is one of the poorer areas of what many – even an American I met on the train to Berlin – call 'the greatest city in the world'. The bistro and café culture is just as I knew it would be, intoxicating, even if you only order a demitasse of coffee.

But you are also struck by the raggedness and shabbiness on every corner. Poverty long ago lost its capacity to shock me, or so I thought until today. There is something woebegone, utterly bereft of self-respect, about the poor of Paris, perhaps because they are a highly conspicuous and wretched minority amid fashionably attired passers-by. It is the contrast that shocks, and seeing it today rebuts any belief in the incremental progress of humanity after re-reading George Orwell, on the first page of *Down and Out in Paris and London*, as he describes their predecessors of 1933 thus, 'The Paris slums are a gathering place for eccentric people – people who have fallen into the solitary, half-mad grooves of life and give up trying to be normal and decent'.

Their presence is as much part of the 12th *arrondissement*, where they hang around the market and beg, as the culture of *café* and the world's finest bread. Near the Place d'Aligre this Sunday morning a 200-deep queue of well-heeled Parisians wait patiently in the drizzle outside a bakery whose fresh, crisp aromas bewitch my nostrils almost intolerably. The baguettes that emerge, lovingly cradled in silver foil, from this *boulangerie* are veritable works of art. I expect you'll want to know whether the poor get any bread? They do; and not just crumbs but, the more enterprising ones, half-loaves. This is just as well. They cannot afford circuses.

On the footpath of Boulevard Diderot this afternoon a middle-aged woman with an oversize coat and a plastic bag brimful of daily necessaries yowls at my chair, 'T'ai ri-aaaargh! *T'ai ri-aaaargh*!' I have no idea what, if anything, the words mean. Clearly she spends her timeless days in Orwell's 'half-mad grooves of life'. I pity her – from a safe distance.

904–912 km

This Monday morning I begin searching in earnest for a place to rest. The Lux is adamant I cannot prolong my stay. The Hotel Garden ('*Complet*'). Auberge International des Jeunes ('*Complet*'). Half a dozen other lodgings, whose names I don't even bother to note down, '*Complet, complet, complet, complet, complet, complet*'.

As afternoon grades into evening, my early confidence sags. Apart from the availability question, some hotels are giving a French impression of their own, that customers in wheelchairs are an alien life form, and even if they had vacant rooms (and they're not saying there are) it's unthinkable they would consider letting them to the likes of me.

About eight in the evening, near the Place Léon Blum, I come to the fifteenth hotel of my search, the Royal Voltaire. And here Georges, the young creative manager, sees his policy of never turning away a potential guest sorely tested. Like many others I have found, his hotel has a lift but my chair will not fit in it. Georges asks me to follow him, but I cannot. He has to push me up the 40-degree angle to the first-floor car park before I can reach an equally bare anteroom, really a puny loft. I'm welcome to sleep in either place. Choice already! With an admirable sense of propriety, he is too embarrassed to charge me anything. This would be like having my own squat. For a while it seems as though the toileting arrangements might be based on the same principle, but a quick look is reassuring. Georges drags a mattress onto a quartet of beer crates and I try transferring my body from the chair to this improvised surface, but it is too unstable to take my weight. I tell him I'll take it, without the crates, if nothing better turns up. As no one else is remotely likely to want to sleep in a loft next to the garage, he agrees I can come back as late as I like to claim it, and informs his receptionist of the deal.

At 11.30 pm I phone to say that, after covering 16 km today under my own steam, I have found a place: the Hotel Acacia, a kilometre away, at an irreducible €44. My chair scrapes against the metal sides of the lift and I can barely get the chair into it, let alone out of it. In the morning the receptionist tells me that the *patron* wants me out, he is afraid the lift will be irreparably damaged. I acknowledge his concern and get back in the hunt.

912–932 km

Today, Tuesday, my search plumbs its lowest point. As might be expected when you have nowhere to stay, haven't had a bath or a shower for two days, and are eating on the run, minor irritations assume greater importance than they ever ought.

In the morning, the No. 56 bus from Place Voltaire to Place de la République starts to move off after the driver has seen me waiting to board. The bus has a 'disabled' sign *and* a ramp that simply needs unlatching. Ignoring me, the driver tells a passenger, who tells me, 'He says he hasn't got a pallet'. The technology doesn't require one, or didn't he know that? I tell him off for false advertising before we go our separate ways.

At lunchtime – which I had convinced myself would be a hypothetical concept today – I greeted Nunzio outside his *trattoria* and he insisted I draw myself up to the table and wait. After five minutes he brought out a plate of steaming hot spaghetti. With a flagon of *grappa*. When I'd finished this, he followed up with *entrecôte* and chips. And more *grappa*. And then refused to take a sou, or even a eurocent, in payment.

Not far from the friendly hotel whose manager would have let me sleep next to the car park rather than see me on the street, its antithesis – which I shall abbreviate to Hotel B.S. – shows a more malign face of Paris. Owned by an upper-class Moroccan family, the hotel is dominated by the adult daughter of the clan, ironically named Mercy, aggressively shrill and possessed of a flair for the melodramatic. It's obvious enough early on that the B.S. is that rare creature, a hotel with a lift I can use and a price not too far above my budget. But Mercy insists all its rooms are *complet,* before registering other new arrivals and handing them room keys.

Around 8 pm the evening shift staff of the Novotel, near the Gare de Lyon, grant me permission to 'use the facilities'. For the next few hours I see the *sans-abris*, the homeless of Paris, with the eye of pity and an unaccustomed awareness of how close the cosy mansions of this city are to its rainswept gutters.

When I return to the B.S. around midnight, my quest still unfulfilled, Majid the nightwatchman describes the ruling family as 'Jekyll and Hyde' and assures me they have plenty of empty rooms.

It's raining hard and closing in on 2 am when I decide that, as Orwell has already written the definitive book about living on the streets of Paris, the Novotel foyer is the only hand I hold in this game of marked cards. By and by, the night owls finish their and head up to their rooms. By positioning myself behind a pillar that blocks the line of sight to reception, I hope to survive until dawn. Towards half past three, just as I'm dozing off, the night duty manager, Branko, gives me a rude awakening.

'You must go. Go now,' he commands. Answerable to higher authority, he insists he cannot accept my continued presence. In a very French moment he says, 'You do not respect my position'.

'*Au contraire*,' I tell him, 'you do not respect my position.'

'And what is that?'

'That I have no position.'

Picture Branko unamused.

After some time, he relents. OK, I may stay until 7 am, not a minute later. Oh, and I'm welcome to watch the overhead TV. Branko doesn't seem to notice but at this late hour the screen is blank. Between seven and eight o'clock it rains again and I avoid a soaking only by sheltering with the dispirited souls in the bowels of the Gare de Lyon.

932–944 km

By Wednesday afternoon I have looked at 21 hotels and other establishments without success and am back at the B.S. Earlier in the week I acted on a suggestion by well-meaning Parisians that I should contact my embassy (though certain that finding abodes for Aussie backpackers would rank fairly low in an Australian diplomat's job description).

I was in the foyer, trying to detect a hint of mercy in Mercy, when a phone call from the embassy came through for me. It was an attaché with the exciting revelation that he had tracked down a hotel in the 11th *arrondissement* – one of the few to have escaped my attentions – and, wonder of wonders, a room in this establishment could be mine for just €99 (A$165)! Clearly, it was years since the diplomat had been backpacking but, thanking him for his efforts, I promised to present myself at the Belle Epoque and see if a large tariff reduction was out of the question. The manager gave me the room for €55, the most expensive night of the journey but a bargain by Paris standards. He probably assumed that the call from the embassy meant I was some sort of VIP (Very Insistent Paraplegic). Only Wednesday and Friday were possible. I must continue the search on Thursday.

Coming out of the lift, which I had entered facing forwards, I fell backwards, never thinking that the lift would stop 25 cm above floor level. Luckily, my chair and backpack cushioned the fall but now I was lying in a darkened corridor and no one could hear my calls for help. This is a bad week, I recall thinking. What to do? Using the chair as a battering ram I opened the heavy door and crawled out to the fire escape, hauled myself up a couple of steps and swung myself back into the chair. We don't call ourselves *Homo sapiens* for nothing.

949–953 km

Recalculating how much I saved by being on the streets for part of a night and in the Novotel foyer for the rest, I can now see my way clear to paying €68 for a night at the B.S. But once more I've underestimated Mercy's mercilessness. Cornered by her previous refusal to drop the price, she now turns vengeful with a frenzy, accusing me of milking my paraplegia for all it's worth. This I fiercely resent, as I've asked for no special treatment. Immediately she flares up. I must quit the premises at once or she will call the police.

On seeing me stay put, Mercy starts wailing like a banshee, 'Get out! Get out of the hotel, you are a barbarian!' ('*Vous êtes barbare*!') When the police arrive, they patiently listen to both sides but, as this is private property, advise me to leave. Adding today's quota of visits to twelve more hotels and even short-term apartments, I have notched up 33 attempts to find lodgings over half the area of Paris. 'Is there anything else I should do?' I ask.

The gendarmes urge me to follow them back to the station. And thus begins a most amazingly patient ringaround (don't they have crimes to solve? I wonder, but keep the thought to myself) which after five hours culminates in success. It is almost 10 pm when I arrive at the Hotel Cosmos, in the Rue Servan not far from the Acacia, just in time to obtain the last room in the house.

It has taken nearly a week and I've hardly begun to see the things I came to Paris to experience. Then again, the consolation is, I have seen an awful lot of Paris, more than most visitors ever will. Tomorrow I return to the Belle Epoque, and for the last six nights of my time in Paris I will sleep at the d'Artagnan hostel out east in the 20th *arrondissement*. My search is ended. Finished. Over. *Complet*.

955–959 km

Back at the Belle Epoque, a Frenchwoman from the country asks a dumbstruck receptionist for a timetable showing *bateaux mouches* departures to the Place de la Bastille. This is the equivalent of a blow-in to Sydney asking when the next ferry leaves for Bathurst. He has no answer for this one.

Pavel Nevzorov, one of the Moscow students met in Kem and an occasional correspondent, has fallen in love. Or at least it looks that way from this email, phrased in his characteristically expressive English, which would not look out of place in a novel.

> Friday 28 September. 8.35 pm AEST
> The Russian sour-colour-face was opened in a new way for me recently.
> The woman I have met in August.

The Louvre is the most famous museum in the world and, despite having seen some great ones these past five months, I expect it will be the best. None of the attendants cautions the camera-toting flash Gordons. When I ask one why this is he informs me that on 1 July the photography ban was lifted 'because we couldn't enforce it'. I start with the large-format French paintings in the Salle Daru, beginning with Delacroix's triumphant *28 July 1830: Liberty Guiding the People* and Jacques-Louis David's equally memorable depiction of Napoleon crowning himself emperor.[26]

But for everyone who stops in front of these works there are dozens who swarm into the Salle de la Joconde to lay eyes on the world's most famous painting. For many, it is the only one they have come to see.

Directly behind the mysterious Mona, I am confronted by an equally impressive depiction of youth in no way inferior, so far as I can tell, to what Leonardo has achieved with Lisa Gherardini. Titian's 'Man with a Glove', formal title *Portrait d'Homme*, seems to be whispering, *You want mystery? I'll give you mystery.*

Titian's subject is more mysterious than that of the man from Vinci; we haven't a clue who he was, only that his portrait was completed 'towards 1520'. And it is clear that the decision of the Louvre authorities to place him behind, but facing away from, Lisa is the only possible reason the whole world passes him by.

When I come face to smiling face with the Lady herself, what hope have I of seeing what thousands of others have missed? A realistic one, it would appear, because they've also missed the clue provided by the young man who spends his nights with her in this darkened chamber. And, while they know her face well enough, none of her many admirers – probably yourself included – seem to have noticed her hands. Observers down the centuries have argued that her eyes pose a question, and now I think I know what it is. *I dropped one of my gloves somewhere around here. You didn't see anyone pick it up, did you?* At long last her secret is out.

It's late in the evening when I surface in the Louvre courtyard next to the famous glass pyramid, and I head straight back to the hotel because tomorrow I must be up before dawn. Time to give culture the boot. The 'one day of September' is at hand.

961–970 km

Cyril, the Belle Epoque's receptionist-manager, tried hard to understand when I told him about Australian football and the significance of this day. I could only compare it with France's hosting the World Cup of soccer, or rugby, and even then I'm sure we both missed the point.

My 5 am wake-up call left me one hour to push the 3 km to Les Halles and the Café Oz, which is really a bar. As I pushed across pre-dawn Paris this wet, braw morning it was hard to picture the excitement among 98,000 fans gathering at the MCG, the highest attendance at an AFL grand final in years. But that was not going to stop me from trying.

On the Rue St Antoine, which I almost missed (it's one of eight roads that converge on the Place de la Bastille), I met a family of power walkers decked out in Kangaroos beanies and scarves, a true display of fanatical devotion since the Roos weren't even playing today.

Perhaps 150 people, most of them wearing Geelong colours, were waiting for the bar doors to open. When they did, I secured a front-row position in return for telling those at the head of the queue what the weather would be like at the MCG today ('overcast but no rain'), intelligence relayed by a woman at the end of the queue who'd been talking on her mobile to a friend at the ground.

By quarter-time (Geelong 5.7 37 to Port Adelaide 2.2 14) the sleepyheads who arrived closer to 7 am had brought the spectatorship strength in our own Great Northern Stand up to 250. Laconic Australian humour would announce itself from time to time. Late in the third quarter Geelong were thirteen goals ahead and streaking away when a male voice somewhere in the ruck behind me could be heard to say, 'They're not playing well, Port Adelaide'. Then a disappointed female spectator told a new arrival, 'There's been a bit of fighting but you really want a mêlée'. (And we say pardon the French!)

After Geelong had trounced 'the Power' by an all-time grand final record margin of 119 points, a result that sent this crowd delirious, I conducted my own post-match interviews. It's more than a game for any fan who cares, but for the expatriate what is 'more' tugs at the heartstrings. Paul Dillon, 30, once of Swan Hill but away from home for eight years, said he felt 'the magnetism of Australia growing stronger' (I've always said we're a lyrical bunch beneath the surface). 'I'm going from an Australian pub in the morning to a friend's wedding in a 13th-century chateau this afternoon,' he told me, scarcely needing to spell out that no one back in the wide brown land would be spending the day like this. And then Paul, an instant media celebrity, did a second interview, with Natalie Vella, from Melbourne and new in town, who within weeks would be presenting contemporary Australian music to Internet users in Paris.[27]

In the last chapter I started to tell the tale of how drowning my camera led to a personally guided tour of Versailles. Siegfried Karbe, the friend I found through that débâcle, told me that he and Ingrid had a son living and working in Vaucresson, a few kilometres from Versailles: so, before arriving in Paris, I had emailed him to ask whether we could meet up while I was here.

The royal palace with the most glittering reputation of them all was originally a hunting lodge for Louis XIII. His son, Louis XIV, transformed and enlarged it, and made it the seat of French government. We can appreciate Versailles better than Louis XIV could; its magnificence only increased during the reigns that succeeded his. Coloured marble from the Pyrenees, covered with gilt bronze, has me mentally discounting other splendours as second-rate.

In the Louis XV Room Goetz Karbe directs my gaze upwards, where the entire ceiling is covered with 142 figures in a work it took three years to execute. The preponderance of gold, porphyry and other precious substances in the Royal Chapel is so dazzling that for the first time in my life I regret not wearing sunglasses indoors. At the end of the parquetry corridor we wheel left into the Hall of Mirrors, where the First World War peace treaty was hammered out. One can imagine Billy Hughes hurling verbal mortars at the illustrious over there, as perky and pesky as a blowfly in a bottle.

And then we enter the King's Bedroom, created for Louis XIV in 1701, where he lived and slept and gave daily audiences from his bed – those legendary *levées and couchées*. Nearly a century later, on 6 October 1789, Marie-Antoinette used the (not so well) hidden doorway in her South Wing bedroom, camouflaged by a Gobelin tapestry, to flee the bloodthirsty horde.

Afterwards Goetz and his wife, Beate, treat me to a traditional German meal and good conversation; they even suffer me to give an amateur piano recital. Then Goetz drives me back to Paris and, dismissing my attempts to conserve his petrol and time, shows me several landmarks up close. The Eiffel Tower, the Pompidou Centre, the hollow cube at La Défense known as La Grande Arche. We circle (make that circumnavigate) the Arc de Triomphe, on the world's biggest roundabout; and at 60 km/h disappear into the Pont d'Alma tunnel where, exactly ten years and a month ago, Henri Paul sped into oblivion at 160 km/h. A great chip of concrete is still missing from the thirteenth pillar on the left, and in ten days' time inquest jurors will come here all the way from England to inspect it too.

970–980 km

Notre-Dame de Paris didn't need Victor Hugo to immortalise it. The most celebrated of Gothic churches would probably have lasted aeons anyway. Gloom-loving Quasimodo won't be making an appearance on this gloriously sunny Paris Sunday, and anyway you can't hear his bell-ringing for the deafening peals of organ music.

Today there is an Australian element to the Mass, with a guest choir from Sydney's MLC school. Somehow I doubt that an invitation like this would have gone out to the old Methodist Ladies' College. Rebranding works miracles.

One of the side chapels, I see, invites parishioners to partake in CONFESSIONS, DIALOGUE. Dialogue? This is very post-Vatican II. In the brilliant sunshine outside I pass dreamy minutes wandering through John XXIII Square before crossing Archbishop's Bridge over the Seine. Then I head up the Rue St Séverin, a tourist alley in the Latin Quarter, where the prevailing French impression is of a foreign legion.

I'm not wandering now, but searching – for the fabled Left Bank. The Rive Gauche, it appears, was never on the riverbank, so I head 'inland', wheeling in a giant circle but one that uncovers no trace of this legendary scene of cultural ferment, not to say debauch.

Towards five I make out the Café de Flore, haunt of Paris's literary élite since the day it opened in 1885. Sartre, de Beauvoir, Camus and Picasso ate here – on separate occasions, except for the first two. A block away is Les Deux Magots, frequented by Ernest Hemingway, although he, too, could sometimes be seen at de Flore. Other habitués included Lawrence Durrell and Truman Capote, Leon Trotsky and Zhou Enlai. Brigitte Bardot is said to have preferred the terrace.

The crowded interior makes me glad I brought my own seat. The waiters, predictably, wear vests and bow ties. A club sandwich costs €17 (A$28), lemonade €8 (A$12). J-P. Sartre developed his philosophy here but, judging by the interval between my arrival and that of a waiter, today's aesthetic preference is for non-existentialism.

And it is here, now I've ceased to trundle after the Left Bank, that I learn why this was a futile pursuit. An article in today's *Observer* laments that the ebb tide of independent bookshops has sent the Left Bank the same way as the Champs-Elysées which, once 'the most beautiful avenue in the world', is now dominated by 'luxury goods brands or universally known chain stores'.[28] It so happens that M. Herbert, a news-stall holder quoted in the article, is the boss of the vendor who sold me the newspaper. Having gone a-hunting for the Left Bank only to stumble across its corpse has come as a shock. Herbal tea at Les Deux Magots – a little cheaper there at just €4.50 (A$7.75) – will be the perfect reviver.

This evening I push from the Tuileries Gardens to the Place de la Concorde, dominated by an obelisk Napoleon's troops stole from Egyptian Thebes and by a giant Ferris wheel, Paris's answer to the London Eye. And then it's a sprint up the Champs-Elysées – not completely dead while the Lido dance troupe is still kicking – to the Arc de Triomphe.

Twelve roads meet here, making the Bastille look straightforward by comparison. Choosing with care, I take the Avenue d'Iéna downhill to the Seine, directly across from a modern wonder of the world (whatever the latest list may say). However many times you have seen it on television – and at some of its most glorious moments, such as the night of the 'false millennium' when it rivalled even the Sydney Harbour Bridge for pyrotechnic wizardry – the sight of those Promethean steel feet splayed across the terrain will always send your senses into a spin.

It is quarter past ten when I arrive. A 'special needs' customer liaison is sent out to explain that under French law I will not be permitted to go beyond the first level owing to the risk of fire. I protest the unfairness of this policy and ask whether she couldn't come up with a better reason for denying me *égalité*. Well, the officer says, there are 600 stairs between the first and second levels. 'That's more like it,' I say. When the steel-cage lift reaches the first floor, the tourists troop up 27 steps. I know. I counted them while bumming my way up to the mezzanine-floor lift the 'service' officer would rather I'd not known about. Peering up through the criss-crossing girders can be every whit as exhilarating as gazing on this city of a million lights, where blues, greens, reds and yellows sparkle and glisten. But the view, let me tell you from experience, is better from the second level.

985–987 km

On the Île de la Cité, where Paris began, you can find Sainte-Chapelle, part of the oldest remains of the first French kings' palace. What makes my visit truly memorable, though, is that I get to tag along with a group led by the best tour guide I have ever met. Vicki-Marie does not just describe Ste-Chapelle. Her voice rises and falls as she invites you to share her fascination with it. And her questions throw a searchlight on the motivations of key, but long extinct, personages.

I cannot improve on her delivery – even her longest sentences are crystal clear – so let me just quote, 'The year is 1226. The Crusades are not yet over. The throne falls to Louis IX but because he is just eleven years old his mother, Blanche of Castile, runs the kingdom until he comes of age.' Vicki-Marie's eyes dart around the group to see we are all following her. Until now France has been an alliance of convenience involving Burgundy, Toulouse, Blois, and sundry other duchies and counties.

The Seventh Crusade, from 1248–1254, is the making of King Louis. First he gets taken prisoner, then pays a ransom and at the end of the Crusade returns to France, faith undimmed and in possession of a prize worth more than victory itself. In exchange for his king's ransom, the Emperor of Byzantium has given him the most precious relic of Christ's Passion, the Crown of Thorns.

'So, now, the king brings himself to the Capuchin monks' domains in a simple white tunic, on foot, barefoot, all the way here with pieces of the tablecloth from the Last Supper, pieces of the Holy Cross containing the nails that pierced the hand of Christ, and – most symbolic of all – the Crown of Thorns; and he is going to tell the vassals giving him trouble that he has a letter from the Pope stating that these are sacred objects and that the holder of these objects is in good favour with the See of Rome and, as the See of Rome derives its authority from Jesus' promise to Peter to build his Church on 'this Rock', he is in good favour with God Himself. Now who are they to argue with that?!'

We are now at the door of the chapel itself. 'You walk in. Your eye goes to heaven.' The ceiling indeed seems to float, the star-filled sky of its gold and azure design hovering over the lancet windows below. Physical pillars of the church represent its metaphorical pillars, the Apostles.

'This and Chartres are the two most exceptional examples of stained glass in existence,' says Vicki-Marie, and to see what surrounds us is to believe her, 'the first traces that have come down to us of French stained glass.'

Just my luck, there was a go-slow at Pigalle Post Office today where I went to collect a parcel from Australia at poste restante. Only later do I hear of it, but the collection of poste-restante mail is supposed to be exempted anyhow. Two counter staff riffle through the registration book while I am thinking, Three weeks should be long enough for it to have arrived in a First World capital. Both of them miss the entry, which on their second attempt I happen to read upside down (a skill acquired during my salad days as a journalist when proofreading hot-metal galleys required it). Stung by the absence of an apology, I jest that perhaps I should be paid for detecting the item in question, and one of the staff turns snooty, insisting, 'We have helped you.'

994–1003 km

Now at the d'Artagnan hostel, Hiroyuki – a Japanese roommate newly arrived in Paris for university study – apologises when introducing himself. 'My English is very dangerous … ah, difficult.'

At precisely 2.02 Paris time (12.02 GMT) on 2/10, I stop and reflect. I have now pushed exactly 1000 km since my journey across Europe began 154 days 9 hours 1 minute ago. Which averages out to 6.5 km per day. I am on the Avenue de l'Opéra, and mark the occasion by photographing King Edward VII (or rather Edouard VII, the hotel) directly opposite.

Dusk finds me at the Quai des Tuileries waiting for the Batobus, a River Seine cruise vessel. A couple of sharp-eyed passengers respond to my gesture of helplessness – there are a couple of dozen steps down to the gangplank – and ensure I don't miss the boat. As the lights of Paris come on, a thunderstorm rumbles its way towards us and raindrops are soon spattering our watercraft. We pass under spans which gleam romantically, and our passenger liaison, Viviane, recites an enchanting nursery rhyme, even if it does lose something in translation, 'And she flows, flows, flows; And she flows night and day; For the Seine is a belovèd; And Paris is her lover.'[29]

1014–1016 km

It's only a twenty-minute push from the hostel to Père Lachaise, the world's most famous cemetery. An information board near the entrance that lists 107 numbered 'personalities' is dedicated to the memory of 'those who have passed away', as you would expect in a cemetery, before adding 'please respect their memory'. Why do they feel the need to say so?

Two young guys, who at a guess have no romantic attachment to anyone but share a fierce love of music, stand looking at the board, each holding a bouquet. I can't help asking, 'Who are they for?' but the answer comes as no surprise. 'Jim Morrison.'

Escoffier, the famous chef, lies here, a man who – heresy though it is to say so – almost certainly brought more pleasure to more people than Morrison, but no bouquets are left for him.

And so to the first resting place of Oscar Wilde … and, yes, the last. The dozens of red hearts and kisses on his modernist tomb could be seen as playful and loving, but the feeble attempts at wit – 'L'importance d'être Oscar' – are not.

One of the dead here is not a 'personality' at all, but notable nonetheless for having been born at the *fin d'un siècle* and died at the *fin d'un autre*: Martha Bourgeois (1900-2000).

As I clatter along the cobblestones trouble lies ahead. In the lowest nook of the cemetery, far from any exit and with all the graves up impassable rises, I accept the impromptu offer of an English visitor to find and photograph Edith Piaf's tomb, and hand him my replacement camera. Do I *regrette rien*? Well, I almost regret something. After five minutes, with the Englishman lost to sight, I call out guiltily, mindful of the need for respect, and only after an anxious minute does he reappear. (Piaf's tomb is difficult to find because it has no inscription, not even 'Piaf', but French visitors guided him to it.) When I express relief that he didn't steal the camera, the man replies nonchalantly, 'Yeah, I realised I could have nicked off with it and there was nothing you could have done. But then I thought about it, and realised I'm not that type of person.'

1023–1024 km

When it comes to punctuality I haven't found SNCF, the French railways, any worse than Die Bahn. My Amiens train leaves the Gare du Nord bang on time. At Amiens I am met by David. It was he and his wife, Pauline, whom I met at breakfast in that Rotterdam hotel more than 500 self-driven kilometres ago; and they will be my hosts this evening at their *pension* in the Picardian village of Bellerive.

We adjourn to the local bar. In a French bar, at least in Picardy, new arrivals come up and shake hands with those there already. David likes this social rite, agreeing it creates a much nicer atmosphere than you often get in an English pub.

In ten years here David and Pauline have built the old farmstead up from a state of acute dilapidation. Poultry appear at the window, the garden nestles beneath a lightly trafficked road and countryside which, from here due south to the capital, consists largely of wheat and cornfields. This is how you imagined rural France would be. Homely. Welcoming. Happily not Paris.

1025–1029 km

This misty morning I visit the Clearing of the Armistice, 7 km from Compiègne – surprised to learn there was a second armistice ceremony here, on 22 June 1940, attended by Hitler. Inside the building an exhibition commemorates France's answer to Baron von Richtofen, air ace Georges Guynemer (1894–1917), elevated to the Legion of Honour at 21 and killed on 11 September 1917, at age 23.

At this sombre spot on this sombre day, my mood lifts only on seeing that a signwriter has misplaced a crossbar in the last word of a public notice nailed to a tree, changing not just a C to an E but the whole meaning of the notice, which now reads, DON'T LEAVE VALUABLE OBJECTS IN YOUR EAR.

A historical explanation board in the charming Amiens district of St Leu underscores the importance of canals to the local economy. In the 19th century, watermills (*moulins*) were established all along one canal, it states, which was flanked by houses belonging principally to tripe dealers, dyers and fishmongers. 'Bath-houses upstream,' we are informed, 'were used for both hygiene and adultery.'

1031–1036 km

Like Ste-Chapelle, the 13th-century pile of Amiens Cathedral was built as a showcase for relics, or in Amiens' case a solitary relic, 'part of John the Baptist's head', brought back from the Fourth Crusade. For 800 years it has been venerated here. A church booklet says 'a thorough inquiry has been made by historians and scientists to warrant its authenticity'. *But how could they be sure?*

A Frenchwoman, I think she was, about 60 – certainly old enough to know better – ignoring the sign saying NE PAS TOUCHER, FRAGILE kicked the outer tile of a recent floor covering with her shoe. The tiles had been laid to reflect the window and wall above. Whether she thought, Touch doesn't include kick, or that, being of recent vintage, it was not due the same reverence as other objects in the church, I couldn't presume to know.

But I chided her, '*Ne faites pas ça*. You see the sign?'

'It is nothing,' she countered.

'Not nothing. It is terribly wrong.'

'If you say so.'

'Not if I say so. The church authorities say so. *Il faut les respecter*.'

At which stage a thunderbolt cleft the ceiling – one of Europe's loftiest – in twain, striking her dead. Her body toppled on to the pristine tilework, smashing it to pieces in eloquent testimony of God's special wrath reserved for elderly illiterate peasants and avatars of the avant-garde art world alike.

Now that's what should have happened ... Actually, she turned on the heels of her well-exercised brogues and departed in audible silence.

The Anzac Hotel receptionist in Amiens told me I'd be back. 'There is nowhere to stay in Villers-Bretonneux,' she said. Still I checked out and headed to that town of 5000 east of Amiens which was wrested by Australians from the Germans in April 1918, dealing a blow to their last great offensive of World War I. Ever since, so I've been led to believe, Australians have been welcome here. Maybe the hotelier is right, but I'm willing to take a gamble. If my efforts to find a place to rest in Villers-Bretonneux come to naught, I am going to see if that place – in a town that is taught to love Australia – will come to me.

The first piece of fortune in this game of chance could not have been whistled up. This just happened to be the day of the annual school fête, and there was no shortage of residents milling in the quadrangle. Villers-Bretonneux Ecole Elémentaire Victoria, established in 1923 with donations from the State of Victoria, now teaches 130 children ranging in age from eight to twelve. Met at the entrance as if I were a long-lost friend and taken into the quadrangle, I found myself stifling tears on seeing the words NEVER FORGET AUSTRALIA spanning the yard.

More luck came my way, as the mayor – visiting the school for the fête – agreed to speak to me. Hubert Lelieur, his town's leading representative for 25 years, fondly recalled his visit to the twin town of Robinvale, Victoria, in 1984. How realistic was it, I asked, to keep Great War memories alive now that the combatants had all gone to their graves? '*On ne va pas oublier*,' he said. 'We will not forget. For our children, it is their history. They [the Australians] were the creators of their liberty. It signified the re-entry of France into the world, the rebirth of the nation.'

Interview over, M. Lelieur let me photograph him. To his right sat a small boy, head on knee. Given the mayor's remarks about the young, I thought it would be good to get them together. The lad was sheepish but eventually sloughed across to the mayor, who placed a hand lightly on his head and looked grim-faced while I took the snap.

Noting down their names for the caption – Victor, age five, and M. Lelieur, 75 – I thanked them both, then turned round to see the boy's father grinning broadly. Frederick introduced himself before letting me in on the joke. 'The mayor is a conservative, I'm a communist, and I'm standing against him in the next municipal election. You have done me a great service. That photo will be very useful in my campaign.'

Then I hit the jackpot. 'Hey, would you like to stay at our house tonight?' The invitation I hoped for had come from an unexpected quarter but I accepted it with alacrity. By the time a friend of Frederick's came round this night to watch one of the most important matches, and what turned out to be the best one, of the rugby tournament – France versus New Zealand – I had learnt quite a bit about my hosts, and a fascinating lot they were.

Frederick, from a traditional French family, was married to Manuelle, from the Kabyle – an Algerian minority – who said their 'mixed marriage' had brought out racism among 'some locals'. It was not the first marriage for either, and they shared the household with six children: Victor, Valentin, Fanny, Orlande, Leïla and Loona. Manuelle's father, who is still alive, won the Cross of Military Valour with Bronze Stars three times for combat operations in Algeria and was admitted to the Legion of Honour in 2004.

The rugby match was grand – and I don't even understand the game. At half-time, France, 13-3 behind, would have been unbackable (if bets were allowable after a match had begun). A great second-half fightback by *les Bleus* secured a slim victory over the All Blacks.

And what was Frederick's plan of action if he were to become mayor? To extend Villers-Bretonneux's welcome beyond the Anzacs, he would like to interest young Germans in the battles and the fate of their grandfathers and great-grandfathers, whose bones also lie in the soil of Picardy. Yet he would be shrewd enough not to hard-pedal this aspiration during the campaign.

I see on its ticket covers that SNCF doesn't wish its passengers *Bon voyage* but *Bonne chance* (Good luck). Maybe it's just me but I find this less than 100 per cent reassuring.

1042–1047 km

Another great city, another great cathedral. Rouen occupies a special place in French hearts because it was here their national heroine, Joan of Arc, was martyred. Rouen, my first taste of Normandy, has more character than Amiens. It *feels* more medieval. Its cathedral spire, at 151 metres standing just shy of Cologne's, is the loftiest in all of France.

Awaiting inside, lest I forget my part-Viking heritage, is a reminder that the Normans were Norsemen. The sarcophagus of the second Duke of Normandy, supine in a side aisle, bears a citation worth quoting, 'Here lies William Longsword, son of Rollon. He established the frontiers of Normandy and died, victim of the snares of treason, in 942.' Not everyone betrayed him, though. His faithful hound lies at his feet.

Luftwaffe bombs dropped on 19 April 1944, the eve of Hitler's 55th birthday, spared only one chapel, on the southern side of the church. Fifty-five years later, part of the church was reduced to rubble again. A plaque explains, 'The tornado of 26 December 1999 that struck the North of France was particularly violent and disastrous to the Cathedral of Rouen ...' One of the roof monuments (the 25-metre-tall north-eastern *Clocheton de la Flèche* weighing 28 tonnes) dropped through the ceiling, destroying part of the 15th-century choir stalls, and restoration work continued until mid-2000.

Claude Monet was a regular visitor here and the tale of one of his greatest series of paintings captures my imagination. In 1892 he arrived to pursue his most ambitious project yet, dedicated to Rouen Cathedral. Monet boldly proclaimed his goal, to see if light 'can exert its disintegrating power on an architectural mass as solid and as immovable as this Gothic cathedral'. I like the way he posed the question as one might for a scientific experiment rather than a work of art. But, then, impressionism *was* an experiment of sorts, a self-conducted course in artistic Enlightenment.

In the spring of 1892, and again a year later, the artist was working on fourteen canvases at a time, moving from one to the next. In the end he had 30 paintings of the 12th-century church's western façade, of which he selected twenty for an 1895 exhibition. The politician Georges Clemenceau wrote an article lamenting the French Government's failure to acquire 'these twenty paintings which together represent a great moment in art ... a revolution without gunfire'. What an unexpectedly avant-garde sentiment from crusty old Clemenceau. The soldier backed up his words with action, buying one of the works and donating it to the state.

Monet had set up his easel in an empty apartment over a shop opposite the cathedral, premises he was soon forced to quit. Shortly thereafter he had to move from a second studio which the owner, a draper, wanted for a fitting room. Then another draper, a little further off, not only gave Monet a room with a view but agreed to build an extension just for his use. How like a parable this is – of the artist twice rejected by mercantile minds that regarded him as a nuisance, only to encounter a businessman of rare visionary spirit.

Boat-like Jeanne d'Arc Church dominates the town's market square next to the spot – a desolate square of dusty earth – where she was burned alive on 14 May 1431.

Downtown this morning I phoned ahead to book a place on Saturday's tour to the D-Day beaches of Normandy, and got through to Monsieur Bacon, the proprietor of Normandy Tours (in Bayeux). His reaction was unexpectedly brusque, and he tried to bluff me, 'We have legislation in France that doesn't allow me to take you. You must travel with another company. I will not take you.' And he hung up.

I rang back to appeal to his better nature and point out that hanging up is '*très impoli*'. Before I could tell him so, he hung up again. The third time I rang, the woman who answered was reasonable enough but M. Bacon grabbed the phone from her and said, 'I respect the law [the law, if I understand him correctly, that discriminates against the disabled] and I have nothing to add.' Fairly seething, I hatched a Plan B.

1051–1057 km

As our bus rolls down to the Atlantic coast, villages are dotted along the banks of the ever widening Seine. We are in Normandy, the land conquered by Norsemen eleven centuries ago.

In a family-run hotel opposite the bus terminal in Le Havre – where the husband, Christian, is an award-winning chef – wife Jacqueline has a ready-made solution that converts my disappointment at the lift being too small for my wheelchair to unbounded admiration for her ingenuity. She places a wooden chair inside the lift and sends me up in it, then one of her sons takes my wheelchair upstairs to have it ready for my arrival. Now why didn't I think of that? If I had, her technique would have saved me five days in Paris.

Unusual graffiti spotted on a shop window in downtown Le Havre: LA RICHESSE AUX RICHES! (Wealth for the Wealthy!) Odd to see inequality being defended rather than condemned. Perhaps, in these counter-revolutionary times, we can expect more of the same? I daydream of a world turned upside down, where placards read DON'T SOAK THE RICH, LEAVE THE POOR HIGH AND DRY, subtitled THEY CAN LEAST AFFORD IT, and millions chant MAKE POVERTY THE FUTURE.

Epiphany. Pink clouds fleck the sky far out to sea nearly an hour after the sun disappeared from view. Dogs frolic on the shore, oblivious to the roseate hues of the slow-dying day as I approach the lighthouse at the end of the pier, 730 metres from land. Left and right gulls wheel, and squeal. A duckboard is surrounded on three sides by a pebble beach (but of ducks there is no sign). It is not quite deserted, young men with bicycles make tracks, couples in love walk hand in hand. The world has exhaled and, for just this moment, catches its breath. But I have been 73 days without sight of the sea – so perhaps it's just me.

1059–1065 km

In most people's eyes, I suppose, the remarkable thing about my visit to Etretat, on France's Alabaster Coast, would be that I hitch-hiked there – or, to use the French, *fait de l'auto-stop*. Having auto-stopped as a wheelchair user in much more difficult territory – Vietnam, Saudi Arabia and Zimbabwe – the crux of the story was not how I got there but the belated discovery that I needn't have thumbed a ride at all. When Christian told me yesterday that *autocars* went to Etretat, I – who learnt French for six years – should have realised that *autocar* was not the same as *voiture* but I thought he meant a privately hired car costing perhaps €40 just to take me there – and that would never do.

I tramped 5 km, mostly uphill, from the suburb of Ste Adresse to a garage past the airport. A helpful mechanic there tore up a cardboard box and wrote on one of the pieces,

ÉTRETAT
ENGLAIS

In no mood to correct his spelling, I held the card up to the oncoming traffic – which quickly became the outgoing. Half an hour – and five cars a minute – passed. After a little while, thinking that a passenger who didn't speak the driver's language might be considered undesirable, I covered up the ENGLAIS with one hand. Within a minute, a van with a GB (Great Britain) sticker whizzed by – another missed opportunity.

A few minutes later, one vehicle did stop – a car driven by Karim, an Algerian immigrant from the outskirts of Paris, where the car burners were active in the bonfires of November '05. Karim was returning to Paris, where he goes to university, and decided to take the lengthier, scenic route. My luck.

It's a very peaceful place, the Alabaster Coast, with its soughing of waves on a sickle-shaped strand. I was just admiring the common sense behind a sign on the cliff that warned, '*Préservez votre vie*' ('Guard your life') when someone innocently told me the *autocar* was leaving in twenty minutes – and it turned out the *autocar* was none other than a regular bus service. Four hours I'd taken to get here when I could easily have done it in 45 minutes. And the charge – not that Karim would accept any petrol money – was all of €2 (about A$3.30).

1067 km

The first bus of my journey from Le Havre to Bayeux this morning crosses two great bridges across the broad estuary of the Seine. The second one, the Normandy Bridge (1995), is the world's largest suspension span. Only months later will I realise why it looked strangely familiar. A scale model was one of the exhibits at Munich's Deutsches Museum.

Just after 10 am I cross into the Western Hemisphere. A helpful passenger tells me exactly where the invisible meridian is. (The driver, asked to let me know when we crossed 0°, had given me one of those priceless French expressions – the pursed lips creating a doughnut mouth, the shrug of the shoulders conveying 'I don't know' and 'What is it to me?' all in one.)

The second bus driver, from Caën to Bayeux, is a pain in the neck. As I prepare to use my bus-boarding technique, he asks, 'Why don't you take the train?' Hauling myself up the bus steps, I have a question of my own, 'Why not make the bus friendlier?'

1072–1083 km

A fiftyish ex-army man from London – an unregenerate Little Englander – provides unintended amusement at this morning's breakfast table in a Bayeux *pension*. He is an habitual utterer of unconsidered remarks that reek of maladjustment to the failure of the French to be English.

After we've been served oven-fresh baguettes, he pipes up, 'When do we get some decent bread?' We swallow hard, but he's clearly feeling alienated. A pause, and then … 'I say, do you think they'd serve porridge if I asked?'

The cost of today's outing to the landing beaches where Operation Overlord began is justified by one immortal line, when our tour guide, Ed, quotes a Canadian D-Day veteran who once told him, 'You didn't worry about the bullet with your name on it; you worried about the one addressed "To Whom It May Concern". '

Needless to stress, the tour to *les Plages du Débarquement* does not occur with the tour company that refused to take me … but I have plans for them.

From County Wicklow – 'a Catholic da, a Protestant ma' – Ed takes us first to Pointe d'Huc. Through an occasionally brash exterior a remarkable humility can be discerned. As Ed says, 'It took me four years walking these beaches before I had a vague idea of what happened down there'. Yet he conveys his distilled wisdom in four hours.

The Allies surprised the enemy, Ed explains, by attacking while Rommel was away in Germany (he had gone back for his wife's 50th birthday). Questioned about the different shapes of impact craters, he points out that naval artillery shells leave oval craters, aerial bombs circular ones. It makes sense when you think of it (but I never did).

'Omaha Beach was the one landing indispensable to the success of D-Day, the loss of which would leave a 35 mile gap. It was close to an unmitigated disaster,' he declares and then goes on to detail why. Standing on top of a German bunker, Ed says 225 men were told to attack this point at 6.30 am on 6 June 1944. 'Lieutenant-Colonel Rudder had been told he could call for 600 reinforcements. But his duty commander, an Englishman, had drunk a whole bottle of whisky the night before. And the order wasn't given on time.

'It was ten past seven before the first [2nd Battalion] US Ranger's boots hit the beach here. Only fifteen of the Rangers got to the top of the cliff. What the Americans didn't know was that the guns had been removed inland, to a barn behind a farmer's field.' There the Germans used hedgerows as 'inverted trenches'.

The largest seaborne invasion in history, its scale staggers the imagination even today. Later, at the Memorial Museum of the Normandy Battle, I will see figures that are beyond comprehension: a force strength of 2.9 million, 660,000 airborne and 285,000 on the sea; 7774 aircraft flown.

Before you know it, we're back in the van with military precision, heading for Vierville (Omaha Beach). Ed informs us that none of the German bunkers was pointing out to sea, 'whatever *Saving Private Ryan* says'. The aperture allowed a gunner to fire obliquely on landing craft within a 12 mile range. So many of the paratroops were blown off course that there weren't enough left over from Utah and Sword beaches to drop on Omaha, retarding the invaders' advance.

The reason Omaha, Juno and the other sites were chosen was that they were among only five beaches along this line of coast where you could get vehicles onshore. The coast of Brittany, Cherbourg and Le Havre was too jagged; the Germans had Calais and Normandy better defended; and sites further south were not practicable because they had to be within reach of fighter cover from Britain.

The last stop of the tour is the American cemetery at Colleville-sur-Mer, overlooking Omaha Beach – a very moving site, with 9387 crosses and Stars of David in a section called the Garden of the Missing indicative of the sacrifice it took to regain a foothold on the Continent. It is fitting that the tour should close with a view of the eloquent dedication on the monument there, TO THESE WE OWE THE HIGH RESOLVE THAT THE CAUSE FOR WHICH THEY DIED SHALL LIVE.

If Normandy suggests D-Day, Bayeux – the first town retaken by the Allies – echoes to the drumbeat of an earlier battle of consequence for the world. The Bayeux Tapestry, depicting the victory of William, seventh Duke of Normandy, over the English at Hastings on 14 October 1066 – 941 years tomorrow – is sometimes characterised as a medieval comic strip, but only the Norsemen's descendants were laughing.

While the events retold on the 68-metre-long ribbon are familiar enough to any student of English history, the story of the tapestry itself was new to me. In the Middle Ages, Bayeux Cathedral burnt down twice without harming it. During the Revolution, in 1792, it was used as a tarpaulin to cover a cart loaded with weapons bound for Paris until a captain of the Republican Guard saved it and stored it in his office.

One of the less celebrated scenes set me thinking about religion's subservience to the military in the Middle Ages (and not just then). A cleric – a man of the cloth in both senses – is shown carrying a mace into battle. God's vicars on earth were not permitted to shed blood, but bashing people senseless was another thing.

All round town leaflets advertise that this is the annual Day of the Pig, with the centrepiece of festivities a '*marché gourmand*'. The leaflets depict a pig smiling under a spotlight – obviously one that hasn't read the leaflet. According to the fine print, one lucky pig will be named Cochon de Bayeux. I visualise the winner getting a sash and a reprieve until Christmas. Tomorrow night, it says in even finer print, the highlight will be a traditional banquet of savoury pork, put on by Bayeux chefs.

Saturday evening, in a local brasserie, it's do or die for France and England – this time at the Stade de Paris rather than Hastings. Old men with red, white and blue warpaint on their faces will not be enough to toss the English this time round.

Near the end of the match I catch a young man hurrying towards the exit. From the camera he has been using, it is easy to guess a local journalist is on the job. 'I think I have a story for you,' I shout above the din. The civic air is thick with news, no doubt of that, but I don't want to talk about rugby or the Day of the Pig. It's M. Bacon I wish to focus on. In the next issue of the town's newspaper, an article by Yann Scavarda appears under the headline (again translated) 'I wouldn't have believed it possible here'.[30]

On reading the article, which it is pointless to quote here since you already have 'the guts' of it, I did discover one thing I hadn't known: in French, 'to hang up' the phone, as M. Bacon did, is to *brutalement raccrocher* the device. *Oui, oui, oui,* I squeal, all the way home. That's much more like what happened.

1083 km

I was sleeping when John Howard announced the election date. Presumably Kevin Rudd wasn't, but it is still hard to believe the wily old campaigner won't rescue his increasingly cracked chestnut from the fire.

1089–1090 km

Angers, 7 km from the Loire, is a pleasant enough town. But its best vantage point is nowhere in its charming lanes or well-stocked shops, but above it all – from the chateau that shares its name. This acropolis, first occupied by the Gauls, was later controlled by the Counts of Anjou – who organised resistance in the ninth century to Breton and, subsequently, Norsemen invaders.

Seated beneath one of the chateau's time-ravaged bastions – and there are many to choose from – your overwhelming impression is that the Anjous didn't like visitors calling unannounced. 'Seventeen towers built on a rocky promontory made Angers the best defended fortress of St Louis' kingdom,' a brochure confirms. 'In the 12th century the Anjou dynasty, under the more familiar name of the Plantagenets, reigned from the Pyrenees to Scotland.'

If that power was on the wane, the process must have been imperceptible. In the mid-15th century, King René reigned over Hungary, the Two Sicilies and Jerusalem as well as his dukedoms of Anjou, Bar and Lorraine. Talk about plans to dominate Europe: these counts were nothing if not ambitious. 'The dukes of those times were enlightened princes and art lovers, and developed a dazzling court life. The many periods they spent in Naples influenced both their lifestyle and their conception of architecture.' And so Europe, considered as a volatile compound of Northern and Southern elements, is seen to have a distinguished pedigree. The love of indulgence, the so-called Mediterranean view of the world, is kept in balance by the cool-headed austerity of the Northerner. Or so the theory goes.

An inexpert group of railwaymen deputed to lift my chair from the train at Ste Pierre des Cours, near Tours, managed to warp the tyre so that it would no longer roll straight. Fortunately, one of their colleagues at Tours station escorted me to a nearby bike shop where the warp was straightened out.

1097–1105 km

Tours is right up there with Freiburg and Bremen as one of my favourite European cities. Easy to get around, a hotel close to the station – and the Loire undeniably picturesque with houseboats scattered along its banks and broad bridges spanning them.

On an autumnal morning in the park, I sit under a broad-leaved tree of impressive stature – an old lady walking her dog in the park tells me it is a *platane*, a plane tree over 100 years old – and wonder who thought it was a compliment to call this city a mini-Paris. *Au contraire*, Tours is clean and relaxed, what Paris aspires to be but can never be, because of its congestion and 'superior' attitude.

Embarrassing moments tonight in Tours' sedate Brasserie de l'Univers. My weary frame was resting on the banquette in the dining hall under a splendrous stained-glass ceiling from the late 19th century when the braying of 'Aussie, Aussie, Aussie, oi, oi, oi' was heard from the front terrace. Shrinking mouse-like into the red plush, I nibbled at my double-scoop strawberry *glace*. Chauvinist rantings were suddenly drowned by a bull's roar, 'Helen, don't give the mongrel a thing!' Just when I thought this immature party – average age probably 60 – were incapable of outdoing this outrage, a full-throated chorus issued forth. Boozily off-key and unidentifiable to start with, it soon morphed into a version of *The Road to Gundagai* at 150 decibels. I crept out, doing nothing to let on that I was their compatriot. And you know what? In many ways, I didn't feel like one.

1108–1113 km

In Martyr's Square, Orléans, stands a statue of Joan of Arc, who grew up here and delivered the town from English besiegers in 1429. Damaged in World War II, the statue was restored to the citizens of Old Orléans through the generosity of those in the New.

There is something magical about France. A woman in front of a perfumery on an Orléans pedestrian mall presses into my palm a brochure – and, after a perfunctory '*Merci, non*' from me responds '*un petit cadeau, monsieur*'. It turns out to be a magnetic compass. Something useful for the journey – and from a complete stranger! Back in Martyrs' Square the sun comes out and the merry-go-round cranks into life. *Oui*, there is something truly magical about France.

On 17 October, Day 170, I notch up 17,700 km while in Old Orléans and, by the time I depart Vierzon down the line – the connecting station almost in the centre of France – for the more luxuriant, more vibrant South, the total overall stands at 17,717. There is no time to consult a numerologist. I would prefer to buy a lottery ticket on the strength of it but can think of, oh, seventeen good reasons not to.

Here we are in the geographical centre of France, whizzing south. And what is my lasting French impression of the heartland? Grassland, in jarring shades of green, grazed by cattle that give our passing train the bovine equivalent of a Gallic shrug.

CHAPTER 9

Chic Just Happens

THE SOUTH OF FRANCE and MONACO

Time spent:	19 days
Distance covered:	2829 km
Distance pushed:	172.3 km
Average speed:	3.250 km/h
Journey distance to date (excluding Andorra):	20,953 km

1113–1117 km

The southbound train arrives in Vichy three hours ahead of a national rail strike, the first in a rolling series of *mises-en-grève* directed against President Sarkozy's plan to swipe public servants' early-retirement cushions from under them. I recall David, mein host in Bellerive, telling me, 'In my next life I'm coming back as a French civil servant'. I, by contrast, strike it lucky. The first likely-looking hotel I call at happens to have a spacious ground-floor apartment flanking a courtyard, costing just over €30 (A$50) a night.

There is a delicate subject I am keen to broach with the good people of Vichy. 'How does it feel to live in a city that capitulated to the Nazis?' Obviously it will not be polite to ask straight out, yet I am not here long. To discover what Marshal Pétain's collaborationist Government may mean to the local populace these days is a puzzle with no clear solution. It will come to me.

1118–1124 km

At breakfast in the courtyard this morning the hotel's co-owner, Annette, is not in the least put out by my prickly question. Mention the collaborators, she says, and young people will nod in recognition, but the choices of that era do not weigh on them. A common refrain runs, *'Pétain, il est mort'*. Their interest in the subject, she adds, is just as dead as the marshal himself. Their elders, of course, remember – but the town itself is neither haunted nor daunted by this chapter in its history. Famous Vichy water, Annette reminds me, springs from a source that is fast-flowing and cleansing, like the passage of decades.

Vichy is proud of its 'beach', a handsome strip of sand alongside the local Lac d'Allier. From a park above the strand I hear a distinctive clinking. Following a trail through the park I emerge opposite a grid of petanque rinks, or *clos*. It has been a quiet ambition of mine to encounter this pastime somewhere in France. Men spectate, their rangy arms on the metal fence demarcating the rink. A couple of them explain elements of *les boules* for the ignorant stranger's benefit.

The differences from lawn bowls, a sport my father still plays in his late 80s, are obvious enough. For a start, *boules* are thrown, not bowled. Players' stances express their individuality. One man waddles round like a duck, flapping his 'wings' before hurling the small, light (700 gram) silver bowl at the gravel surface. Reverse spin, I see, is not confined to cricket. Equivalent to the bowls jack is a small pip, or pivot, usually orange-coloured, called the *bouchon*, at which you aim your projectile.

After agreeing to show how it's done (only to add some jollity to their afternoon), I retire – gracefully, I hope, but at any event backwards – to the 'pavilion', a club bar at a reasonably safe distance from the *clos*. There, at an outside table, a lifelong resident of Vichy is already enjoying a beer, something rare enough to be notable in wine-besotted France. Five months in a wheelchair after a recent accident (he now uses a walking stick) serves as an icebreaker.

Did I say the answer to my impertinent Vichy question might come to me? Well, it does now as Roget Faure – seeming to sense my purpose before I ask anything – starts to speak of what it was like to grow up with the Gestapo living in his house. Faure was only twelve when their jackboots marched into his home – 'not my neighbour's house, *my h*ouse', he emphasises, the indignity of it still rankling six-and-a-half decades on.

'Pétain,' he surprises me, 'was not pro-German.' Well, I observe, they removed his name from the Verdun Memorial after World

War II, so someone must have thought he was. In the manner of wise old men whose opinion is impervious to arguments from those who were not there, he repeats, '*Pétain n'était pas pour les allemands.*' ('Pétain wasn't for the Germans.')

Of de Gaulle M. Faure says, 'He led the Resistance from England'. It could be he is praising the Free French leader; it could be he is damning him. Then, allaying any suspicion that he has grown *faux* nostalgic about the Occupation, he says, rheumy-eyed, 'They were like this in our house' (and at this recollection he points an imaginary sub-machine gun).

Did different soldiers treat him differently? Were there 'good' and 'bad' Gestapo? A pause, then, 'There were good ones, there were bad ones. But they were in *our* house!'

No one could fairly accuse Vichy of whitewashing its history, yet ... General de Gaulle's call to arms, '*A Tous Les Français*', issued from his London exile, is a common sight in public places nationwide even today. Only here do I see it consigned to obscurity behind a bush. At another public site I spot a remarkable historical error in a name plate on Avenue General Dwight D. Eisenhower. He was not the *Chef des Armées Alliés*, 1939–45, as it says. America didn't enter the war until Pearl Harbor. Surely even a Vichy schoolchild would know that.

1127 km

At the entrance to a dogs' sandpit beside Vichy's Grand Marché is this catchy little sign: NOS TROTTOIRS NE SONT PAS DES CROTTOIRS. *Merci de les respecter.* Or, in cultivated English, OUR PAVEMENTS ARE NOT SHITHOUSES. *Thank you for respecting them.*

1131–1137 km

One train takes me to Clermont-Ferrand, a second to Lyons, and a third – delayed 40 minutes by the erratic strike action – delivers me to Grenoble in the late afternoon. Tonight is the World Cup rugby final.

In bistros and brasseries France has been tuned in for weeks – up in the north for the international cachet, here in the South with genuine enthusiasm. Just as I'd envisaged, Grenoble in the shadow of the Alps – home of the 1968 Winter Olympics and a sports-loving city *par excellence* – has plenty of big screens up for the occasion. A street-corner brasserie becomes my grandstand of choice.

Twenty seconds after kick-off, a group of youths swarm in – half-interested in the game since it is the *grand finale*, but if the French themselves had been playing they would undoubtedly have been three times as numerous, ten times as raucous.

An intense first half – what else would you expect from South Africa and defending champions England, who beat Australia in Sydney back in '03? – but rugby players routinely ascribe victory to special inspiration and, in the end, the physical presence of Gordon Brown at the Stade de France is no match for Nelson Mandela's pre-match video address to his national squad.

Spot on half-time a three-pointer puts *l'Afrique du Sud* on 9 against *Angleterre* on 3. After the break the Springboks pronk their way to an emphatic 15–6 victory. In the bar the Frenchmen promptly rediscover their passion for the game, the ancient enemy having been conquered again. Oh, and this will be the furthest thing from their minds right now, but what does that say about European unity?

1139–1149 km

It's a strange sort of railway strike when the staff turn up for work – and do work – but, when some of the trains arrive an hour or two late, and at short notice, they are spurred into short bursts of activity and work much more quickly than usual.

This is a day of contrasts in my dealings with the SNCF. The departure from Grenoble was fraught, with 'assistance staff' temporarily mislaying my luggage (it turned up in the stationmaster's office) but the rest of the team, boarding me and then inspecting my Eurail pass, nothing short of professionalism personified. At Valence TGV – a three-year-old station as grand as a medium-size airport, standing in splendid isolation near the foothills of the French Alps – I had to wait 75 minutes for the connection to Nice. And it was here I experienced the contrast.

Valence's '*bonne équipe*' (good team) treated me like a VIP customer, beginning with that oft-forgotten word, 'Welcome'; being resourceful instead of bureaucratic – when one of the lifts refused to come they unlocked the one normally reserved for staff – and ending, or so I thought, with a complimentary coffee plus a ham-and-cheese baguette. But customer service officer Said, originally from Casablanca, still had an ace up his sleeve. Ten minutes before the TGV – Very Fast Train – from Paris arrived, he upgraded me to a first-class seat on the silver bullet to the coast – a dream that the need for thrift had forced me to abandon.

Just after a quarter past four this Sunday afternoon the TGV emerges from a tunnel and there, unheralded, is the Mediterranean Sea, filling the picture window, glistening in the autumn sun. I have returned to the 'centre of the Earth'.

I note with quiet satisfaction that it has taken 144 days, almost five months, to cross Europe from north to south – from Gamvik to Marseilles, whence the train will continue on to Nice. If my French fellow passengers appear indifferent to this epic achievement – *Can't they tell from my appearance?* – at least the folks back home should have been suitably in awe. In Grenoble this morning I phoned home. (A partial transcript follows.)

'Later today I'll have crossed Europe from the Arctic to the Mediterranean, Mum.'

'That's nice, Ken.'

'Tonight I'll be on the French Riviera, at Nice.'

'That's nice, Ken.'

'No, not nice, Mum. Neece.'

Today, 21 October, I attain another traveller's 'milestone'. Counting up all my previous journeys outside Australia, today marks six years of my life spent on the overseas road.

A wise friend long ago christened me 'an international vagrant' and I really don't mind, although to travel so far you need more money than a vagrant usually possesses. But, whatever country you go to, you are likely to run into other Antipodeans. Why are Australians and New Zealanders such inveterate globetrotters? I long ago concluded that it is at least partly because most of us have relatively recent European roots.

Excepting Aboriginal and Torres Strait Islanders, we Australians belong to families (the Desses were just one) that arrived in the Great South Land within the past few generations. We boast – or used to – of being multicultural. But our dominant culture is so homogeneous that it is natural for us, living on our island nation, to wonder, What is life like elsewhere?

With our many importations from Europe – from democracy to the cappuccino – it would be tempting to study the ways of foreigners through the prism of our own society, or from the comfort of a computer desk or armchair. But there is no substitute for being there – and I suspect that Aussie backpackers, and even more affluent travellers, feel this in their bones.

1149–1159 km

John Cage – whose silent musical 'composition', *4' 33"*, proved him a master at eloquently expressing nothing – is quoted, in translation, on a wall of Nice's Museum of Modern and Contemporary Art. '*Même quand il ne se passe rien, il se passe toujours quelque chose.*' Which is to say, 'Even when nothing is happening, something always happens'.

The truth of this paradox is one I keep encountering every day of the journey. Along with something else: anything that happens here happens with style. Call it *chic*, the French do. Paris may think it has a monopoly on *chic* – but when the time comes to let its tresses down where does *le tout Paris* prefer to holiday in style? The South – and, more specifically, the Côte d'Azur, that strip of Mediterranean glamour and leisure resorts, spiced with intrigue, that is perched on the coast running from the Italian border south-west to Toulon. Countless people who have never been there know the names Menton, Antibes, Cannes, St Tropez.

Even at this time of year, the Mediterranean has a reputation – not thoroughly deserved – of being ablaze with sunshine. If Paris *chic* happens to be a strapless dress, on the Riviera (poor things) they often go without.

Nice is a lushly flowering Garden of Eden, a paradise of pine and palm, where the knowledge of evil is often better advertised than the knowledge of good. Even so it's literally on the side of the angels, or at least the bay of the same name (Baie des Anges).

Wandering along the Promenade des Anglais at night, seventeen beaches visible by day are lost to view. But behold a stupendous arc of light where humans have lived for 2000 years. The lights are brightest, the shadows darkest, in the Vieux Nice quarter, where at any moment you expect a gun battle to break out, or Graham Greene – despite having been dead nearly twenty years – to appear at his regular table. Not all the tales these walls could tell would be pretty, despite the surface sheen. All Nature runs wild in steamy Nice, human nature not excepted.

Overlooking the town is the ancient Roman city of Cemenelum, now home to Gallo-Roman ruins. Many Southern habitations are the longest-settled in France. (Whisper it not in Montmartre.) Overlooking the ruins, in a 17th-century Genovese villa, is a museum bequeathed to the city by the leading post-impressionist Henri Matisse (1869–1954), who began his painter's life at exactly the same time as Picasso, and – like him – worked prolifically until the end. He 'discovered' Nice at age 47, but the museum brochure exaggerates in saying he 'settled here for the rest of his life'. He certainly kept coming back, and regarded it as home, but to say Matisse 'settled' anywhere is to misunderstand the man. At the age of 60 he left Nice for Tahiti, where he saw out the Thirties. He would later muse aloud, 'I had a great desire to appreciate the light on the other side of the Equator …'

In 1947 Matisse designed a Chapel of the Rosary for the Dominican community of Vence, a hill town not far from Nice. This followed his meeting with Monique Bourgeois – *Wait a minute, could she have been a relative of the old lady in Père Lachaise …?* The Riviera and reverie, you see, are never far apart.

Matisse's pencil sketches – such as his study of a geriatric, *Academie – Etude de Vieillard*, from the mid-1890s and obviously done from life – truly tantalise. As does the *Portrait de Madame Matisse* (1915), which depicts her wearing a hat that prefigures the Sydney Opera House by more than half a century.

SNCF. South, North, Comédie-Française. Of course that's not what it stands for,[31] but it might, given how French advertising is done with style, too – and this from a railway network priming itself for a showdown with the Government. My ticket envelope features an ad showing a man tied to a chair in his living room. The room is bedecked with party balloons, his head with coloured bird feathers, suggesting a birthday party interrupted. The text says, *'Qu'est-ce qui peut vous empêcher de partir?'* 'What's stopping you leaving?' Once again, when you least expect it – you know how it is – *chic* just happens.

1160–1169 km

If your natural walking pace is 5 km/h, you will soon leave laggardly old me – shuffling along at 2.4 km/h – in your wake. (No need to get your calculator out, I've done the maths.) Now, if Monaco, the world's second smallest nation, were a perfect square – instead of a straggling strip of land 3 km long by, on average, 600 metres wide – it would take you just 68 minutes to walk your way around its perimeter; even I could circumnavigate it in a respectable marathon world record time. And they call this a sovereign state. Ha!

Well, at least it is a state with a sovereign, the latest in a line – the House of Grimaldi – stretching back 750 years. Prince Albert II, despite the diminutiveness of his realm, is far more impressive a character than many a more powerful supremo. Monaco jealously guards its independence – some would say because as a tax haven it needs to. Yes, it has its own phone code (377) and Web suffix (mc) but somehow, you feel, the claim to a place in the sun must rest on more solid foundations.

This chapter joins the style élite in treating the principality as part of the French Riviera. If Monaco had all the paraphernalia of a sovereign state, none could be more Ruritanian. Take the railway. SNCF trains run here on SNCF tracks. A navy, *peut-être*? But if there were a Monégasque – lovely, bizarre adjective – Navy, its home port would have to be the marina. What geopolitical minnow could take it on? Liechtenstein is landlocked and Malta a long way off.

For a comic-opera state, though, Monaco has had its share of tragedy. Even the most ardent republican might be forgiven for choking back a tear or two at the saga of Grace Kelly, the film star who turned her back on Hollywood for the prince of her dreams.

As we shall see, Monaco is replete with reminders of the princess. But it is also famous for other reasons: the Grand Prix race through its narrow winding streets; its casino, whose elegance and period charm a hundred Las Vegases could never equal; and its high life, in both senses – its precipitous rise from the Mediterranean to the Alps, and extravagant economy, which puts even Norway's in the shade. Oh, and every day there are sightings of Elvis. Just read on and see if there aren't.

But will it be possible for me to explore Monaco at all? And how can I ever afford to stay there? If Paris hotels demanding more than €50 a night could upset my financial balance, what will it take to break the bank in exclusive Monte Carlo?

This sunny late-October day I took the 9 am bus from Nice. All along this coast, the kaleidoscope revealed more pastel-pink mansions, sun-spangled waters and an elegant sufficiency of Nature's own curves and switchbacks, cove after bay after inlet all the way until we passed through a narrow road tunnel that whizzed us out of France and into the sovereign enclave.

On Monte Carlo's main street, Boulevard des Moulins, I kept one eye peeled for possible lodgings while the other went window-shopping. When I spotted a €1200 price tag next to a pair of crocodile shoes it gave me quite a shock … I'd never realised they wore any. The shopkeeper, Michaela, on seeing my gobsmacked visage through the window, tried to humour me. Was I interested in buying? 'Well,' I said, 'I don't think I have €1200 on me right now.' She suggested I buy one shoe now and its fellow in two months' time. *Drôle d'idée*!

Finding a hotel here makes Paris seem simplicity itself. I tried three: the France (friendly but *complet*), the Versailles (unfriendly but *complet*) and, at the latter's suggestion, the admirably accessible Terminus (even friendlier than the France but … you guessed it). Monaco thus becomes the first country I've ever visited without sleeping in. My three days there were punctuated with late-night retreats to, and early-morning sorties from, Nice.

Even the prospect of visiting it filled me with despair until a café manager pointed out an off-street pedestrian tunnel leading to a bank of lifts that take you, via more tunnelling, to the upper town.

On every hand, panels headed '*Parcours Princesse Grace*' (the Princess Grace Tour) present black-and-white photographs from the public life of the micro-state's former First Lady. One, from April 1956, a week before they wed, shows the Sovereign Prince 'taking

His yacht, the *Deo Juvante II,* out to meet His fiancée, Ms Grace Patricia Kelly'. Somehow I find it unlikely Grace Kelly was ever addressed as Ms in her lifetime.

Passing another shop window – something it is difficult to avoid doing in Monte Carlo – I notice a yacht advertised for €3.6 million (about A$6 million). Judging by the glossy photos, it is worth every penny, but that kind of outlay would make the crocodile shoe pinch.

To visit Monte Carlo, and not the casino? Unthinkable. But a budget traveller has no cash to throw away on the baccarat table or roulette wheel. This casino is so exclusive it even charges €10 (A$17) just to enter. I'd been a high roller ever since replacing my orange-foam seat with a state-of-the-art gel-filled cushion, but I knew a single night here could spell the end of my European travels. And then I had a brainwave ... Flashing my passport ID at the receptionist, I mentioned my big idea. She giggled, then whispered to her colleague, who also giggled. I was sure one of them was going to call a liveried guard to throw me out. But on regaining her composure the first receptionist merely waved a hand in the direction of the betting halls and said, 'I like Australians. You can enter *gratuit*'.

Free! As free as the beggars you never see in Monaco, at least as free as the bin scroungers of Vieux Nice, but with so much more chance of getting rich, I wheeled into the plush-carpeted betting hall before she could change her mind. At its far end sat a bespectacled man in a zoo-like cage. Apologetic for troubling him – which seemed to amuse him – I introduced myself as a long-distance traveller crossing Europe on a budget, before launching into an explanation of what I wanted to do.

'In English we have a saying "to bet one's bottom dollar",' I began, repeating myself in French to avoid any misunderstanding, '"*se parier le dernier dollar*".'

'Tonight I've brought one American dollar with me and' – his amused smile now broadened into a horse laugh before I could declare my intention – 'I would like to bet this dollar at the casino. Nothing more, just the dollar.'

'You won't be able to do that on the games tables,' said L.E.J. (his initials are on the voucher he exchanged for my greenback). 'But,' he brightened, 'it will be perfectly possible on the slot machines.'

The voucher stated that I had 66 eurocents to play with. This was duly rounded down to 65¢ when I handed it up to the gentlemen in bow ties at the high counter in the *salle* of the one-armed bandits. Upon explaining my purpose once more, I expected to be ushered into the anteroom formerly kept for gamblers who had lost their worldly wealth, where they were left alone with a pearl-handled revolver. (These days, instead of a graceful way out, the casino's least successful clients are furnished with a towelette of the kind normally favoured by airlines, packed snugly inside a pouch all too easily mistaken for a condom sachet.)

But, no, they all had a jolly good laugh before swapping my voucher for tokens, and Gilles, the youngest 'client liaison', offered to lend me his personal assistance with the enterprise. We proceeded to one of the many fruit machines (they doubtless sound more grandiose in French) that populate the room like tin soldiers in well-drilled formation. Gilles inserted a €5 note – not part of the stake, just to operate the machine. 'And now,' he said, feeding tokens into the slot, 'each press of the button' (the equivalent of pulling a lever) 'costs 5¢, so your 65¢ gains you thirteen chances.'

'Lucky me!' I commented, a trifle prematurely. 'And just suppose I'm successful with my dollar. Tell me, Gilles, how much could I win?' After a couple of seconds' lightning calculation, 'One thousand eight hundred euro.' My brain raced: A$3000! Not bad for a night's work ... I felt Lady Luck would be sure to smile – if only she could avoid laughing outright.

After two or three non-results I resorted to another button – the slot-machine equivalent of AutoDial, thinking, Perhaps I am trying too hard. Two more tries and my luck turned. Three lemons in a row, followed by the jingle of coins. Three euro.

'What do you want to do?' Gilles put me on the spot. I needed no studio audience to make my mind up for me, 'That's easy. I vowed to bet my bottom dollar, and at the moment I've only wagered some of it. I am going to bet the whole dollar – and nothing but the dollar. Play on, my man.'

After 22 stabs at glory the machine cleaned me out. I took defeat with good grace, consoling myself that I'd found a novel way to cut my losses. Not since their great varnished doors first swung open in the 1890s, I felt sure, would these neo-Classical chambers of Mammon with their marble statues and crystal chandeliers have witnessed such a scene.

Had Gilles ever heard of a gentleman called Kerry Packer? A polite shake of the head. He was too young to know of the late media mogul's gambling renown. On learning something of the legend, he said loyally, 'Ours is the only casino in the world where we will never say, "You cannot keep playing here because you have won too much." Never.'

How much was the biggest win in the slot-machine room? This he could answer. 'Eight hundred thousand euro.' (That is A$1.3 million at the then current conversion rate.) 'I suppose you can't give me the winner's name?' 'He was an Italian gentleman – a really nice guy, but he was already rich. He was like a child, so happy he was – and he has a photo of himself being presented with his cheque.'

'That's nice,' I said, suppressing a blush of envy. 'What happened to him?'

'Oh, soon afterwards he lost €2 million playing craps.' (At least I think he said craps.)

My mission was complete – I had bet my bottom dollar – and, seeing it was nearly midnight, I was anxious to be off. If I missed the last train back to Nice my wheelchair was bound to turn into a pumpkin, and where would that get me? But Gilles detained me a little longer, disappearing into the next room to fetch a waitress who bore aloft a stylish 33 cl glass of Coca-Cola on a silver platter. Normally this would have cost € 7 (A$12), but Gilles said he had found my visit very entertaining and, presenting me with the Coke and a Monte Carlo commemorative pen – both 'on the house' – and ('but really, you shouldn't have') a lemon-scented paper towel, he declared, '*Même quand on perd, on gagne.*' 'Even when you lose, you win.'

Say what you will, the Monégasques are not without a sense of humour: 100 metres from the casino stands a neo-Classical *non-pareil*, the Hotel Hermitage. Room prices are graded from 'low season' – during which the cheapest room in the house costs €360 (A$600) a night – to 'very high season', at New Year or any time between mid-July and mid-August, when the most expensive room in the house (named, simply, The Suite) costs 'from €1995' (A$3325) a night.

Correction. Some rooms are costlier still. Even the Hermitage Hotel blushes to advertise how much it charges during the Formula One Grand Prix in late May. Prices during this Very Very High Season are obtainable, its schedule teases, '*sur demande*'.

1172–1176 km

Another photo – in retrospect the most poignant – shows Grace accepting plaudits at the opening of the Princess Grace Theatre, a restoration project close to her heart. Soon afterwards there was mourning – as there would be when another princess died in a car crash fifteen years later. But in 1982 no one talked of a conspiracy to murder, mystery Fiats or dynastic division. This princess had already claimed her realm, even if it was one of far inferior magnitude to that of England.

A new exhibition at the Oceanographic Institute – The Arctic, 1906–2006 – commemorates the work of Albert II's great-great-grandfather, Albert I, who was an Arctic explorer from the Mediterranean. In an elegy for the Arctic that doubled as a searing critique of petty politics among his subjects, the first Albert wrote, 'I love the North whose attractiveness takes me far from acts of injustice and of covetousness, in the unadulterated splendour of the scientific spirit'.

The prince made 28 expeditions altogether, four of them to the island of Spitsbergen, where reels of his 1897 expedition – among the earliest cinema documentaries – can be viewed through stereoscopic boxes that resemble binoculars. Albert I wrote of his 1899 expedition, 'I succeeded in sailing west and north to Spitsbergen as far as latitude 80° 37' where the ice field blocked my path, and I returned to the south by the Greenland Sea'. I don't know about you but my blood tingles with excitement at such writing. In it real life imitates art, for if I had told you Jules Verne wrote that would you not believe me?

Albert's scientific zeal occasionally competed with an appetite more familiar among European royalty. Again from 1899, 'Sometimes some species were caught in my trap in great numbers:

for example, one of my traps that had been lowered to a depth of 393 metres arrived back on deck with 1775 red prawns inside: a true wealth for my laboratory as well as my table.'

In July 2006 the reigning prince led his own expedition to Spitsbergen to study the impact of global warning on marine life. A blown-up photograph by Albert II of the same Spitsbergen cove hangs alongside one taken by his forebear exactly 100 years before; and here is something instructive: whereas then the cove was ice-bound, now it is ice-free, open sea.

But who are the Monégasques? Aware of how brief my time here is, I take a short cut by asking a hotel executive who has worked in the principality for years. 'You have people belonging to Monaco with their blood,' she says. 'Monaco is attached to the Family, it is an extension of their family, the prince's Family – and to their little piece of earth. Others want to be seen as Monégasques, and try too hard to prove it, because they don't have roots in Monaco.'

Madame then offers a critique of the enclave that explains why she has asked for anonymity. 'There are sharks out there and I am only a clownfish. But I am not afraid of the sharks because they will give me a certain amount to eat when they have enough to spare.'

So what do Monégasques think of Big Brother France? One thing I ought to know, she tells me, is that, whatever its family quarrels, Monaco looks down on *all* its neighbours. Villefranche is inexpressibly posh, Nice vulgar, Menton dead. 'They go to sleep at eight o'clock.'

1182–1183 km

Grace loved the rose – and a snippet of free verse she tossed off one day is chiselled for posterity in front of a statue of the lady herself in the Princess Grace Rose Garden, unhappily sited next to an airport.

> *What is special about a rose that it seems far more than a flower?*
> *Perhaps it is the mystery it has gathered through the ages.*
> *Perhaps it is the joy that it continues to give.*

Rose patches bear the names of family members – Rainier, Stephanie, Caroline. Some are unaccompanied by blossoms. For all

I don't know about floriculture, they are out of season. Cary Grant is not appearing this year but, in case you were wondering where Elvis had got to, he is here. So, for that matter, is Charles de Gaulle, but that one keeps well away from the Grimaldis. (They never were the best of friends.)

1185–1187 km

Surprise, surprise. Monaco, playground of the rich, has proved the cheapest country of the journey so far – simply because every expense has been spared in the matter of accommodation.

Today I attend the Changing of the Guard at the Palais du Prince, only to learn upon arrival that a decision may be made quite late in the piece to cancel the ceremony, weather not permitting. On my way back from the ceremony, which goes ahead despite drizzle starting five minutes in and falling steadily to the end, I meet a formidable but friendly lady of 70, Isabel Smith from Kent, protected from the persistent rain by nothing more than a plastic sheet.

Her view of the Continent is that of the old Tory party base. 'I like Europe, I really do. I like my neighbours, but I don't want to live in their house.' She visibly shudders at the thought of an ever-closer union. 'Those people who died (in war) would have been horrified to think that there would be a united Europe.'

1189 km

Back in Nice, the morning brought forth another classic faux pas. Wanting a clean towel for my shower, I asked the hostel's duty receptionist, Alison, for a *serviette hygienique*. I mean no disrespect by this, but she laughed like a hyena. What's so funny about trying to dry your body with a tampon? I think it's sad.

1197–1198 km

Freshly arrived in Cannes, I saw an ostentatiously rich man inspecting a city map. Clueless as to what direction my *pension* lay in, I politely asked where on his map the relevant street (the Maréchal Gallieni) was. He conspicuously ignored me, flicking one hand at my importunity, as if dispensing surplus cigarette ash. Compare this with an unsolicited offer of help – 150 metres on from that first encounter – by a ragged Kurdish youth from Kirkuk, whose family must have been through terrible times. The meek shall inherit the Earth, right? I can't wait ...

My *pension*, did I call it? It was a spartan dwelling but at €9 (A$15) the room cost a record low for Europe so far. Transfer to the appointed lower bunk was accomplished only by performing a Fosbury flop from the chair so my head passed just under the sagging upper-bunk netting. That night I spent in the dingiest digs of the entire journey, worse than anywhere, including the Russian *peripheria* – and this in luxurious Cannes, no less. I 'shared' the room with a short-order cook who had sticky-taped a large-as-life photo of Kim Basinger on the wall; whose worldly possessions appeared to consist of portable stereo speakers and enough clothes to half fill a wardrobe; and who never came home.

1202–1208 km

Apparently I should have applied in writing two months in advance. Frère Pierre-Marie, who revelled in the slightly sinister title of the monastery's guestmaster, was apoplectic. '*Vous imposez!*' he growled. His eyes flashed with anger. I could only respond, '*Vous avez raison*' ('You are right'), conscious of the promised reward for meekness but willing to pay my share of the burden until my time came to inherit the Earth.

Pierre-Marie said with undiminished vehemence, 'I will get you a room for the night.' Only later did I discover that those eyes which flashed lightning could twinkle with humour and dispense the sacrament with compassion. The storm passed, his natural sunniness beamed forth and I warmed to him.

At lunch and dinner silence is enjoined and observed, a trial I at first found onerous but valued so much by the end of my stay that for weeks afterwards the sound of voices in a refectory at breakfast time annoyed me.

Half an hour by spume-churning ferry from Cannes, Abbaye de Lérins is a Cistercian monastery situated on St Honorat Island – a retreat for the faithful, a point of interest for the historically inclined and, yes, a destination for day trippers. While the priests would say they live by faith, their monastery thrives on visits from the outside world and the purchase of olives, wines and liqueurs sourced from its vineyards.

I arose early in answer to the bells announcing Vigils at 4.15 am. (I've always felt there is no real point in visiting a monastic community and not attending its observances); and at half past five went back to sleep until the breakfast summons. After 9 am Mass I followed the only trail around the island, which is mostly wooded but opens into a clearing where 900-year-old Trinity Chapel stands. Near today's monastery is its abandoned predecessor, converted into a fort by Spanish invaders in 1635.

1214–1216 km

Salt-encrusted ancient port, purveyor of a famous fish stew; France's main sea link with North Africa; her oldest city, and one of the oldest in the world; the one that lends its name to the national anthem; stronghold of the National Front; a place that simultaneously greets and repels immigrants. Marseilles has its own subset of French impressions that long precede first acquaintance. Yet you never know quite what to expect …

My initial impression is of its beauty. At Vieux-Port I am facing an oblong harbour with restaurants strung like bangles along its left and right arms. Evening lights have just come on, casting a rainbow of colours over the water. A floodlit medieval castle rears on high. It is not hard to see why people are prone to fall in love with Marseilles at first sight. Who knows? I might even succumb myself.

But tomorrow will bring reminders that, after six months' journeying, I am definitely in the South of Europe. In too few cities are transport systems accessible and integrated – but there are more in the north of the Continent than the south. An extensive Métro system underlies these streets but to me it is beyond reach. (This matters when you're staying at a hostel on the outskirts of a sprawling city.) Pushing round town, I see that Marseilles is bidding to be the European City of Culture in 2013. More strength to its arms, disabled ones included.

1220–1226 km

At the outset of my Cook's tour round the inner city, I stumbled on a food fight. Well, not exactly, but at the Vieux-Port morning fish market where large silver catches expire on the ice before your eyes – no question, these fish will be fresh before they're frozen – two tenants almost come to blows. They're dressed in plastic aprons, the better to wash down the (fish) blood, but onlookers assure me they're in earnest. The cause? One of them had caused his barrow to trespass 3 cm into the other's assigned space.

The History Museum of Marseilles – the only museum I've ever come across inside a shopping mall – chronicles the first 1000 years of this city's story. Marseilles – we have it on Aristotle's authority – was founded as a Greek colony, Massalia, in the sixth century BC. Celts, known as Ligurians, already lived here. Soon Phoenicians and others added to the rich mix – what you might call the ethnic bouillabaisse. From a museum leaflet I discover that the fascination with Northern Europe occurred much further south, and much earlier, than I would have supposed. Pythéas – a traveller, savant and astronomer from this town – explored the North Atlantic coast *circa* 330 BC, going further than anyone before him.

In 1983 I flew in a Cessna – the only plane owned by Druk, Bhutan's fledgeling national airline – from Calcutta to the Bhutanese capital, Thimphu. During a passage of violent turbulence the captain's voice came over the intercom, reassuring us he had once been personal pilot to the prime minister of Malta. I remember thinking, What did he do so wrong that he's now working in this backwater of international aviation? Today a similar thought occurs when I perceive the following notice – in English, oddly – in the window of the Shanghai Restaurant: 'Mr Han, the senior chef, holds the professional certificate issued by People's Republic of China. He worked in the Embassy of China in France. He is willing to serve you now.'

Which is more than I can say for a certain old man at the bouillabaisse restaurant on New Bank Quay. I couldn't leave Marseilles without sampling its most celebrated dish. But it is costly, more than €20 (A$33). Six months into the journey, I have spent nigh on €11,000 ($18,000) and now I have an extra incentive not to splurge, as I am just €18 ($30) over budget.

As if on cue, I see a chalkboard offering a half serve (still quite a lot) of the famous dish for €11.90 (A$20) – a bouillabaissement bargain if ever there was one. The stern old man (I assume he is the owner, he has that proprietorial air) stands squarely in the entrance, and when I point to the chalkboard item of my choice he announces, 'I have no right to serve you'. And, what is more, 'We do not have toilets for the disabled'.

'I am not looking for a toilet,' I counter. 'I have just been to the one at the museum.' Even as I speak, a disturbing idea occurs to me. Is there something I should know about this fish soup, that I will need to go to the toilet straightaway? This shot across the bows leaves him physically and figuratively unmoved. I put my brakes on (the equivalent of digging in my heels, which I find too anatomically challenging) and feel my voice rise. 'If you don't serve me the bouillabaisse, I will call the police.' This brings out the restaurateurs from next door to see what all the commotion is about. At this point, a man in early middle age who has been standing behind the till while this impasse deepened indicates with a wave of his hand that I should draw up a table.

As his old man retreats into the shadows, the son commences to fawn. I hand over €12 – to ensure my fresh catch doesn't escape back into a sea of hostility – and the fish arrives shortly before the rich red spicy broth, with side dishes I am instructed to dip into it. The younger man soon shamefacedly returns half the amount, so – to the disbelief of anyone familiar with Marseilles – I can attest that bouillabaisse at €6 (A$10) is a possibility. Then again, I doubt the circumstances would ever repeat themselves.

1229–1236 km

Arles may be a quintessential tourist town, but the summer crowds are a distant memory by the end of October. Here by the swirling Rhône I can explore this elegant habitation at my ease. The principal attractions of this World Heritage Listed town are its architectural remains from Roman and medieval times – many of them wonderfully well preserved.

I visit several hotels but their architecture defeats me. The closest approach to success is when I make it clear to the lady of the house I'm quite happy to haul myself up steps if someone could bring my chair up to me. She asks me to come back at 6 pm but our conversation has roused her husband from his *sieste* and he is grumpy.

'What's going on?' he demands. She explains.

'*Jamais*. No way. You cannot stay in our hotel,' he says.

After nearly three hours of searching, I seem to have run out of two-star options. So, I think, why not ask the impossible? (Occasionally it works.) And, at the first three-star hotel I sight, the greatest good fortune of the journey befalls me. The *hôtel particulièr* (private hotel) d'Arlatan – three stars but deserving of five – encapsulates Arles' cultural history within its own stone walls. This is not a place I would have dreamt of staying in (actually I *would* have dreamt of it, but nothing more) were it not for the lack of alternatives.

Hélène drops the price to €40 – from a tariff I will leave to your imagination – and doesn't seem to mind when I ask to stay two nights. I am staying in the former townhouse of the 15th-century Counts d'Arlatan de Beaumont, rightly renowned for its antique furnishings, refined comfort and tranquillity. The Lords of Arlatan built this mansion over one of the ancient world's grandest civic basilicas. Luxuriating in the bath this evening, I gaze at a wall fragment from the reign of fourth-century Emperor Constantine.

Next morning I breakfast in the most sumptuous of settings. At any moment I expect to hear a troop of horse commanded by Jean d'Arlatan arrive in the courtyard below.

Outside Le Havre I saw that city was 'twinned' with St Petersburg and Southampton. Tours has seven 'twins'. Now, I see, Arles has nine *jumeaux* in as many countries. Isn't it time someone in authority practised civic birth control?

In spite of its antiquity the majestic oval of Arles Amphitheatre is a new wonder to me. One of fifteen Roman stadiums, of which the Colosseum in the Eternal City is the best known, this one measures 136 metres long by 107 wide, and was built *circa* AD 90. To think this massive monument has stood for nineteen centuries impresses me mightily.

A brochure titled The Roman Amphitheatre of Arles contains a couple of amusing observations. One is 'Stagehands would set up décors or make animals appear by using trapped doors'. And Two: 'The public delighted in watching gladiators or animal fights as well as hunting spectacles.' (You can just picture a member of the delighted public asking anxiously, Where did I put my glasses?)

1239 km

On a day like this I begin to see how daunting it is to get people thinking like Europeans (whatever that might mean). In a laundrette I meet Stephan, a Croatian steel-mill worker employed here for eight months – because here he can earn much more than he could back in Zagreb. Still, Man cannot live by bread alone.

'This place is shit,' he says.

'Arles?' I respond, doubtfully.

'France.' Stephan is proud that he speaks virtually no French.

'What is shit about France?' I ask him in English.

'The food. The food is shit.'

'But,' I counter, 'the food here is some of the best in the world.'

'Yeah, I know. But they give you salad. Salad is OK,' he concedes, 'but not every day.'

I assume Stephan's culinary preference is for something unsophisticated and straightforward, and am about to point out that the butcheries here sell horsemeat – but think better of it. As he removes his clothes from the dryer and prepares to leave, Stephan speaks the only *français* sentence I hear from him though it is really too weird for words. He has one thing more to say about the French, he tells me. 'They should speak English.' To an outsider, Stephan may be a European. But he's an insider, in Europe, and nothing of the sort.

If horsemeat doesn't tickle your taste buds, how about wolf in a provençale sauce? Over lunch at an Arles brasserie today I mention to the waiter, who speaks some English, that I have seen on the menu *filet de loup avec sauce provençale* and, having prided myself on translating the name of an Arles CD shop called Le Loup des Steppes as nothing other than Steppenwolf, would like to know whether fillet of wolf in a provençale sauce is a local delicacy and, furthermore, just how easy is it to catch a wolf these days?

He laughs the laugh of one in the know. 'It is the same word,' the *garçon* admits, 'but ours is a fish, like a sea bass.' What a lucky escape! I could have ordered wolf and sent it back out of ignorance (though a provençale sauce can make any dish delectable).

1242–1246 km

> Sur le pont d'Avignon
> L'on y danse,
> L'on y danse.
> Sur le pont d'Avignon
> L'on y danse tout en rond

We learnt the French nursery rhyme at primary school. And here today – a mere handful of decades later – I am on the bridge itself. At one point, in a case of life imitating lyrical art, a five-year-old French girl in golden plaits performs a jig on its pebbled surface.

The Pont d'Avignon was begun in 1177 when a Provençal youth, Bénezet, began to raise funds for its construction, saying he had received a divine call to do this for the glory of God. Originally, the span was almost 1 km long. Raging floodwaters destroyed most of the bridge long ago. So you proceed along it, over halfway across the Rhône, and there – unless you are extremely unwise – you stop.

Both the bridge and the 14th-century Palace of the Popes, the biggest Gothic palace in existence, also here in Avignon, are on the World Heritage List. Unfortunately, the interior entails too many staircase ascents and descents to make a comprehensive visit practicable for me. But, with help from a few other visitors, I get as far as Guards' Hall and the spacious central courtyard.

For nearly 100 years, from 1305, Avignon became the new Rome. The primacy of Rome for Catholics was challenged, not, as it had been since 1054 by the refusal of the Orthodox to recognise the Pope; nor, as it would be in 1517, by a Luther; but by a simple act of shifting house, after the Pope himself, Clement V (a Frenchman), moved the Holy See here. Over the next seven years he created 24 cardinals in three mass promotions. Twenty were French, thirteen from the South. Their resultant influence enabled a succession of French popes to be enthroned. According to an official brochure, they decided to make Avignon 'the capital of Christianity'.

Apart from the question of whose Christianity we're talking about here (the Orthodox in Armenia and Ethiopia, or the Copts in Egypt, would doubtless be offended by the presumptuousness of the phrase), I pause to reflect how repugnant the very notion of a 'capital of Christianity' would have been to those who heeded Jesus' words 'My kingdom is not of this world'.[32]

Later pontiffs built on. The edifice we know as the Palais Vieux, surrounding the cloister I can only glimpse from the courtyard, was built at the behest of Benedict XII (1334–1342). Clement VI (1342–1352) added two immense, ornately decorated wings, which make up the Palais Neuf. Then in 1376 Gregory XI packed up the papacy and took it back to Rome. But the Great Schism in the Western Church between Roman and Avignon factions persisted for decades after that.

1250–1257 km

Like Arles, Nîmes dates from Roman times. In its ancient Forum the Maison Carrée – a veritable mini-Parthenon and one of the best preserved of all Gallo-Roman temples – has been standing literally since Jesus was a boy (AD 2 or 3). It is easy to believe that it would collapse tomorrow without the scaffolding, and the concrete backing and filling, that partly obscure its clean lines today.

In 1992 Norman Foster's firm of architects was refurbishing the site at the same time as it was restoring the Reichstag. I am glad to see that even Lord Foster resisted the temptation to put a glass dome on this one.

Nîmes' Roman amphitheatre – smaller than Arles', really a boutique stadium of its day – is said to be the best preserved in the world (though I have to say, I don't see much difference between the two).

The audioguide, though lacking the solidity of an official guidebook, manages to convey the 'sense of theatre' that accompanied a second-century gladiatorial contest here. (The brutality of such entertainment is not so easily conjured up, for which we should probably be grateful.) VIPs sat in the front row, shielded from the sun by vellum awnings – which reminded me how inequality seems to have been long accepted as the permanent state of man: think corporate boxes at today's stadiums.

At great expense, we are informed, First Magistrate Titus Julius has had lions brought from Roman provinces in North Africa. The lions don't fight each other but *venatores*, men who fight them, run around the arena – a comic image, that – in an effort to tire them out; and sometimes even wrestle them with their bare hands.

Apparently, the thumbs-down sign is a Hollywood myth. 'If the gladiator appeared to lack valour, the crowd would call for him to die. The Magistrate, called an "Editor", turns to the crowd who will call "Mercy" or "Cut his throat". The Editor decided.' [*Sometimes the old traditions are the best.* – Ed.]

1259–1262 km

Toulouse lacks the crime-ridden reputation of, say, Nice or Marseilles. But it is no Utopia, as I saw for myself tonight. Ric, met as I was going into a supermarket, was friendly enough. 'Do you want a drink?' he asked – and, perhaps relieved that he hadn't begged for money, and also because I had just been thinking of visiting a bar, I said yes.

He trumped that plan by buying a couple of beers from the supermarket, and we adjourned to the steps of a neo-Classical public building about 100 metres away. After handing me one of the tall cans, Ric began to talk.

'I've just arrived in Toulouse today.'

'So have I.'

'I was living in Paris. They let me out of jail yesterday.'

'What were you in for?'

'The worst thing.'

'And will you stay here?'

'Awhile. I know people here.' The convicted murderer nodded to a blue sedan parked unobtrusively in front of us. 'Watch.'

A man got out of the car and walked over to a white van which had parked almost simultaneously on the side street opposite, whereupon Ric turned commentator. 'There are police in the van. They're dealing in cocaine. You will see nothing.'

Ric's last remark struck me as something a hypnotist might have said; and the scenario he was sketching certainly had the capacity to mesmerise. But I did see something. The blur of a retreating hand that held a bulging envelope, perhaps a Manila folder, that is all.

St Sernin Basilica is far from being Toulouse's only outstanding public building but it is the one that points the visitor back to the city's distant origins. The world's largest extant Romanesque church – 115 metres from façade to apse, all brick – St Sernin is an important stop on the pilgrimage route to Santiago de Compostela in north-western Spain. Sernin, the first Bishop of Toulouse, was martyred *circa* AD 250 when he was dragged by bulls from the Forum – still the town's main square, now the Place du Capitole – along the road to where this basilica would later be built.

For three days I abandoned Toulouse for a detour to Andorra – travelling there and back by bus. Andorra is so distinct – a nation with its own traditions and place in the world – that my experiences there merit a chapter of their own. When I arrived back in Toulouse it was lunchtime, and I knew just where to go.

1283–1286 km

By the time I reach Les Halles covered market, lunch is in full swing. Months ago a French chef working in an Oslo hostel recommended the *cassoulet* in far-off Toulouse – not the sort of advice one forgets. Downstairs is a fish market; upstairs – which I reach by the goods lift – are a succession of good, bustling and economical restaurants. In the queue I get talking to a youngish French couple. They later keep a place for me at their table – a mercy in the crowded circumstances – and when the meal is over, before I can say *Je suis content,* they have paid for my *cassoulet* and unstintingly shared their bottle of red, requiring only that I reciprocate when they are in Melbourne. I am humbled by their generosity.

It is eight o'clock on a late autumn night on the far side of the seasonal divide – and feels like early winter. Shivering a little, I sip a Turkish coffee in the Place Arnaud Bernard, the large public square that is the hub of Toulouse's populous North African community. What is Europe to these people? Here I may pick up clues. The main concern I have is not that they will tell me what they want me to believe but that they will not trust me enough to say anything at all.

The restaurant owner, Ben Arfa from Tunisia, finds most Europeans in Toulouse pleasant. 'Some are tolerant; others are rude with their silence. But then they don't come here often so I can live with them, or' – the witticism makes him chuckle – 'without them.'

While we are speaking, four motorcycles ridden by police officers screech into the square, stopping with a beautifully executed three-quarter turn. Many eyes focus on them from the perimeter of the square, but they act as if oblivious to their surrounds. When they are gone, Kaaki – a young Moroccan sitting at the table across from me – spits, 'Pigs!' It is not the first time this epithet has been applied to members of the constabulary but it has added venom when expressed by a Muslim. 'No one is doing anything and they come here and talk about us,' complains Kaaki. 'They do not speak to us, all to make us afraid. But we are not criminals, we do nothing wrong. We have no fear of them.'

1290–1292 km

A concert takes place this evening in the Place du Capitole, to support this city's bid – against Marseilles, as mentioned, and one other French city – to be the nation's candidate for European Capital of Culture 2013.[33] A bemused octogenarian *Toulousain* who has come to the square, it seems, out of either curiosity or habit tries to bop with the rhythm of an Afro-rap group testing the sound system, but succeeds only in looking pathetically out of place (and time). An hour later I am on a train heading through green, green Gascony, westwards – the direction my journey has taken since Monaco.

1294–1299 km

Before I left St Honorat, Frère Pierre-Marie had recommended that in Lourdes I might like to stay at a convent. Now that would be an experience to dine out on, I thought, and said yes. Pierre-Marie – eyes now twinkling – even recommended a nun of his acquaintance at Lourdes (and by now I knew him well enough to permit myself a smirk, but asked no questions). Even if her function was similar to Pierre-Marie's, at least her title wasn't guestmistress.

A taxi from the station brought me to the Maison d'Accueil Assomption, where Sister Ghislaine de Clercq was waiting. Sister Ghislaine – Belgian by birth and vexed by the continuing tug of war that threatened her homeland – turned out to be a kindly, bespectacled nun of seventysomething years. She explained the hours of prayer, silence and dining – some of which overlap in unexpected ways – and, after showing me to my room, thoughtfully arranged my bedclothes. It isn't every day a nun makes your bed so I asked if she minded my taking a photograph. As Sister Ghislaine peered up from her perfectly executed hospital corners, a knowing glint in her eye told me she was no fool.

I was at Lourdes for less than twenty hours on my headlong rush across Europe, but time slowed down to meet me. When it comes to the commercialisation of religion, surely few places can match this. On Boulevard de la Grotte, leading down to the sanctuaries, one of the largest shops is the Palais des Rosaires (the Palace of Rosaries). Its shutters were down today, though, and painted on them were the words FERME DIMANCHE (Closed Sundays). Surely the proprietor was missing a marvellous business opportunity here?

What lies at the root of the belief in Lourdes' significance? That in a grotto here over several weeks in 1858 the Virgin Mary appeared eighteen times to Bernadette, a girl of simple faith. On her fifteenth appearance Mary said, 'Go and tell the priest to build a chapel here'. The chapel arose long ago – and construction still goes on.

As I am in the grotto, moving respectfully past the clammy rock which millions of hopeful hands have touched in the past century and a half, dozens of the prayerful are seated 10 metres away, many fingering rosaries. A slow procession passes from left to right. The sepulchral silence is suddenly broken by an American woman, who says to her husband, 'Can you hear the water?' (Everyone could before she spoke.) Ten seconds go by, and no one has dared caution her. She cries out again, 'It's still coming!' As though the flow of centuries would stop just for her ...

1301–1310 km

The train to Biarritz never gets there. At Bayonne, 10 km short of the seaside resort, the conductor tells everyone to disembark. A general hubbub ensues, and a ramp appears from nowhere to carry me down to the platform. What's gone wrong? Nothing to worry about, says the conductor. The stationmaster at Biarritz ends his shift at 6 pm and, since our train would have pulled in at ten past, no one would have been there to wave the red flag, so we're alighting here and every Biarritz passenger will arrive in a taxi, free of charge.

I see on a magazine billboard that Monaco's Prince Albert II will wed next year and wonder if anyone else has recognised the mathematical sequence that will create. His mother, Grace, weds Rainier in 1956; she dies tragically 26 years later; her son weds his sweetheart 26 years later …

From the lookout on the well-named Rue Perspective the Atlantic is one colossal force of Nature in the raw. At this southern extremity of France the Côte des Basques is craggy and colourful, Biarritz architecture *simpatico*. You can actually see where it breaks away at a right angle – where France ends and the Basque Country, formally in Spain, begins.

For half a century Biarritz has attracted surfers from all over the world. Down by Miramar Beach, on the coastguard information board, someone has chalked up next to Observations, '*Bonne journée*.' ('Good day.') Somehow I don't see the half dozen surfers I saw enter the water ten minutes ago, now reduced to two hardy souls, agreeing.

Wheeling along Prince of Wales Boulevard, I stop for a chat – the sort of thing that happens easily enough away from big cities – with Ida, 78, who is dressed in a tweed outfit of smart cut. A lifelong resident of Biarritz, Ida – whose childhood memories include life with a family of White Russians her mother took in after the Bolshevik Revolution – says she couldn't imagine living anywhere else. At the thought of those vanished days, she casts a look of keen regret. 'The beautiful people have gone.'

Not while she is still here, I think, but try to redirect her thoughts from past to future – my immediate future. What does she think of Spain and the Spaniards? Ida gives the topic serious consideration before issuing her *pronunciamento*, 'The Spanish have a love of life. You will find they dance, sing and play music at the drop of a hat.'

I receive a fantastic farewell from France, a country not always easy to comprehend, even if French is what I have in mind when I tell people I speak one-and-a-half languages. The whole Biarritz *auberge* team take me to the railway station and see me off to Hendaye, on the Spanish border. I take it that by turning out *en masse* they are not saying a final goodbye, merely *au revoir*, but that may just be my parting impression.

CHAPTER 10

An Avalanche Without Snow

ANDORRA

Time spent:	3 days
Distance covered (to, from and in country):	407 km
Distance pushed:	15.8 km
Average speed:	2.679 km/h
Journey distance to date:	20,329 km

1263–1265 km

The minibus to Andorra leaves at nine in the morning: three days later the return journey commences at 5.30 am. Only a stroke of luck decrees that in both directions the bus departs close to where I dwell.

This speck on the Continent lies almost 200 km by road from Toulouse, southward and upward into the Pyrenees. As woodland replaces pastures half an hour or so before we reach the border post, we pass through the hamlet of Foix. Traditionally the Count of Foix was Andorra's joint head of state, along with the Bishop of the See of Urgell which includes territory on the southern, or Spanish, side of the border.

Since 1993, Andorra – occupying just 464 sq. km, not much more than 20 km by 20 km, making it Europe's fifth smallest country – has been a 'parliamentary co-princedom', a gesture to the democratic age that hasn't pleased all Andorrans, as we shall see. Now the co-princes are the bishop and the French head of State, at the time of writing Joan Enric Vives Sicilia and President Nicolas Sarkozy.

An official map of Andorra makes a droll error in stating, 'The country extends over an area of 464 square metres'. It's not quite *that* small. But being located between Spain and France has served it well. A co-principality since the 13th century, Andorra is the only country in the world with Catalan as its official language. I am surprised to learn that only 40 per cent of Andorran residents are ethnically Andorran.

There are two post offices in the capital, Andorra la Vella, which lies two-thirds of the way across the country from where we will enter – a whole 37 km from the border, or less far than from the centre of Melbourne or Sydney to the *nearest* outer suburb. At one the staff are Spanish-speaking; at the other, French-speaking. Inexplicably, it's €11 cheaper to post a Christmas present to Australia from the 'Spanish post office'. Not for the first, or the last, time I find myself asking, Where but Andorra would this happen?

And where but Andorra would the owner of a *pensión* – after assuring me over the phone that the price for a single room was €31 a night – move me on arrival to a double room because it would be more comfortable, and then ask, 'How much do you want to pay?' Flustered by this rarely conferred power, I stammer, 'Twenty-six euro a night?' to which she counters, 'We'll make it twenty-five.' Done deal.

My first impression as I push through this capital of 20,000 residents is of a clean modern town so small it makes Monte Carlo look sprawling. Andorra boasts 2000 shops that, according to the city map, 'have very long opening hours and are not closed at the weekends'. Indeed one suspects that the tills in Shopper's Paradise would never stop ringing if the Government had not legislated 'dates of compulsory closure'.

At times you get the impression that Andorra is one gigantic (well, not *exactly* gigantic) duty-free shop masquerading as a nation. Yet a senior Andorran official protests that this country is 'an independent nation, not just a department store'. Only upon leaving do I learn that in a corner of the department store (or independent nation, if you must) a bomb is ticking.

1266–1272 km

You know a place is not really jumping when the main news in the national paper is a 25-year-old story. *Bon Dia* 'leads' today with heavy unseasonable rains turning the streets of the capital into an all-engulfing torrent of water – on 7 November 1982.

I turn to the sports pages. Andorran culture is predominantly Spanish, with the odd nod north. For example, Andorra has its own rugby XV. That they're not very good hardly dents people's pride in being part of the competition (in south-west France). Nor are its soccer team world-beaters. But who could expect them to be, given that the nation's population of 82,000 would fall well short of a capacity crowd at any of Australia's biggest stadiums?

In Catalan 'fire brigade' is 'bombers'. To see a red van with flashing blue lights and BOMBERS painted in large capitals on its side can be disturbing.

Casa de la Vall (Valley House) must be the most relaxed, as well as the smallest, of the world's parliaments. (The debating chamber would measure no more 10 metres by 3.) The Conseil-Général has been in existence since 1519, meeting in private homes and churches until it moved to the Casa de la Vall in 1702. Of course this was not a full-blown democracy – neither bishop nor count would permit that. But it was, and remains, closer to the people than many a foreign assembly.

At the adjacent secretariat, Caroline makes an appointment for three o'clock this afternoon, noting it in her personal diary. Where else but Andorra could you approach the parliament with so little protocol? Just as I'm heading down the stone path, up comes a serious woman of 60 or so, her hair in a bun, feet clad in sensible shoes, leading a two-person TV crew from Lithuania: a pert presenter and her shaggy-maned cameraman.

Roser Jordana – the country's director of tourism, it emerges – lets me tag along. She is brisk and businesslike; you can tell she has done this shtick so many times that her mind may be clicking over to her next meeting even as she chaperones us through the old stone building.

'Animals were stabled in the foyer in the old days,' she announces and, if the Lithuanians are impressed by this fact, they don't show it. We enter the chamber of the legislature's president, or *syndic*, adorned with frescoes donated by chapels throughout the land. 'The session starts with the ringing of a bell, which ushers in the Mass,' she says, indicating an altar at one end of the debating chamber. 'We are a Catholic country. They [the politicians] are supposed to pray to the Holy Spirit to give them clear thinking.'

In 2006 Andorra played host to the Small Countries Olympics, and the fact that this Pyrenean principality was the fifth smallest of the seven participants[34] has not changed Ms Jordana's well-rehearsed rodomontade that bills her homeland as 'the biggest of the small countries'. It is at this point in her spiel that questionable, or just plain wrong, statements pour forth – claims no one appears ever to have challenged. 'We are the oldest democracy in Europe,' she asserts, which would certainly be news to the Icelanders, not to mention the Greeks. When I pipe up about this, she bristles. Roser Jordana has delivered this monologue countless times. There can be no dispute.

Gabija Luneviciute interrupts Ms Jordana to mention that the hirsute Albinas's camera has been malfunctioning for the past three minutes and none of her monologue has been captured on film 'so we'll have to do it all again'. I have the distinct impression she wants to stamp her sensible shoes on the 18th-century floorboards at this point. Instead, she sneaks a look at her watch and says to the presenter, 'Cameramen are a pain in the neck.' Clearly expecting some sisterly sympathy for this view, instead she is met with the stoniest of stares.

'Well, don't you think Monsieur Sarkozy is wonderful?' she asks in a forced attempt at breezy conversation. You can see Ms Luneviciute's lips move, but this has nothing to do with Sarkozy. She is rehearsing her next question. Ms Jordana gushes heedlessly on, perhaps convinced a well-delivered recitation can stand in for a discussion any day of the week.

'He's a little dictator, that is for sure,' she declares. 'But I love Napoleon, so I love Sarkozy. France needs order, and he is going to be the one to bring it to them.'

At last comes word that the camera is working. *La Tourisma* preens a little, and awaits her cue. Uh-oh, says Albinas, it's playing up again. Patience please. Ms Jordana's feet are killing her. Taking the weight off them, she utters a most revealing line, 'Now I am sitting in the chair of a counsellor!' The lady would seem to have ambitions. But something is wrong with this picture, even apart from the camera trouble, and Ms Jordana knows just what it is.

Bouncing up from the seat on our left, she shifts to the more comfortable-looking one opposite, forcing Albinas to move his tripod. 'Now I am in the prime minister's place.'

False starts over, she runs through her spiel with just as much polish as before, almost verbatim, and has just repeated the canard about Andorra being Europe's oldest democracy when her mobile phone starts to play *Blue Danube.* Ms Jordana tut-tuts at the distraction but insists she cannot stay because she has a 1 pm appointment. Ms Luneviciute now challenges her interviewee, on film, about her assertion of Andorra's democratic pre-eminence. The directrix quivers but cannot help rising to the bait. 'Not only is it the oldest in Europe,' she now avers, 'in fact, in the world, I would say.'

Downtown later in the afternoon I run into the dynamo on her way to the office and she invites me in for a chat. It would be churlish to say no to one of the most fascinating characters met on this trip. I begin by asking whether Andorra's is the smallest parliamentary chamber in the world. 'Monaco's is very small,' she parries, and then comes the thrust. 'Of all the small countries, we are the largest.'

Speak of the refugee influx during the Spanish Civil War and you've pushed her nostalgia button. 'Franco was very good to Andorra,' she recalls, eyes misting over at the thought of the good old days. 'Their children have grown up here. All these people are here, living their lives. We saved their lives, you know.'

Democracy has not exactly captured her heart. 'People of my generation find it hard to see any advantage. I lived in the time when there was really one power. In the old days you could just chat informally with someone and things would get done.'

One point still worries me. I want to know, How long will those of Andorran extraction put up with being a statistical minority in their own country? Ms Jordana's reply again demonstrates why she will probably never win a diplomatic posting. 'I think Andorra needs immigration, but we are strictly selective. I don't want to compare humans to animals. But if we have immigrants we have to know how many people we can absorb – and some of them are just like animals, in fact worse than animals.' It's not like the old days, of course, when animals were stabled in the parliament, but Ms Jordana is too polite to mention that.

In the National Library today I looked up the newspapers for March 1993. The voting statistics therein were revealing. While the Constitution gained 74 per cent approval nationally, the highest yes vote was in the national capital (78.5 per cent), with the lowest (64 per cent) in the country town of Ordino.[35] Which only goes to show that rural conservatism is a fact of life in mini-states just as much as it is in Australia, China or the United States.

This evening, mooching through la Vella, I notice something different about Andorra. Here, in any given, or even potential, encounter between vehicle and pedestrian – or vehicle and wheelchair, come to that – the vehicle stops and the less powerful entity takes precedence. On the rare occasion someone even threatens to reverse this order – as when a young motorcyclist was speeding along this evening oblivious, though there was scarcely any risk of collision – a police officer commands the potential offender to halt (which this one did, quite sheepishly) simply by glaring at him. What a wonderfully civilised country, I thought. Where but in Andorra …?

1273–1277 km

Where but in Andorra can you 'walk in' off the street and get yourself a ten-minute interview spot on national radio? This morning I'm in the studio at 9.30 for a pre-recorded interview with Montse Buil, an enthusiastic young FM station announcer who conducts the interview in English for translation into Catalan.

By bus today to Ordino, that heartland of conservatism all of 8 km away. Once there I am visited by an epiphany. Imagination tells me this is what Tibet in summer must be like. In the high Pyrenees it's nearly winter, and a thermometer reads 21 °C. I am on a public balcony in this attractive hamlet drinking in the view of a sunlit valley. In it the prettiest trees you have ever seen shine golden and orange. Their autumn tints contrast with the dark green of mountain firs carpeting the saddles like the soft down of moss. The gentlest zephyr twirls ventilation ducts like mandalas on the sloping roofs of multi-storey buildings. The perfection, the rightness, are so timeless that the only reason *not* to wish you could go to heaven is the realisation that you're already there.

For a small country, albeit one of the bigger smalls, Andorra has an eclectic mix of museums. One highlights tobacco; another perfume; a third bicycles; a fourth, now merely the National Museum, was once the Museum of Stuffed Animals – and there are others.[36] But, for sheer eccentricity, none can compare with the one I visit today.

Ordino's Museu de la Miniatura is a one-man show … Nikolaï Siadristyi, a Kiev-born 70-year-old, is claimed as the founder of a totally new art form, micro-miniaturism. It strikes me as incontrovertible that his artworks must be 'the most diminutive objects ever made by the hand of Man'. An adventurous Andorran family – the Famille Toni Zorzano Riera – travelling in Ukraine in the 1970s 'discovered' the artist and his work.

As in other museums, works here hang on the walls but, being invisible to the naked eye, they are positioned behind microscopes. By raising myself, palms on top of my tyres, I can see them as easily as anybody. The first of Siadristyi's marvels I behold is a pure-gold model of a Roman chariot constructed within the eye of a normal-sized needle. The bowstring on the charioteer's arrow, says an explanatory caption, 'is 400 times finer than a human hair'. *The Peace of the Unwise* is a human hair 3 mm long with the word 'PEACE' engraved along it in five languages. The artist's most celebrated work, *The Flea with Horseshoes*, is described as 'a golden life-sized flea with golden horseshoes' inspired by the Russian folk tale of a craftsman who placed golden horseshoes on a flea as a present to the tsar.

Andorra often seems like a postcard brought to life. So what is wrong with this picture? Something about the beauty of the afternoon is troubling me all the way back to Andorra la Vella. By the time the bus drops me in the city centre I know what it is. No snow, and it's almost winter. Tonight I drop into a ski shop on the Avinguda de Meritxell. The store manager, David, confirms my suspicion. 'We are really worried whether we're going to survive the season. We won't if it's like last year. We had just a little snow in December, and no falls in the New Year until the middle of

February.' Tourism – mostly in the ski season – has traditionally been Andorra's top money-spinner, to which even shopping comes second. Global warming threatens the whole basis of Andorra's prosperity.

1279 km

In the minibus on the way back to Toulouse I discovered that one of my fellow passengers was an English corporate headhunter, Philip Price, a resident of Andorra for the past five years. As we headed back into France amid striking landscapes, Philip unfolded an equally dramatic scenario. The country's very existence would be under threat, he said, if the next two winters were as warm as last year's. Confirming the ski-shop manager's gloomy account, he pointed out, 'The Pyrenees are not as high as the Swiss Alps ... They can have all the snow cannons they like, but if there are no natural falls dedicated skiers will stay away in droves. If that happens – and with global warming it's on the cards – it will be catastrophic for Andorra.'

As Andorra disappeared in the rear-vision mirror of the minibus it dawned on me that, were I to pass this way five years from now, two nations along my route through Europe – this co-principality and Belgium – might have disappeared. But only Belgium's doomsday scenario was being bruited abroad. Andorra, the only high country in south-western Europe, is perched on a precipice. For the rest of our road, Philip's thoughts were a closed book but I couldn't help wondering if there was a word in any language – Catalan best of all – for an avalanche without snow.

CHAPTER 11

Broken Railway, Smokin' Bar

NORTHERN IBERIA (NORTHERN SPAIN, NORTHERN PORTUGAL)

Time spent in country:	15 days
Distance covered:	3256 km
Distance pushed:	165.2 km
Average speed:	3.044 km/h
Journey distance to date:	24,209 km

Whenever I thought of Spain I saw blood. The blood of Aztecs and Incas shed by the conquistador, the sacred blood that true believers adore. The blood of the matador, blood of the bull. Tomatoes drying under a vermilion sun. The red of the Spanish Socialist rose. The blood of priests shed by Republicans, the same colour in the end as that of the democrats shed by Fascists. Innocents' blood spilt by al-Qa'eda on 11 March 2004, a murderous act of racism (blamed on ETA) that galvanised Spain into giving its marching orders to a Government that had marched troops off to Iraq ... to shed blood. None of this blood would be avenged.[37] Rich is the mixture that flows in Spanish veins, bled dry – in a single horrifying year of 'ethnic cleansing' – of the blood of Muslims and Jews (many of whose descendants now howl for one another's). The pain is so expunged that on both sides of the Atlantic they celebrate an *annus horribilis*, 1492 – the year when Christopher Columbus set sail for a better world than this. Though, in the end, for all the gain (the loot and plunder, the shame on Spain), his expeditions only spread the stain.

But this, I hear you protest, is too grim a picture – and of course you are right. Where are the fiestas, guitars and siestas, tapas and paellas? Bring on the flamenco dancers, open up the bodegas, rock on the Costa del Sol. Barcelona remembers its Olympic party, forgets the stadium 'executions'. Who gives a damn? You only live once.

At Buchenwald and in Gamvik, not to forget Versailles, we have seen how the refinements of civilisation are to be found alongside the most barbarous savagery. But here's a difference between the Iberian neighbours: while Portugal has repudiated its past, Spain has quite literally buried its own. Six hundred mass graves from civil war times are said to exist, unvisited, unmarked and largely unknown. A people who once crossed oceans now refuse to look under their feet.

The Pyrenees, which isolate Iberia from the rest of the Continent, have made Spaniards and Portuguese seem less typical of Europe – with all its sanguinary spirit – than they really are. Even today it is possible to write, '... the Spanish, like the British, sometimes refer to Europe as if it were somewhere else'.[38]

On this very journey I witnessed a small but perfectly formed example of such provincialism – cultural apartheid, if you prefer – which keeps the various peoples of the Continent in their 'little boxes', inhibiting the creation of a really unified Europe. The episode will sound trivial, but is worth pondering. A Spanish family were taking breakfast in a hostel north of the border. The five-year-old boy saw a plate of croissants and was clearly tempted. Seeing this, Papa shook his head in stern disapproval and, if I understood correctly, was saying, 'No. They are not normal.' It took a few seconds to realise that he didn't mean they were stale but, rather, 'They are not what we have for breakfast.'

To outsiders, Portugal and Spain have long looked exotic, inward-looking and obsessed with their own affairs to the point of ignoring the rest of the Continent. This was the image the Iberian 'brothers' projected when they went one way under Fascist dictatorships while the rest of Western Europe was going in the opposite, liberal democratic, direction. It was the image they projected in the middle of the last millennium when the two Great Powers of Europe persuaded the Pope of the day[39] to apply the wisdom of Solomon and divide up the world between them, half and half. (You can't say fairer than that.) The image was always part illusion. Scientists and artists, pilgrims and poets were ever more far-sighted than politicians – they generally are – and, although the Pyrenees stand between Iberia and the rest of the Continent, the trails and passes over the mountains are ancient and well worn.

My first Spanish landfall being in the Basque Country, many here would say I am not in Spain at all. The famous people of 'defeated nations' go unrecognised beyond their borders. Who knows the name of the first person to circumnavigate the globe? That honour belongs to a Basque – Sebastian Elcano[40] – but often goes instead to Ferdinand Magellan, his commanding officer, who got himself killed in the Philippines.

Proudly independent Basques see the Spanish as the Spanish used to see themselves – conquerors on horseback, *a caballo*, carrying the sword of self-styled righteousness in one hand and the Bible in the other. They see less of Cervantes' Don Quixote – the fanciful daydreaming Spaniard who gets stereotyped by Anglo-Saxons, even to this day, as lazy, feckless and undisciplined.

Basque and Catalan nationalists see the Castilian knights of Spain much as Cuban and Filipino nationalists saw them until a new conquistador, the United States, drove them away at the end of the 19th century.

Yet in South America, earlier in the century, Madrid had bowed to the spirit of independence in other nations far from the Spanish mainland. There is much to admire in the Spanish spirit, even as one recognises the love of liberty for one people can go hand in hand with a dark desire to enslave others.

One state or contending nationalities? Spain's predicament over Catalan and Basque autonomy mirrors that of Europe in relation to its member nations. The Basques have their story, the Catalans theirs. They see themselves on the receiving end of Spanish history. The Spaniards – they are the ones on horseback – inevitably draw a different lesson. If everyone in his own way is right, no wonder the European is an endangered species.

1310–1319 km

Even a simple thing, such as where your train from the border town of Hendaye is bound, can become a complicated issue in the Basque lands. You say San Sebastián, they say Donostia. Within five minutes you're reminded in the friendliest possible way that respect for the local people demands you speak their language, not the occupier's. Believe me, I was going to. Regrettably, the beautiful Basque word for 'thank you' – *keskarikasco* – is not easily committed to memory. For best effect, divide it up into syllables. Kess-curry-kuss-koe. Even on the third day here, I find myself mumbling, Keskasa – , Kerikas – , Keskica … The Basques are invariably amused; effort counts for more than result. A train passenger, eager to acquaint me better with this orphan in the family of languages, grabs my notebook and scribbles other useful phrases in it – *agur* for *adios* (for goodbye); *kaixo* for ¡hola! (hello); *silla de ruedas* (wheelchair), this last one the Spanish term. For such a helpful gift of words I just can't thank her enough … or, at least, well enough … in Basque.

And still the Vikings pressed southwards, overrunning the Cantabrian coast before the first millennium was out. In Basque eyes the Spaniards are just the latest in a long line of invaders stretching back to the Phoenicians and Romans. Today they come from all directions, descending on the Playa de la Concha (but only in summer, I note with satisfaction). The Beach of the Shell may be less extensive than Broome's Cable Beach but its perfect scallop shape makes it unquestionably the most beautiful strip of sand I have ever laid eyes on.

A three-hour search fails to turn up anywhere I can stay. All the *pensións* here are on upper floors. Press the buzzer out front and, if the owner is in, you will be lucky if he or she speaks English. And then, of course, you need goodwill more than luck. Just as the odds are shortening on the prospect of a night in the cold outdoors, the owners of a family-run *pensión* with a lift to their first-floor rooms come to my rescue. The couple's English-speaking son, John – he prefers the English name to Juan – is a law student. Filled with youthful zeal about the Basques' national rights, he tells me that to achieve nationhood any people must have three things: language, culture and territory. 'And for us the third will come.'

In a tapas bar tonight all discussion is dominated by the public spat between King Juan Carlos and Hugo Chavez at a conference in South America. The Venezuelan leader accused the king of siding with Fascist sympathisers – he named former Spanish PM

José María Aznar – at which point the irascible old monarch told him, 'Shut up.' Basque nationalists – predictably – are impressed by Chavez's chutzpah; Spanish nationalists regard him as a buffoon.

1323–1327 km

Nerea, the waitress at Sidreria Donostiarra restaurant, squirts 'hard cider' from the barrel (though, having imbibed it, I think 'easy cider' would be a more fitting description). After I've bought the cheapest entrée on the menu – a delicious cod omelette that should have cost me €7 but that the house reduced to €3 – the chef offers me a complimentary steak, pleading that the omelette was smaller than normal. I can't help noticing that the steak takes up the same proportion of the plate as the egg-and-fish dish – 100 per cent.

On this dismally wet day the *pensión* is full up, and I am back on the street searching for a night's lodging. At the risk of being mistaken for a beggar, I even approach strangers for guidance. 'Have you tried Urban House?' says one. On the first floor of a residential block, this *hostal* is so laid-back you wouldn't know it's there. The management of this latter-day hippie haven is laid-back, too. Most of the time you can't see the NO SMOKING signs for the smoke.

1334–1337 km

Founded on 10 June AD 68, León has lived through two gilded ages – one as an outpost of the Roman Empire, the other as a medieval orb of Castilian glory. This handsome town reveals the occasional token of its antiquity: in the evening I pass a building that incorporates the surviving fragment of a Roman wall.

William Longsword, Duke of Normandy, and Harald the Severe of Norway would have been also-rans if there had been a European award for Funniest Regal Name of the Dark Ages. One of León's proudest buildings, St Isidore's Basilica, which I visit today, supplanted a humbler church founded on the site in AD 966 by order of – all hold your sides now – King Sancho the Fat.

The basilica was later rivalled by León's cathedral, commenced in the reign of Ferdinand III. Wisely eschewing a nickname, Ferdinand was crowned King of León and Castile here in 1230. My visit lasts long enough to contain a highlight and a lowlight. Cocooned inside the chapel, I let my eyes wander to the mesmerising geometric ceiling and the altar shimmering in candlelight, as I feel the thrumming of some deep harmonic chord from a distant pipe organ.

After emerging from the chapel I sit peering up at the spectacular mass of stained-glass work – 1800 square metres in all – when the cathedral calm is shattered by a squalling child of five or so years who is capering and yowling, totally uncontrolled by his mother. When I venture to hush him, she finds her voice. 'Tranquilo! Tranquilo!' she spits. My chastisement is cut short as her mobile phone goes off, in plain disregard of the signs in five languages enjoining silence in the House of God.

1346–1351 km

The bus journey from León, 400 km from the Castilian plateau down to the Atlantic coast, ushers you into the land of the Gallego (pronounced hal-a-hoe). The whom? While everyone has heard of the Basques and Catalans, even if their famous individuals are unknown abroad, the Gallego are a forgotten collectivity. These inhabitants of the Iberian peninsula's 'top left-hand corner' – long thought to be of Celtic origin (anthropologists now doubt they were) – may be better known as Galicians. Oh, and one of their descendants has achieved some individual renown: Fidel Castro, the collectivist *commandante*.

La Coruña is a triple-fronted city. One frontage overlooks the sea to the north-east, a second faces due north, the third due west. The city occupies a peninsula shaped like a hammerhead shark patrolling the wild Atlantic. It has two names, just like San Sebastián/ Donostia – La Coruña to the Spanish, A Coruña to the Gallego – and locals will interpret what you choose to call it as your position on the vexed issues of national unity and ethnic autonomy. (Or you could just act the part of an ignorant foreigner. It always works a treat for me.)

Tonight completes 200 days of travel. In 500 hours of straining sinews I have now pushed myself 1350.7 km/h – 575 km in the first 100 days, powering up to 775 km in the second. (This means I've added 2 km to my average daily distance of late.) When you combine the distance pushed with the distance travelled by public transport, I've covered 21, 946 km since setting out last May, almost 110 km per day. At the 100-day mark I was almost €2 a day over budget; now I'm 62 eurocents (or A$1.03) under it. Avoiding all those French restaurants and similar acts of self-restraint have manifestly paid off. I try not to wreck all this progress with one blowout. But I must say the skewered delicacies at one of (L)A Coruña's tapas bars tonight are particularly appetising.

1353–1359 km

This afternoon I make for the outskirts of town, to the Tower of Hercules, the oldest working lighthouse in the world. These days the Roman tower from the second century AD is automated. I am pushing my way up the long approach path, leaning into the wind, when the unmistakable strains of *Waltzing Matilda* waft my way. Did I take a wrong turn somewhere? Halfway up, a man in his late 20s is puffing that great Gallego invention, the bagpipes, for all he's worth. On drawing within earshot I ask, 'How did you know I'm Australian?' My surprise is reciprocated by Franck, or Francisco (like the town and the people, he goes by two names). 'I didn't,' he replies. 'I just like the tune.'

One thing I should know about the Gallego (or Galicians), Franck tells me. Like the Japanese and Icelanders, they are renowned for longevity. 'Ten people in my street are 100 years old,' he says, almost boastfully, 'and the oldest is a woman of 109.' But quantity goes with quality. 'The old folk don't go into nursing homes. They are out doing manual labour, cultivating potatoes and tomatoes.' Or indoors writing, I later reflect, on seeing the bust of a Gallego writer in a public park, inscribed Murguia (1833–1933).

Franck offers a tantalising hint on his ancestors' possible migration routes when he tells me the Gallego word for 'bagpipe' is *gdita*, the Bulgar name *guida* and the Turkish *gaida*. Having said which, he swaps his *gdita* for a Gallego piccolo (a lively musical phrase in itself) and in doing so inspires the thought, If pan-Europeanism is a pipe dream, maybe true Europeans dream of pan pipes.

My hostel in A Coruña charges another record low, an unbelievable €7, which will not be bettered by journey's end. Guests are supposed to pay €10.30 (A$17) a night if they're over 30 but the receptionists accept my word that I'm 29. My word that I'm 29 is 'twenty-nine': others' word for it is 'self-deception'. I'm comfortable with being 29 – not surprising when you consider that I've had 24 years to get used to it.

It was nearly dark when I reached Santiago de Compostela, the terminus on Europe's most heavily tramped pilgrimage route, and after dark when I made it to my appointed hostel, Monte de Gozo, which, as its name suggests, is on a mountaintop. But, heresy of heresies, I was to miss out on visiting the burial site of St James that others came thousands of kilometres to see, because the only bus to Portugal would leave at 10 am and just now I hadn't a day to lose. The bus driver dropped me at the foot of Monte de Gozo. After straining myself to the maximum until the road became too steep, I waited for some minutes – 300 metres shy of my goal – until I flagged down a driver who gave me a lift the rest of the way.

Monte de Gozo offers three varieties of accommodation: hotel rooms, comfortable hostel rooms and basic rooms for religious pilgrims who have schlepped across Europe to get here. Perhaps it was because I looked rough around the edges; more likely it was the sack of wet laundry I'd been carrying since France, where the dryer at the Biarritz hostel had stopped in mid-cycle. The first I knew of my presumed identity was when the receptionist – staring at me and then at my humble sack – asked in puzzled tones, 'Aren't you a pilgrim?'

1362–1368 km

Moses came down from the mountain with ten fresh, crisp commandments. This non-pilgrim descended Monte de Gozo carrying the same old wet laundry on his lap … Right, there's no comparison.

Braga, in Portugal's northern Minho region, is steeped in Roman and medieval history. But what will always fix this hill town in my memory is the extraordinary friendliness shown to me by a local family. I was still lugging my wet laundry load – this time across the town's main square – when an amiable but sensible-looking woman, Maria Teresa Almeida, approached and asked whether she could help. Normally I say no, but I did need clear directions to the *pousada da juventude*, the youth hostel. Maria Teresa accompanied me there but didn't leave it at that. Waiting only for her husband, Eduardo, and 13-year-old son Henrique, she offered to drive me to Bom Jesus do Monte, site of a popular hillside temple and pleasure gardens 5 km out of town. It was already on my list of things to see but arranging transport there and back would have been tedious, so her unexpected kindness was gratefully received. The steps into Bom Jesus chapel (to say nothing of the grand staircase cascading below it) rendered it as inaccessible as the 19th-century funicular to the gardens, but Maria kindly bought me a booklet as a memento.

Before reaching Southern Europe I knew there were differences between the Portuguese and Spaniards but could not have told you what they were. Now I'm here, the Portuguese tell me that they regard themselves as Spain's 'poor relations'. This perception is supported by hard economic facts. Portugal's relative poverty is a boon for tourists: this is a destination where your euro goes further. Tonight's soup course costs €1. Across the border it would be three or four times that; in Paris, seven or eight.

1370–1375 km

This morning a poor man in an orange T-shirt selling Braga's *Metro* newspaper in the rain overrides my initial response of '*Não, obrigado*' with a winning sales pitch. 'You should take it anyway,' he tells me. 'It comes with a dictionary. Portuguese is the hardest language but it's a lot of fun to learn.'

Many towns in Old Europe boast a coffee palace so venerable it has become an institution, and not to visit it would disqualify you from any entitlement to claim you had seen the town that boasted it. In Braga that institution is A Brazileira, well described as a 'mildly decadent corner bar attracting effortlessly stylish regulars'.[41] Notching up a century this year, its octagonal gilt-edged mirrors with the stylised motif of an old lady sipping coffee (you can see her real-life descendants reflected in them) create an atmosphere, yes, of mild decadence. Well, it is only ten in the morning ...

This sodden Monday morning I embark on a self-conducted tour of Braga – an eclectic tour of Old Town landmarks. But, not for the first time, it is an unexpected sight – and, sometimes, a sound – that creates the indelible memory. A legless beggar warbling *Ode to Joy* on a flute. The 90-year-old man with cratered features emerging from a pharmacy in nattily furled cravat, gripping his handmade cane – a picture that appears to have escaped into the real world out of the pages of an Edwardian photo album.

After the tour, a pleasant surprise. Maria Teresa comes to pick me up from the *pousada* and take me to the bus station, in a steadily intensifying downpour. We part like old, rather than day-old, friends. Imperious, impervious, impatient, the bus driver turns out to be possessed by speed devils. In bleak fog and blinding rain we hurtle along the arterial at 110 km/h, which may or may not be the legal limit but is well beyond the safe one.

Of all the towns on my long, long haul, none is less suited to the wheelchair traveller than Porto. Almost all the streets in Portugal's second city are lengthy inclines. Tramcars heave, as cars chug, their way up here. My only option is to take deep breaths and keep in mind that this is not a race. I will get there when I get there – or fifteen minutes later. As if to compensate, I am spared the usual battle for a place to stay. In the centre of town I come across a luxurious old-style hotel with long carpeted corridors, elegant foyer and a dimly lit reception counter – in a word, classy. On Day 206 I am given the old iron key to Room 206. Oddly enough, what is modern here often doesn't work as well. Management has embraced an automatic lighting system with excessive zeal. Every few minutes, plunged into darkness, I am forced to wriggle about to generate enough heat to bring the light back on. But my annoyance is offset by several factors: the marble floor, the wood-panelled bedroom and the low-season price – reduced, only slightly, to €35 (the same room costs €100 in the high season).

1379–1382 km

One of the most picturesque of many picturesque streets in Porto (Oporto to the English gentry) is Rua Mouzinho da Silveira. In a typical liquor store on this street there they all are in the window: ruby, tawny, white, Fonseca, Moscato … in a shop itself aged in oak, all the products 'that gave this city its name', as an advertising poster from 1920 put it.

When it comes to bottling knowledge, the Museum of Port Wine on the River Douro waterfront leaves you thirsty for more. Housed in an old port depot, it used to offer tastings but, alas, does so no more. Porto is a port built on port. In 1718 the creaking of ox carts bearing casks of the smooth scarlet drop, as well as coal supplies, from the hinterland prompted the council to order that the streets be paved – with cobblestones. The museum itself confirms Portugal's poorer-cousin status, having been built as the Casa do Cais Nova (New Quay House) for the Saavedra family of Spanish nobles in the late 18th century. With the coming of the 19th century, port's popularity created a homegrown aristocracy, the vintners of the Upper Douro, men with country estates who reinvested their profits in city properties as well – neo-Palladian edifices that were christened 'port wine architecture'. Like the feta of Greece and the champagne of France, Vinho de Porto was appropriated by these producers who, in modern parlance, went all out to 'protect their brand'. Coopers, caulkers, rope-makers, boatmen – the last of these so conscious of their importance they took to calling themselves 'mariners' – all floated on the rising port tide.

Perhaps the museum's most entrancing exhibit is its copy of a painstakingly intricate map of the Douro. Giving our longitude as 8° 53' W, it was hand-drawn by a Scot, John James Forrester, who was ennobled as Baron de Forrester by King Dom Fernando in 1855 for just such detailed cartography after a dozen years spent plying the river. Mindful of the Vikings' southward thrust, I find thought-provoking a digital image of the *rabelo*, a specialised vessel adapted to perilous Douro conditions and of a type that, 'while not unknown in the Mediterranean, is more common among Nordic peoples'.

Just before 7 pm – a trifle late for afternoon tea – I made my entrance at the Café Majestic, Porto's own coffee palace. Trying to steer my way between two rows of tables without disturbing any of the patrons, I managed to stop a dozen conversations at once when the rim of my right wheel caught the edge of a tablecloth and brought three wine glasses – fortunately empty – and an assortment of small china plates crashing to the floor. The waiters were forgiving. My bill came to €1.80, the surprisingly modest cost of an *americano*. I would not have been surprised at ten times the charge – with a separate bill for smashed crockery.

Across Iberia at this season the weather is the news. On TV this evening I see that the heavy rains which were lashing western Portugal have intensified as they moved east into Spain. My next stop, Salamanca, has suffered flooding, and a tornado has struck Seville. The rain in Spain may fall mainly on the plain, but it comes from the Portuguese hills.

So what do the Portuguese think of their neighbours? They are shallow and frivolous ('not serious'), says Alfredo, a bar owner here in Porto. 'You cannot trust them. They make a promise and forget it.' Even worse, he adds, they are obsessed by money (a common enough complaint of 'poorer cousins' about their more affluent relatives). Responding to the same question, an anonymous man at the bar shrugs his shoulders and tells me, with the world-weariest of looks etched on his face, 'They are our brothers. It is good we keep a little distance between us. Do you know what I mean?'

1383–1387 km

Any storm in Oporto makes this city an ideal micro-climate lab. The highs and lows of the topography tend to make all weather local. In the ten minutes between our departure from the depot to the outskirts of town, bound for Spain, our bus is drenched at first by showers, and then in sunshine.

If Portugal and Spain are ever looking for a common symbol, a sight you're likely to come across anywhere on the shared peninsula, they could do worse than opt for legs of cured ham hung on hooks from shop ceilings. (I am reminded of this by several examples of the phenomenon in Salamanca.)

Not all Portuguese are poor. On the bus from Portugal I meet a self-confident and generous entrepreneur, Eugenio. Portuguese – although resident in France for the past few years – he is moving to Salamanca to take over an established bar he has bought there. Formerly in charge of a team of disabled basketballers, Eugenio obviously admires anyone who gets out and does something in spite of a physical incapacity. I look at things differently. As one who enjoys travelling, the question for me is not whether to see the world but how. Before we are across the border, Eugenio – who says he has a personal fortune of €40 million (A$67 million), and who am I to doubt him? – issues two invitations. The first is to visit his restaurant tonight (where, after my arrival, he pays for all the food and drink I order, refusing even a modest contribution); the second invitation, extended to me, my parents and their dog, is to stay with his family at their Portuguese villa overlooking the Atlantic, with all airfares paid. This invitation is still outstanding. It's not that I doubt his genuineness, just that the gesture is too overwhelming to take in.

At Eugenio's restaurant I witness a scene worthy of a comedy classic, though manners forbid me to laugh out loud. An Italian family of three occupy the table opposite mine and, when a Spanish waiter appears, the po-faced mamma points to their five-year-old daughter and tells him, 'We want to eat her, and then we.' Only after intense thought does it become clear that they would like their daughter's order to be served before theirs.

1388 km

Three hours by bus from Salamanca, I found Madrid – flat as a tortilla – bewildering from the outset. At the metro station next to the bus terminal, the same *señor* who sold me a train ticket then summoned the security guards to prevent me from using an escalator (there were no lifts) to reach the platform. When I asked why, he said it wasn't safe. There was no insurance cover if the *guards* were injured.

1397–1406 km

This morning I make a beeline for the Australian Embassy, to vote in tomorrow's election verdict on twelve years of John Winston Howard. My democratic duty done, it's high time to embark on the prescribed round of sightseeing. In Madrid no obligatory destination could outrank the Prado, up there with the Hermitage and

Louvre in the top flight of Europe's art museums. Spanish humanity trumped officiousness after a few moments' hesitation. The young attendant at the entrance started off by saying, as she must have done hundreds of times, 'For a ticket you need to go to [some building kilometres away]' and then stopped short and, perceiving that I was travelling in a self-powered vehicle, relented. 'No, OK, you go in.'

The nation's artistic heritage, on display here, demolishes the impression that – in cultural matters, at least – Spain developed in isolation from broader European trends. A Titian in the collection portrays Carlos at the decisive Catholic victory over Protestants at the Battle of Mühlberg (1547). There he is on his horse, *a caballo*, jut-jawed and ready to do battle, and it takes a while before I twig that the king known to Spaniards variously as Carlos I and as Carlos V is none other than the French monarch Charles V, who must have commissioned this triumphal scene for propaganda purposes. The Titians and Velázquezes of their time were dependent on the conservative nobility and equally conservative Church for their supper, but the income enabled them to travel and create a Europe of the mind, a common heritage.

Cultural genius, like the geniuses themselves, knew no borders. Rembrandt might be a Dutchman, Goethe the first citizen of Weimar, but all Europe soon laid claim to them. Velázquez, Goethe and Dostoevsky, each in his time, travelled to Italy. Van Gogh did not stay in the Netherlands, Titian came to Spain, El Greco's name and history speak for themselves. In this sense Europe has been more than the sum of its parts for centuries. Without doubt it is the politicians who are lagging behind. Velázquez's Fables – a temporary exhibition due to run for three months but opened only this week – showcases one such genius. If I could choose just one work that demonstrates Diego Velázquez's ability to sum up what is typical in an individual's face, my choice would be *La Venerable Madre Jerónima de la Fuente*, a magnificently lifelike portrayal of a crabby Mother Superior. She is carrying a crucifix and a Bible, and that face would crack an egg at a thousand paces.

But this is Spain, and blood will out. In Francisco de Goya's *Christ on the Cross* splotches of blood spatter Jesus' feet, combining with the vivid portrayal of agony to make this an unforgettable work. Goya followed Velázquez in turning out royal portraits – he had to eat, after all – but was not coy about injecting his own opinion of the subject into his work. A 1786 canvas portraying Carlos III as a hunter borders on caricature. The gun dog lies asleep at his feet, his collar bearing a riband proclaiming him 'The King's Dog' (in case His Majesty, or the hound, were in any doubt). For pure horror it's hard to beat *Saturno Devouring One of His Sons*. A work of utter madness, it is brilliantly, disgustingly done. Goya's delight in shocking the observer hints at Salvador Dalí a century in advance. It must be something in the Spanish (lust for) blood. In the world outside these walls, bloodlust escapes from the realm of satire. Posters at bus stops across the city protest against '*violencia machista*' – one of the nation's gravest challenges – which they say has killed 69 women in the past six years.

1406–1415 km

After two weeks of lugging wet laundry across the Iberian peninsula, yesterday evening – at long last – I found myself staying at a hostel with a working washing machine. At least it was working until I put the clothes in. At two o'clock this morning the clothes were still wet, and they were no less sodden at 4 am when I sloughed off to bed. Rising early, I found a local laundry that promised to have the load back to me, dry, by 2 pm, its Saturday closing time. At 10 am, having snacked rather than breakfasted, I was back at the hotel in time for my rendezvous.

At 10.20 am (7.20 pm in eastern Australia), Sky News announces (as the fifth or sixth item of its bulletin): 'John Howard appears to have lost his bid for a fifth successive term as prime minister.' At half past ten the BBC confirms this with the addition of one detail, that Howard is tipped to lose his own seat. A tickertape litany of Coalition losses skitters across the bottom of the screen. Bennelong, Braddon, Corangamite – my gosh, Corangamite! My mind races back to 1975 when I was a cadet reporter at Camperdown, in Victoria's Western District. Then, Corangamite was the second safest Liberal seat in the country and Labor's Camperdown sub-branch had a membership of ten. Who would ever have thought? ...

Three hours later, it's time to retrieve the laundry. And time for the lift from the third level to the ground floor to follow the washing machine into limbo. Somebody down there is stuck in the lift between floors, and I'm stuck on this floor without a lift. Nothing for it, I prop myself against the staircase and begin lowering my body step by step, down three flights. Once a receptionist has fetched my chair, I power myself into it with a samurai-inspired action and hurry off to the laundry, arriving there just as the doors are closing for the weekend. One thing I have learnt from this serial fiasco, Spaniards are not surprised when machinery breaks down.

Of the modern European states, Spain alone has restored its monarchy. This clearly corresponds to the Spanish ideal. Every year on 6 January, in the spacious courtyard of the Royal Palace of Madrid (Palacio Real), the king takes the salute from his military forces – *a caballo*, I do not doubt. The royal family are not exactly short of palaces – there are five in and around Madrid, and a royal monastery as well – but, as the brochure puts it, this is the 'palace for all eternity'. The security guard who accompanies me in the lift to the first floor unaffectedly calls it 'the best palace of Europe' and then, blushing, confesses she may be biased. But, I observe, you can be biased and still be right. The brochure also says that each room is more glorious than the last. Now usually I would discount this as hype, but in the Palacio Real it comes close to being the unvarnished truth. The Hall of Columns has played host to two historic events in recent times. One of them – Spain's 1985 accession to the European Community, forerunner of today's Union – would be judged a shining success; the other – 1991's Middle East peace conference – would not.

A red-carpeted passage brings us to the Throne Room, studded with 18th-century rock crystal chandeliers, gilt-edged mirrors, a gold-sculpted throne canopy and four ornamental lions. An inner voice reminds me that Versailles has no peer; but, amid such opulence as this, there is no shame in coming second. And when I learn that Spain's Carlos III was a grandson of Louis XIV the source of this inspiration seems beyond question.

Majesty succeeds majesty. I pass through the Gasparini Room, replete with Oriental fantasies; and then: the Carlos III Salon, honouring a king who died before it could be completed; the Porcelain

Room, consisting of 134 ceramic panels; and the Gala Dining Room, where it is easy to picture the banqueting table set for 140 guests in November 1879 to celebrate the king's marriage to Maria-Cristina of Habsburg-Lorraine. The glasses that rest on it are of Bohemian crystal, and I crane my neck to view a wonderfully presumptuous scene overhead. Velázquez has painted Christopher Columbus offering a modest gift – the New World – to Ferdinand and Isabella, 'Their Most Catholic Majesties'.

The mood of silent admiration is punctuated by the remark of an American tourist, 'This room reminds me of the Randolph Hearst castle in California.' I suddenly feel seized by an urge to move to Nevada, or the Sierra Nevada, but it's simpler to carry on to the next room, the Salon de Ciné. In the time of Alfonso XIII, just after World War I, the royal family gathered here on Sunday afternoons to watch the latest films. I leave via the Silver Room, where visitors are invited to inspect 'a selection of ordinary silverware of the royal family', the most scandalous misuse of the term 'ordinary' I've struck in all my born days.

Guernica is sometimes called the 20th century's greatest painting. It is certainly one of the most familiar. And, in the Queen Sofia Arts Centre, the work Picasso refused to show in Spain while it was under Fascist rule has found a home. I remember thinking, on my first encounter with this modern classic in a high-school art class at age fifteen, There is more to this than I can possibly take in. On seeing the actual canvas, as distinct from a copy, my reaction remains essentially the same. Picasso was so haunted by the German strafing of Guernica – a Basque town held by the Republicans – that, besides this masterpiece, he produced a host of sketches showing portions of the work before and during its creation. Last night I was in the Puerta del Sol, the heart of Madrid. Tonight, in the same gallery as these Picassos, I see the Puerta del Sol through the eyes of photographer Juan Pando Barrero. A 1937 photo of his showing bombed shops and rubble there brings the horror home. I can almost smell the blood.

1419 km

By rail from Spain to Barcelona, that was the plan. On 11 March

2004 Madrid's Atocha rail hub was Ground Zero, scene of the deadliest terrorist attack on Spanish soil since the civil war. Today its interior has been converted into an artificial 'tropical' jungle, in an inspired flight of architectural fancy.

You cannot just go to Atocha and proceed to the platform, I discover, even if you possess a ticket. First you have to submit to airport-style screening – which you can't really blame the authorities for, given the carnage of that day. I produced my ticket and my passport for identification. The desk officer, who sported a peaked cap, looked tentative and then broke the news gently, 'You will be taking a bus for the last part of the journey, from Tarragona to Barcelona, did you know that?'

'No,' I replied, feeling that the Spanish variant of Murphy's Law was set to strike again but still compelled to ask, 'Why?'

'Well,' he shifted uneasily, 'the railway is broken.' He seemed to be counting on my understanding.

'The railway is broken?' I asked, perplexed by the phrase.

'Yes, the high-speed train crashed last year and the track is not yet fixed.' The railway track, the washing machine, the hostel lift. Do I detect a pattern here?

1426–1428 km

To call Barcelona a Spanish city is to provoke the Furies. We are in the heart of Catalonia, where *Bon dia* opens many more doors than *¡Hola!*; and *Perdoni* excites a certain sympathy its cousin *Perdón* never could. Wherever it belongs, this is one of Europe's most lovable, stimulating, accessible and characterful cities – and it quickly becomes a favourite of mine. (Its metro, unlike Madrid's, gives me little cause to worry whether I will be able to get back to street level at the other end – and that alone is enough to win me over.)

On my first morning here I sit at an outdoor café diagonally across from the friendly hostel where I have been lucky enough to find a room. Flicking through the current issue of *Catalonia Today*, an English-language weekly, I come across an article that seems to say a lot about this country.

Two young Catalans, Jaume Roura and Enric Stern, have been fined €2700 each by Madrid's High Court for burning an image of King Juan Carlos. The judge resisted prosecution calls for their imprisonment, saying he hoped the fine would teach them that they could think freely 'but that they can't attack the basic institutions of the state' [a long-winded way of saying they may not speak freely]. Roura and Stern are quoted as saying they would do the same again, and denounced 'the scorn of Spain and its legal system for the Catalan people'. They were not allowed to address the court in Catalan.[42]

Elsewhere in the paper, an article by columnist Matthew Tree lampoons government plans to teach schoolchildren civility. He points out that so far the only Spaniard to have received instruction on how to be well-mannered was Juan Carlos, who had delivered the Spanish equivalent of 'Shaddapayaface' to Chavez. Nice point, even if it does pander to Catalans' anti-Spanish sentiment.[43]

Those who wish to be reconciled to their history are as admirable as they are rare. One such is Ignacio (Iñigo in Catalan), a receptionist at my hostel who is far in advance of separatists and nationalists of all stripes. Asked whether he is Catalan or Spanish, he replies, 'Both, and a European also.'

What Central Park is to New York, and Circular Quay to Sydney, the long, graceful slope of Las Ramblas is to Barcelona. On this pedestrian promenade an elderly couple waltz to a busker's serenade; electric-orange punks strut their stuff; street performers turn your head (and some of them your stomach); trained monkeys act like humans, and humans return the compliment; while an endless procession of families pause to chat on the most leisurely of strolls to the sea.

On this cloudless day I halt on Las Ramblas to let hand-holding primary-school pupils pass on their way to the waterfront Mall d'España, greeting their teacher as I do so, '*Bon dia*'. Smiling, she responds in English, and, since Catalan is new to me, I ask whether *Per-do-ni* (each of whose syllables I take care to pronounce distinctly) is correct, and she answers, reflexively, '*Si*'. For a good while afterwards I think she has relapsed into Spanish, but languages, like the people who speak them, are influenced by their neighbours, and '*Si*' is Catalan, as well as *español*, for 'yes'.

At the foot of Las Ramblas stands Columbus Monument. The bronzed explorer stands on top of his prodigiously tall plinth, pointing eastwards across the Med. It's a strange way to get to the New World, but maybe not if you're looking for India. And in any case it's better than having him point inland. Opposite his statue, a marquee advertises the Barcelona World Race, a rally for yachts – 18-metre Open 60s – that set off from here a couple of weeks ago aiming to circumnavigate the globe. The competitors are currently off the coast of West Africa and anyone is welcome to come in off the street and check their progress through daily webcam updates. Miguel, who takes queries from the public, informs me that the eighteen competitors include ten French entries, three Spaniards – and one Catalan (I note the separate classification). There is one Australian yachtsman, Andrew Cape, and in the lead at the moment are the French yachts Paprec-Virvac and PRB. Of course no one knows it yet but, by following the race's own website,[44] I will see Paprec-Virvac maintain its lead all the way to the finish line here, on 11 February, by which time I will have rounded the world in 93 days.

1433–1434 km

About 50 km north-west of Barcelona, in the foothills of the Pyrenees, lies 'the spiritual heart of Catalonia', the 11th-century Benedictine Monestir (Monastery) de Montserrat. The monastery materialises through the left-side window of the train coming from Barcelona. At first sight, to my mind, it resembles the Potala Palace in Tibet.

The age of the cablecar linking us to the mountain (77 years) doesn't worry me – so long as it has been receiving regular maintenance. But my mind starts swimming with thoughts of broken railways, non-drying washing machines and other visions of a kind best not entertained in a gondola rising through the air at an angle of 49 degrees.

Among the vertical sardines, my fellow passengers, three friendly looking English-speakers offer to help me out (literally), and when the gondola reaches its zenith they do. University students from Seattle – two Canadians and an American (Matt, Ben and Zak) – they tour the monastery with me for the rest of the afternoon.

Luckily, we have arrived at the 900-year-old monastery with minutes to spare before the daily 1 pm performance by 'Europe's oldest boys' choir' – which I take as a reference to the choir's age rather than the choristers'. As on every other day, the performance ends after seven minutes, on the dot, but the purity of sound lingers long afterwards.

Unexpectedly, the monks turn out to have been shrewd collectors of modern art. Renoir, Monet, Degas and Pissarro are all represented. No moral slide rule appears to have been run over the works before acquisition, although one of them hints at a cautionary tale. The subject of Ramon Casas' *Madeleine. Absinthe* painted at Montmartre in 1892 stares vacantly out of the frame. On the table is her glass of absinthe, her right hand holds a cigar. It all goes to show that good girls have been going to the bad for a hell of a long time now.

1443–1463 km

A sign (of great liberty) is seen in the window of a Barcelona bodega, THIS BAR IS ALLOWED TO SMOKE.

Barcelona has long welcomed the inspired eccentric. Think inspired, think eccentric, think of Salvador Dalí, as well as Antonio Gaudí and Joan Miró, whose hometown was Barcelona. It may not have been Picasso's but it was his launch pad, in two senses: the first place where he made his artistic mark in an eight-decade-long career; and the town from which he launched forth, several times, to explore then unknown reaches of the European art cosmos.

In 1963 the Museu Picasso was inaugurated in a backstreet mansion (Aguilar Palace); with the donation of 1700 works by the master himself in 1970, it spread into new wings in the adjoining Castellet Palace (it helps to have a palace next door if you're thinking of expanding). The great service this museum performs is to focus on the unknown child artist who emerged from his chrysalis here. His first large oil painting – a stunning work, of the type that will always having the naturalists sighing, 'Look what he could have done if he hadn't drifted into abstract' – was *First Communion*, second-prize winner at the Exhibition of Fine Arts and Artistic Industries in Barcelona in 1896, when Picasso was just fifteen.

Another realistic work that those who view it will not soon forget is *Science and Charity* – painted in Barcelona in 1897. In it a doctor checks a mother's pulse as she lies abed, her eyes – and all her fears and hopes – focused on her young son.

It is the best known of Barcelona's landmarks. You either love it or loathe it. Begun a century and a quarter ago, in 1882, it may never be finished. If it were, fewer people might come to visit. *Surely the builders must know that.* Answering the obvious for what must be the thousandth time, a guide assures me that the project is on target for completion in 2040 – but I cannot say she speaks with conviction. The Atonement Temple of the Holy Family (universally shortened to *Sagrada Familia*) is dedicated to St Joseph – San José, Jesus' earthly father (and in November 2010 Pope Benedict consecrated the incomplete structure, albeit as a 'minor basilica'). Inextricably associated with the flamboyant architect Gaudí, it was actually the brainchild of an earlier generation. But it is Gaudí's plans and fantasies his successors claim to be following.

Joan Miró was the last of Barcelona's great eccentrics. I take the funicular up to Montjuïc, where his legacy, the Fundació Joan Miró, stands on a promontory overlooking the city. It is a hallmark of Miró's humour that a painting title will tell you either nothing, or everything, about its theme and contents. Witness his 1951 painting *Painting.* (In the same room hangs a 1925 painting also titled *Painting* but it's easy to tell them apart because they're on opposite walls.) Never afraid to shock, he called one 1938 work *Man and Woman in Front of a Pile of Excrement.* Shit, I think, trying to distinguish the man from the woman from the excrement, he would have done better to name it *Painting.*

Up the slope I push, to the summit of Montjuïc. There is just enough twilight for me to peer inside the Olympic Stadium. You see where Muhammad Ali's archery illusion kindled the Olympic flame, you feel the connection with history.

On Day 211, I have covered a record distance of 20.1 km. My daily average speed – a blistering 4.1 km/h – is at the top of my range. The credit belongs to Barcelona, to its smooth pavements; an outbreak of summery weather; the proximity of each destination from the next; the pure joy of rambling on Las Ramblas; and the long descent from Montjuïc back to the centre, all of which enticed me to clock up the kilometres without noticing. Paris apart – where I averaged 11.55 km per day because the paucity of usable public transport forced me to get out and about – Spain has seen the most freewheeling passages of the journey. I've been bettering 10 km a day here.

1466 km

'Chancers and adventurous rule-breakers have always intrigued, or been admired by, Spaniards.'[45] One would expect that to apply to the Catalans in spades, and be grievously disappointed ... Yesterday I arrived at Barcelona's Barri Gòtic cathedral on closing time and the Gothic landmark's ticket vendor told me when to come back. It's a great Barcelona tradition to go up on the roof, and she said nothing to deter me. Perhaps she thought I would see it was impossible. Well, I didn't; and I don't.

It would take more than a couple of steps into the chapel that gives on to the lift to stop me. When a finger-wagging official closed the chapel door and disappeared, I crawled to a pew in the chapel and persuaded another visitor to hand my wheelchair up.

The door gave way. The officer had dared not lock it, knowing a few people already on the roof would need to come down. When they had done so I slipped through, closeted myself in the lift and pressed the UP button. Now came the business of hauling myself up a steel scaffolding of three dozen steps. The next five or ten minutes were pure bliss, enjoying views of Barcelona's skyline and a Picasso's-eye glimpse of the Mediterranean. I was about to come down when the lift came up for the third time, but now its human cargo was in uniform.

Two police officers – one friendly, the other slightly menacing – trooped up the steps, partly obscuring a grey-jacketed subordinate of the finger-wagger.

'What are you doing up here?' I challenged them.

'We were going to ask you the same thing,' the friendlier cop said.

'Enjoying the views just the same as other tourists,' I replied.

'Take a look around, there's no crime here. You've been called out for nothing. You should be down there catching criminals.' (I pointed vaguely at the street below.) We left it at that – or, to be more precise, they left me to come down in my own good time – though the issue may not be closed for keeps. There is always the risk I will burn in hell for confronting a churchwarden, but you know the drill. No one expects the Spanish inquisition, let alone the Church police.

CHAPTER 12

The End of Europe

SOUTHERN IBERIA (SOUTHERN SPAIN, SOUTHERN PORTUGAL)

Time spent:	18 days
Distance covered:	2062 km
Distance pushed:	131.6 km
Average speed:	2.685 km/h
Total journey distance:	26,271 km

1478–1484 km

Bus sleep usually comes fitfully for me, if at all, but the pace I've been keeping up these past few days has been the most relentless yet, so my brain in its wisdom decides to let my body claim its reward. The first time I awaken we are pulling out of Valencia, having tracked south-west since Barcelona. Our road now veers west before breaking south. The Sierra Nevada, rising darkly, keeps its brooding distance.

You don't often see graffiti by conservatives, but Cordobans obviously live in a different world. UNO – UNESCO CORRUPCIÓN says one of two messages on a brick wall. TV DESTROYS THE FAMILY says the other – which comes with a helpful drawing in case you had no idea what a television looks like. I call it street art; Joan Miró would probably have called it *Painting*.

Cordoba was one of the glistening jewels in the Muslims' empire of Andalusia (al-Andalus) which ruled the south of this peninsula from 711 until 'Their Catholic Majesties', Ferdinand and Isabella, expelled them all – along with the Jews – in March 1492. The Edict of Expulsion marked the greatest tragedy to befall the Jews between the destruction of the Temple of Jerusalem in AD 70 and the Russian pogroms of the 19th century. More significantly for the world we live in, Muslims whose names we all know still voice outrage over the loss of their Western caliphate.

As Robert Fisk points out – and I don't know of any other writer or commentator who has given this fact the prominence it deserves – Osama bin Laden, to name but one, sees a parallel between the Christian reconquest of Spain (the *Reconquista*) and the re-establishment of Israel. Fisk writes,[46] 'What is also clear from his tapes … is bin Laden's almost obsessive interest in history. "… we shall never accept that the tragedy of Andalusia shall be repeated in Palestine."'

In the heart of Andalusia, the immensity and history of Cordoba's former mosque, now its cathedral, the Mezquita, put me in mind of Istanbul's Aghia Sofia. After my rude encounter in León's cathedral, this is one place Spaniards are awed into silence. Maybe it's because there is no sign commanding it … In a passage headed 'The Mother Church of the Dioceses' the brochure handed to me on entry insists the cathedral is not 'a temple of different cultures'. The ancient stones and exhibits in the city's Museum of San Vicente, it says, prove that the Visigoths were Christians (which must have been news to the Romans).

King Ferdinand III (the one that we saw was crowned in León's cathedral in 1230) reconquered Cordoba in 1236. The brochure deplores 'the inconvenience of celebrating the liturgy among a sea of columns'. Pews which take up perhaps one five-hundredth of the mosque-cum-church's interior show that after all this time the Christians have produced a solution that is at least architecturally respectful.

Curiously, they then give themselves a pat on the back for having kept the mosque structure intact. 'It is the Church through its cathedral chapter that has made it possible to keep the former mosque of the Western caliphate, the oldest cathedral in Spain, and a World Heritage site, from becoming a heap of ruins.' How disingenuous of Christian triumphalists. Preservation has surely not been achieved in order to safeguard Islamic heritage?

The Juderia is Cordoba's old Jewish quarter. In 1491 this was a flourishing community, by 1493 a mini ghost town. It seems a ghost town still, but that is because I arrive during the siesta, which is taken very seriously – and somnolently – in the south of Spain. On my way through the Juderia my ears catch the haunting strains of a flamenco guitarist from deep within one of the medieval courtyards playing *House of the Rising Sun.* The lyrics easily rearrange themselves. *There is a house in Cordoba they call the synagogue ...*

To the Hebrews it was the year 5075 – to the Christians 1315, to the Muslims 763 – when this synagogue was built. After 1492 it was converted into a hermitage. Four centuries on, a priest discovered its original purpose when a section of the mortared walls collapsed and – in a signally progressive gesture for that time – it was declared a national monument in 1885.

Today it has been restored, but as an exotic tourist attraction rather than a working synagogue. An original Star of David mosaic graces its courtyard, a candelabrum sits in splendid isolation on a recessed ledge, and extracts from the Book of Psalms line the upper parts of the internal walls. Across the street is a Sephardic museum, whose curator – Angelo – looks after the exhibits as if he himself were Jewish. In Cordoba today, he reveals, there are just four or five Jewish families and no Judaic worship services.

Donkey carts, heavily pregnant orange trees and haciendas obscured by olive groves announce our arrival in 'the real Spain' but then, I reflect, religious intolerance of the type peddled in the Mezquita propaganda is equally real and, in a sense, equally Spanish. Then, in the book I read as our bus barrels along the Mediterranean Highway, [47] I learn that the Vatican recently denied Muslims the right to pray in their old mosque because it is now a cathedral. If only religious leaders' vision were as broad as that sea of columns, eight sets of worshippers could have been accommodated there. No, the age of religious wars is not yet over.

1486–1491 km

Like the Pyramids, the sublime Alhambra which dominates Granada was built by cheap labour – and to last. One of the world's great architectural complexes, the incomparable burnt-orange ensemble in the foothills of the Sierra Nevada has survived repeated waves of religious fanaticism down the centuries – and proved a special inspiration to poets. To enable those who have never seen it to visualise this man-made wonder, no description could conceivably surpass that of the Muslim poet who described the Sabika acropolis 'as a crown and the Alhambra as a great ruby set in it'.[48]

On the bus to Alhambra, I meet a group of young Spaniards, also visiting the complex, who volunteer to help me into those parts of it I couldn't possibly reach unaided, and to give me the benefit of their Spanish perspective.

Few verses can survive transplantation from one tongue to another with their beauty intact. But even in English the sentiments expressed in a Spanish poem translated by one of my new friends, Benigno, have the power to move me:

> Give him alms, my lady,
> For there is nothing so sad
> As being blind in Granada.

The Spanish original of this Francisco de Icaza poem is inscribed on a plaque at the foot of a great bastion known as the Watch Tower. The poem has even more force when you've seen the Alhambra's glories with your own eyes.

Probably the most memorable sight of any Alhambra visit is the Court of the Myrtles, located in Comares Palace, in which an 'Olympic-sized' reflecting pool takes up nearly an entire courtyard, fringed by porticoes at either end, and mirrors their elegant pointed arches in its hidden depths. The palace's wooden ceiling, its craftsmanship and design, its geometric starbursts and optical wave effects, stagger the senses. Work continues, so they say, on the Carlos V Palace, a *Reconquista* masterpiece begun in 1533 – and if this is so (it is proceeding imperceptibly, if the claim is true) Barcelona's *Sagrada Familia* may yet be completed before it is.

Benigno opens my eyes to the way mainstream Spaniards view the phenomenon of separatism. On 11 March 2004 he was in a bar in the 'Basque Country' (he would insist on the quotation marks) when breaking news of the multiple bombings in Madrid interrupted the morning television fare. As the newsreader spoke, Benigno recalls, spontaneous cheers erupted in the bar and 'my blood ran cold'.

The regional bus line operates 32 coaches to the Mediterranean resort of Malaga. Not one has a ramp. All the coaches are rated 'accessible'. Search me.

I thought we were in for a straightforward bus trip (the driver was certainly among the most accommodating I've met) but when, within 30 seconds of our leaving the bus station, a Spanish woman seated near me crossed herself – and on seeing there was no church in sight – I *really* sat up and paid attention.

This soft summer evening outside a fish restaurant in a covered arcade, an Hispanic Bojangles of 70 years – Pepe the troubadour, with a guitar-strumming sidekick who might have been his son (but wasn't) – was serenading nine empty tables until he spied a lone woman sitting at a tenth around the corner. Pepe now gave his all, singing and soft-shoe shuffling his way to her side, going down on bended knee and thrusting his hands skywards in a show of bravura worthy of something far better than the look of unimpressed blankness she bestowed on him in requital.

1497–1510 km

One of the journey's best vistas is that from high above Malaga, in the grounds of Moorish Castillo de Gibralfaro, which has overlooked the Mediterranean since the 14th century. From this eyrie – and even more clearly from the nearby parador – you can see for kilometres along the Costa del Sol.

The only sunny thing about today's bus driver is his Ray-Bans. His tape deck plays music at well over 100 decibels, regardless of the passengers' wishes – and, when I get down at La Linea, it does not come as the shock it should to notice my bags are missing. The cavalier driver, who was hostile from the outset to my boarding his bus, had just left them standing outside. Five sweat-inducing minutes later, the bus office assures me the three items of luggage are safe at its offices back in Malaga; the bad news is I won't be reunited with them until about half past eight.

The looming Rock is a sight long familiar from photographs and

TV programs but when first you see it for yourself it still overpowers the senses. The fact that it *is* different, and special, has aroused my curiosity. Will I find here a cloying cliché, Little Britain without the humour? The first signs are not promising. After being welcomed across the border by an immigration-service equivalent of a British bobby, the first thing that confronts me on the other side of the line is a traditional red phone booth on Sir Winston Churchill Avenue.

Finding a homely and welcoming hotel doesn't take long. The manager's a Scot but the breakfast, he assures me, is English. The only disturbing note is a poster out the front about Madeleine McCann. I suppose that all the rooms on minuscule Gibraltar are like mine, sufficiently close to the Rock that the last audible sound before I drift off to sleep is the screeching of Europe's last wild apes, the Barbary macaques.

1510–1514 km

The Gibraltar most people see comprises the Rock and a precious few monuments around the town but the Gibraltar its 30,000 souls know and cherish revolves around its main street, Main Street.

Given that this is not exactly Washington, you should not be surprised to learn that this morning I ran into Gibraltar's first citizen, the Governor, Sir Richard Fulton. I had just passed the Convent – the former Franciscan mission that has been the vice-regal residence since 1711 – and was asking a liveried guard for directions to the cablecar when His Excellency stepped briskly to his Jaguar, which was purring expectantly under the portico. I will not say Sir Richard was anything other than courteous (he acknowledged my 'Good morning' with a bow of the head). But our meeting was brief, and the fault does not lie with me, you see. The man had nothing to say.

I am puzzling over the apparent impossibility of reaching the platform from which the cablecar leaves for the Upper Rock when members of the Gibraltar Fire Brigade, mingling outside the station opposite, perceive my predicament and rush to the rescue. When the ticket vendor sees a blur of blue uniforms and shiny white helmets, she gives a start – perhaps momentarily thinking the gondola has caught fire – and is so taken aback by the sight of us that she forgets to charge for the ride.

The gondolier, a John Bull type with a hearty sense of humour, announces, 'The cablecar will stop halfway up the Rock (i.e. we will be hanging in mid-air). Do not, under any circumstances, leave the cabin.' When we reach the upper station he turns surveyor, 'That hazy blue line you can see over to the south is the Rif, part of the Atlas Mountains. Across there' – our eyes follow his hand as it swivels right – 'you can see the Straits of Gibraltar; and over there' – another 120 degrees to the right – 'is the Spanish coastal town of Algeciras.' Between the cablecar terminus and the restaurant are several flights of steps – which is all right for everyone else but for me to get from one to the other I must place the palms of my hands on the concrete floor and swing my torso, adopting the gait of a macaque. As I shuffle off, John Bull proffers some well-meant advice. 'Be careful of the monkey droppings.'

Life elsewhere may be a soap opera: here it's more of an English sitcom. Downing an ale at a pub off Main Street, I cannot avoid overhearing an upper-class Englishman at the outdoor table next to mine as he leans over to the young woman at his elbow and tells her in a hoarse stage whisper, 'I might have to marry her instead. You'd better make your mind up.'

Gib has a far more developed European consciousness than, say, Russia. There is even a Europa Road here. Chief Minister Peter Caruana has incurred plenty of flak over the past decade simply because he is patently not hostile to Madrid. (Yet the Gibraltarians cannot be so conservative as the overseas press might have you believe since, just a few weeks before my visit, they elected him to a fourth term in office.) The Chief Minister later tells me, 'We share a Mediterranean culture with the hinterland … evidenced in musical, culinary and religious trends. We are bilingual in English and Spanish.'[49] He backs up these statements with chapter and verse, surprising me with the information that more than half of all Gibraltarians are Catholic, and a staggering 90 per cent-plus speak both languages.[50]

Caruana attended a hearing of the UN's decolonisation committee in mid-October. There was a beautiful irony at the outset when he thanked the committee for rescheduling the hearing.

Evidently, the original date chosen for the meeting had clashed with an act of self-determination – the holding of elections in Gibraltar. Caruana challenged the very concept of independence in an interdependent world, going straight to the heart of the European conundrum. 'If Spain … remains an independent country, even though she has chosen to surrender to the European Union institutions a very large and ever increasing part of her power and control over her own national affairs, why is Gibraltar a colony just because we choose a constitutional relationship with the UK that gives the UK much less power over our affairs than Spain has surrendered … to the EU?'

Tonight, as I arrive in Tarifa, at the Continent's southern tip, a dimly remembered poem comes to mind. Where the land meets the sea, the voice of the land says something like:

> This is the end.
> There is no more of me.

I rack my brain to no avail, striving to recollect where this couplet came from. Anyhow, it seems appropriate these words should rise into my consciousness just now.

1516–1522 km

Am I hoist with my own petard when I conclude that the southern point of Europe is on the Isla de las Palomas? In Norway I refused to accept that the island on which North Cape is situated was part of the Continent. Well, it depends whether you consider the Isla an island. Despite the unchanged name it is no longer one, because a man-made causeway now links it to the Spanish mainland.

Official permission is needed to get onto it. The 27-year-old senior officer of the Guardiá Civil in Tarifa is glad to give the go-ahead, and by the time I reach the rusty iron gate – just past the helpful signs either side of the causeway announcing 'The Mediterranean' and 'The Atlantic' respectively – the gatekeeper has unlocked it. The few barren hectares that make up this promontory would not entice you to go further if this were your first European landfall. A rusting tank and an equally rusty obstacle course, an abandoned soccer pitch and barracks that *look* abandoned are all that remain. There is a reason for keeping it out of bounds, but I discover it only later.

On the stroke of noon my chair is parked on a knoll at the top of a short, steep rise. I am peering due south across the water. To my left, a mere 12 km from this spot, Africa is spread out below. Today is warm, about 20 °C – a breeze is blowing – and, whatever you say, I'm more powerful than ... Roser Jordana in the seat of Andorra's prime minister. I mean, I have all Europe behind me.

Landward lie tens of millions of square kilometres. Not right now but later, in the privacy of my hostel room, I will calculate how far I have come: 25,172 km. When you consider that in a 'straight line' from Gamvik to Cabo da Roca lighthouse the distance would be about 5000 km, I have undeniably digressed. But I long ago concluded that, in travel as in life, it is the tangent that makes the round trip worthwhile.

Unlike the lighthouse at Gamvik, the one on my right is not automated. Its operators, I realise, are normally the southernmost Europeans, but not today, because the lighthouse is undergoing restoration. Suddenly I recall Rita Bastholm, the northernmost European; and a new definition of Europe flashes into my mind – the largest expanse of land in western Eurasia between two lighthouses.

Today, at the very south of Europe, I meet a Christian, but this one is not even a European, or a Spaniard (though he would like to be). Christian is a Liberian member of the work crew restoring the lighthouse – the only member of it who can speak English. He points to a compound on the far end of the 'Isla'. Those buildings I'd mistaken for disused barracks, do I see the barbed wire in front of them? Now that Christian points it out I can. 'That is a detention centre for illegal immigrants,' he says, as though spilling a state secret – which I later realise is exactly what he's doing.

A Spaniard named Germán, in charge of the restoration project, corroborates this later. 'As they're technically in a military zone, they're not subject to Spanish law.' Inside my brain a globe goes on. Aha! I have stumbled upon Spain's very own Guantánamo Bay.

The other thing I can see from here – though I must overlook the detention centre to see it – is the biggest array of wind turbines I have seen on my traverse. Don Quixote aboard Makybe Diva would think thrice before tilting at these monsters – *aeolicos*, in Spanish – as they whirl their way across the Rio de Valle.

By bus to Cadiz. This Atlantic port is shaped like a fist – a sizeable fist, 1.5 km by 1.2 km – enclosing half a dozen barrios. Cadiz lays plausible claim to being the oldest city in Western Europe. According to classical sources, the Phoenician colony of Gades was founded here *circa* 1100 BC. In a soft twilight the good people of Cadiz enjoy quiet pursuits. Some drop a line in the ocean and wait with the stillness of patience; others play the medieval sport of royal tennis. I linger over a great meal in one of the journey's most evocative settings, the Plaza de San Francisco, people-watching between courses.

1524–1531 km

Today an Andalusian musters up the effort to tell me that the Spanish of the north call Andalusians 'the lazy half'. He laughs in hollow self-recognition. With half the men of working age in Cadiz unemployed these days, the philosophy 'We work to live; we don't live to work' has obvious attractions.

A plaque on the façade of Cadiz City Hall commemorates the 500th anniversary of the departure of Columbus' second voyage. I can understand enough Spanish to see that it claims this brought 'evangelisation and culture to the New World'. How amazing that a statement so insensitive to the fact that the Amerindians already had culture – their own – could be made as recently as 1993, the carryover of a timeworn conceit.

In 1778 the Baroque Tavira Tower – because it was the highest lookout in its part of town – was appointed the official watchtower, a vital early-warning post in a city that had recently been granted the monopoly on Spain's trade with the Americas. The tower's uppermost turret houses a camera obscura, a darkened box containing a lens which projects a moving image of the cityscape outside to observers within an enclosed room. Unfortunately for me, the room in question is up several flights of stairs; fortunately for me, the attendant – seeing my position – borrows my camera.

When I return later she has taken several panoramic shots and, after handing my camera back, announces my 'early Christmas present' – a CD on the topic of the other camera, obscura.

Outside Cadiz's cathedral I find strangely affecting the sight of an elderly man wheeling his legless and nearly blind wife in her wheelchair across the cobblestones in front of the church, to the strains of Louis Armstrong's *What a Wonderful World* played by a busker on guitar.

This is the most photogenic of places. Its wrought-iron tracery, shady plazas, palatial mansions and drop-dead-beautiful laneways overhung by enclosed patios put Cadiz in the top rank of European cities for me.

Sometimes the literature is less than informative. This afternoon I lose interest in a brochure that begins, 'Cadiz Museum's 150-year history indicates that the institute enjoys a long tradition …' The museum's prize exhibits are two identical-looking sarcophagi – one containing the skeleton of a male, dated *circa* 400 BC, the other presumably his wife. The first was discovered in 1887, the other only in 1980.

The curator tells me Trajan was the first Roman Emperor of Hispanic origin (reigning from AD 98–117). They say you learn something every day, so that's my quota right there. Ancient sources said that the journey by ship from here to Ostia, the port of Rome, took nine days. Estrabon, an ancient historian with a droll sense of humour, quipped that the population of Cadiz spent more time on the high seas than on terra firma.

1535–1537 km

How we judge by appearances even as we deplore the habit in others. This morning, fresh out of town on the train to Seville, the only other passenger in my carriage looked worse than scruffy. I was disinclined to offer him more than the briefest of pleasantries. Tiago, on the other hand, was eager to talk. A few minutes into our ride, the young Portuguese looked out the window and said matter-of-factly, 'I have slept on this beach my first night in Cadiz.'

The only part of his life story that lodged in my brain was that he was a balloon-tying artist – animals being his speciality – and a juggler. Appearances deceive. I would not have thought the man well travelled. He had been in the Netherlands but stated categorically, 'I didn't like Amsterdam or the Dutch. They are like this.' On 'this' his mobile features snap-froze into a frown. I couldn't help but laugh. The atmosphere had lightened. I put away my book. He spoke with an unpretentious fondness of his ten-year-old son, who has lived with his mother since his wife died in a car crash three years ago. Suddenly I felt a rush of sympathy for someone whom I'd regarded as an annoyance five minutes ago.

When he had said his fill, Tiago lapsed into silence. Idly, he took out a balloon and fashioned a dog from it, which he gave to a wide-eyed five-year-old girl who had just come on board. Her mother looked on indulgently. Then he got up and juggled a few balls while the train moved ahead, blaming its low ceiling when one of them speared astray.

Whereas Cadiz is charming, Seville I find too prettified by half. Its authentic soul is to be found far from the tourist drawcards but it is worth questing after.

Flamenco is often likened to other folk music but it strikes me more as the authentic jazz of Spain, all the more so for its seemingly infinite adaptability to other musical styles and tastes, from bossa nova to hip hop. A pub barn called La Carbonéria hosts flamenco nights every night at eleven (free of charge, but that's how they get the crowds in: beer sales pay the performers' wages). Tonight I beat the crowd by arriving two hours early and securing a front-row seat – my own, of course. The house band, *Quadro Flamenco de la Carbonéria* (Carbonéria Flamenco Quartet), are past masters at rousing an audience to fever pitch. Their star dancer, Anna Japon, has such attitude that by the end of the performance the crowd are clapping in time to her stamping feet and whistling her emphatic and virile movements. Her dancing provides the perfect counterpoint to the extraordinary tone of anguished passion and yearning in the voice of lead singer Juan Murube. After the show the flautist, Mauro Perego, who visited Australia in 2000, smiles broadly on learning that I hail from Melbourne. 'I really enjoyed the shopping in Chapel Street!' he enthuses.

1538–1546 km

Jésus, the desk manager at the *pensión* where I am staying in Seville, possesses the endearing mannerism of saying 'Any problem' when he means 'No problem'.

'Can I buy a Coke?'

'Any problem,' replies Jésus, reaching into the fridge.

I look at my head in the mirror and know this is time for a haircut; I look at my whereabouts on the map and know this is the place. Where else can I visit the barber of Seville without forking out mega-euro at the box office?

To my surprise, no one around town seems to have heard of a *peluqueiro* (loosely translated as a stroppy Spaniard) appropriating the opera's title for his business. So any old barber shop will do, I decide. The first one I come to, La Caballero (The Horseman), is just opening its doors. On seeing this out-of-season tourist, Paco – a rake-thin barber of the old school – raises his eyebrows but, luckily, not his prices. Unlike Gibraltar's governor, Paco doubtless has something to say – have you ever met a member of his profession who didn't? – but, failing a language in common, all is silence save for the monotonous chirruping of blades. Until the moment Paco opens his mouth to sing, that is. Nothing operatic, sadly, just an itty-bitty ballad. But, as he brushes the last stray hairs from my collar, Paco gestures to the wall on my left – where I see some yellow clippings, not of hair but the newspaper kind. And the headline over the longest article says, you guessed it, El Barbro de Sevilla.

As Arantxa seats her tour group in the stands at Seville's Plaza de Toros, I consult a written description of bullfighting ceremonial which I've been keeping since Arles in Provence: *The classic rules of the corrida* [fight] *are established. The paseo* [parade] *opens the show. The toreros parade in their spangled costumes, followed by the banderilleros, picadors and the 'mules' – horses that will drag away the bull's carcass.*

There are compensations for those who cannot occupy a grandstand seat. On a signal from Arantxa, a gatekeeper admits me to the arena, thus affording me a bull's-eye view of the world without the downside.

Up in the stand, Arantxa tells the crowd King Juan Carlos is a fight fan. He has been to this stadium, but not Reine Sofia. 'The Queen doesn't like bullfighting. She is Greek.' As if that explains everything which, on reflection, it probably does.

The fight begins with the entrance of the animal, emerging from the toril [bullpenl, where he has been kept in the shade, into the full sunlight of the arena. The torero waits with his cape, tries to calm the bull's anger to master it and impose his own will. This is the phase of the passes.

I ask Arantxa, 'What is your best argument against the critics who say bullfighting is cruel and barbaric?' She gives me two. 'Bullfighting will always be. It is part of the expression of men's lust for death and violence.' Her secondary argument boils down to this: a man has to eat. She quotes a famous bullfighter who once said, 'It is more painful to feel the horn of hunger than the horn of a bull.'

The second phase begins when the picadors, with their lances, wound and provoke the beast.

'You should know something about it before you criticise,' Arantxa remonstrates. 'Every movement [in the sport] is well designed.'

Next, the banderilleros come to stick their arts into the bull's flesh to excite him and make him fight.

'It's not so easy to kill a bull. You have to pierce it at a part of the flesh between the third and fourth vertebrae. And you have to kill it through the heart. The connection is direct from the spine to the brain.'

The fight ends with the work of the muleta.[51] *The toreador, muleta in hand, brings the animal to the point of exhaustion to finish him off by a death thrust.*

'It is an instant death. People believe that bulls are innocent animals, but they are not. They are wild animals and they will attack anything that moves.' The death of a man in the arena is rare but in Olympic year 1992, with the eyes of the world on Spain, two *banderilleros* were gored to death within a month. One of those deaths still makes Arantxa quail. 'It was quite awful,' she confesses. 'It was televised.'

I ask Jésus his opinion of Portugal and the Portuguese. 'For them Spain is an important country; for us, Portugal is not so important,' he tells me. 'But the ones we see here, they are nice people. For us they are any problem.'

As the regional bus bears me back into Portugal, I am still trying to bring to mind the source and exact words of that poem about the land and the sea. But I reach my hostel room in Faro, the largest town on the Algarve, unable to recall it and unsure why it seems so insistently to matter.

1551-1554 km

In high summer this pretty stretch of coast would be crowded with holidaymakers, a second Costa del Sol. In low winter it is quiet, almost deserted. Perfect. The middle of Faro's main pedestrian mall is covered in a Santa-red carpet. On Sunday morning a plastic Father Christmas – just last night a puffed-up jolly giant 20 metres tall – lies crumpled and deflated on the grass; I know the feeling only too well.

Faro is a 20-minute bus ride from the Atlantic coast. At this time of year the air temperature at Faro Beach – Praya de Faro – is perhaps 11 °C, not bitterly cold but nobody is braving the water. Along the coast, a ribbon of sand glints under the odd shaft of sunlight, but for a more scenic view you must look 100 metres inland, at a broad lagoon called the Rio Formosa. There, runabouts lie at anchor, faithful sea dogs abandoned. For these vessels, unlike their masters, there'll be no more running about this year.

1557–1559 km

Faro railway station ticket hall, 7 am. My ticket is for the 7.38 – a most inaccessible beast – to the interior. Unless someone makes a move soon, I will miss the train. Meanwhile I keep one eye on a brand-new wheelchair ramp that only wants to be unfolded to be ready for use. The stationmaster is here now, gesturing that he intends to ignore its existence and lift me bodily into the train. It's his station; I don't argue. But this would never happen in Germany. One Europe? Not yet, not soon.

Évora is a trial on wheels. World Heritage status is a mixed blessing for the residents of this small, yet historic, walled town in central Portugal. But for me it guarantees an ordeal with every revolution of my wheels – two hours from railway station to upper town across jagged rocks to roll 3 km. Typically friendly Portuguese who warned me I would never see Évora because of its rough surface are owed an apology. Then I thought, I'll prove them wrong. Now I think, How right they were, as I make the slowest 'progress' of the journey.

At the medieval mansion – a *pensão* of great character accessible only with the staff's kind help – Sophia is sympathetic. 'Nothing can be touched. This is because our town is all patrimonial,' she says, flinging the Unesco term as an epithet. It is one thing to keep your streets in a pristine 15th-century state (rough) – and damn the inconvenience to motorists, the elderly, mothers with prams and, oh yes, wheelchair users – but why then, I ask myself, looking around me, are residents allowed to install ungainly Meccano-like television antennas on their red-tiled roofs? Once we start going down this rocky path – and at under 1 km/h in Évora I know plenty about rocky paths – intellectual monsters lurk, ready to waylay you.

1559–1564 km

David, the owner of my *pensão* – the Portuguese equivalent of a *pensión* – is so town-proud that aware of his guest's difficulties in getting out to see the neighbourhood he puts aside other, more pressing, business to ensure I don't miss out on its premier attractions. The building ensemble on the hill overlooking the *pensão* makes those few hundred square metres probably the most historic location in all Portugal – not excluding Lisbon. Whether the edifice they call the Temple of Diana was actually dedicated to the goddess of the hunt is dubious but what is not in dispute is its status as Iberia's best preserved Roman temple. If that sounds like faint praise – it is roofless, after all – we do well to be thankful it is still upright after two millennia.

Nearby is the town's distinctive marble cathedral, simply called the Sé. It showcases an amalgam of architectural styles rarely seen in a single building: Romanesque towers, fortress-style parapets, Gothic entrance and a Baroque apse. David mentions, quite casually, that the Inquisition had its own interrogation chambers here in the church, which celebrated its 700th anniversary in 2008.

Not far across town, outside St Francis' Church – not as old as the Sé but once attached to the royal palace and so endowed with great prestige – there is just enough time to ask David about the antennas before he must head off on other business. I quiz him, 'How did they get past the patrimonial police?' and he informs me of a recent proposal brought before the town council to replace them with one 'super-antenna' for the entire area. 'But,' he laments, 'it was an idea too logical, so it failed.' Perhaps, I suggest, those precious antennas should be declared World Heritage aerials, and added to Évora's list of priceless relics, never to be altered. Deeming this an excellent idea, David notes it down for future reaction.

In a dusty unvisited recess along one side of the building, a destitute crone clutching a single crust of bread feebly attempts to feed a coterie of cats that have adopted her. Exactly midway between the riches and the poverty lies the great equaliser we know as Capela dos Ossos, the Chapel of Bones. Constructed entirely of human skeleton parts, it is inevitably dismissed by many as grotesque. As David explained to me, the 16th-century Franciscans meditated much about their church's location over a graveyard – and this was their response. On a marble lintel under which everyone must pass is the most thought-provoking inscription. WE BONES THAT ARE HERE, WE ARE WAITING FOR YOURS. Skulls are inset among geometric arrays of tibias. One complete skeleton dangles from a wall. A sign in Portuguese hangs above the altar. What wisdom is there? I ask a tour guide, who translates it for my benefit. 'Why are you going so fast? Stop and think. Life is so short.' Going so fast at 2.4 km/h, and more than twice as slow in Évora? This is a clear-cut case of mistaken identity.

Swiftly, the view from the train alters from a field and forest landscape to a picture window filled by the broad, broad Tagus. Lisbon announces itself more impressively than Paris, more imperiously than Madrid. Will it live up to the expectations this creates in the first-time visitor? We shall see. The train service terminates at ultramodern Gare do Oriente, opposite the equally ultramodern Vasco da Gama shopping mall. From world-beating global explorer to shopping mart in just five centuries. *Sic transit gloria mundi.*

1567–1570 km

To understand the essence of Portugal, I've been assured, you must embrace *fado*, the beautiful music of Fate. Portugal's contribution to world music may not have travelled well outside lusophone (Portuguese-speaking) societies, but *fado* explains so much more than I could hope to know from any other source that I cannot wait to share the passion. With its roots in the working-class Lisbon districts of Alfama, Mouraria, Bairro Alta and Madragon, *fado* – which emerged in the second quarter of the 19th century – is described in the Casa do Fado museum as 'a music of daily life, of joy, sadness, love, jealousy, homesickness, faith'.

Like opera before it and jazz in the decades to come, *fado* soared – around 1870 – from its humble origins into the most fashionable of settings. Portuguese aristocrats took their lead from King Dom Carlos (1863–1908), who was taught guitar by *fado* composer and performer João Maria dos Anjos. The fateful music's golden age dawned in the 1930s, spurred on by radio, gramophone records and official censure under Fascist dictator Salazar. His order banning *cegadas*, plays full of *fado* songs dealing with comic, cultural and even political themes, prompted singers to create two sets of lyrics to the same melodies – one for public exhibition, the other *proibida*. Ricardo Rocha, the Casa's tour guide, says a friend of his, Ricardo Almeida, is playing tonight in Alfama. Then he adds, with as much impartiality as he can muster, 'This guy is probably the best guitar player in the world.'

Alfama is in the upper town. How to get there, when it's too close for a taxi ride, too steep to push? I'm mulling this over when a minibus stops in front of me, and I surprise us all by leaving my wheelchair at the kerb and crawling down the bus aisle. Luckily, the driver recovers enough presence of mind to bring the chair aboard before straining up the hill.

Having forgotten where Ricardo is performing, I settle for a restaurant where someone has mentioned that a 'late show' will be starting at half past ten. The singer, Ana Sofia Varela, arrives with a camera-toting friend who turns out to be none other than the wife of Ricardo, 'the best guitar player in the world'.

How many *fado* acts are in this city? There must be dozens,

I'm thinking, and, turning to tonight's guitarist, Pedro de Castro, exclaim, 'What a coincidence!' My naivety incurs a summary rebuke. 'There are no coincidences.' Such is the decree of *fado*.

Ana Varela's voices are remarkably diverse. The music that flows from her ranges from the sweetest fluting utterances to a sound as sharp as a knife in the ribs – but vastly more satisfying.

1575–1577 km

On Friday evening in a downtown plaza by the Tagus, the last thing I expect to hear is an orchestra tuning up. But this afternoon the European Reform Treaty – better known as the Treaty of Lisbon – was signed, advancing closer European integration, not long ago a seemingly doomed cause after the Dutch and French between them scuttled a proposed Constitution. (Irish ratification in late 2009, at the second time of asking, will refloat the treaty after all.) This evening the city is invited to party. The EU leaders who are in town have also been invited but, although they are dining just 500 metres from here, no one seems to know if they will.

Under a canopy on the concourse in front of the European Presidency offices I meet Nicholas McNair, an Englishman resident in Portugal and a classical composer by profession. But his particular skill in demand tonight is his expertise in timing. As the 70-piece Orchestra do Algarve goes through its program, his job will be to press a button a split second before each big musical bang, to ensure it is synchronised with the fireworks.

Before he goes back to the rehearsal I ask Nicholas whether he considers himself more British or European, and he says, 'Definitely European. I couldn't feel so European in England – ' he pauses, then adds, 'I'm joking, of course.' But anyone who has lived in England will know there's more than an iota of truth behind such a slip of the tongue. Naturally I stay for the concert, announced by the theme to *2001: A Space Odyssey*. Bom-boom, bom-boom, bom-boom, bom-boom, bom – starburst! Nicholas has come in right on cue. Then the strains of *Ode to Joy* fill the air – and eyes with tears.

'Europe' is popular here. Portugal may still be overlooked by Spain, for whom it is 'not very important', but the Union allows it to regard its fellow European nations as equals – except that, on this day, Portugal itself becomes the first among equals. And the politicians? No-shows, the lot of them. Having said they signed the treaty for the good of the European people, they're exhibiting a curious reluctance to mingle with their masters.

1580–1582 km

These mid-December days, the weather continues crisp. But tonight, as I overlook Lisbon from the heights, the heavens open. I shelter till the storm has abated before descending the cobbled streets of the Castelo quarter and the narrower lanes of Alfama. The cloudburst has emptied these old thoroughfares, so traffic is no problem. But it is late, and unless I make it to the railway station soon I risk missing the last train and not arriving back at the hostel till dawn. I abruptly call a halt to such pessimistic thoughts. Watch yourself, Ken, you're becoming Portuguese.

1584–1588 km

With help, I board a 'non-accessible' tram from central Lisbon out to Belém (I really am living dangerously now). The joys of this dormitory suburb of Lisbon are bundled together, close enough to enjoy them all in one afternoon and evening.

Mosteiro dos Jerónimos is Portugal's most sacred space, the 'home church' of the nation. To the left, as you enter, is the tomb of Portugal's Shakespeare and Dante combined, Luís Vaz de Camões (1524/5–1580). Keeping him company is Vasco da Gama, not just a shopping mall but, all in all, 'the Portuguese navigator who established the sea link between Portugal and India (1497–1498), thus setting a new trade route which, for over a century, would grant the Portuguese supremacy in the Indian Ocean'.

Less than 200 metres separates this august church from the home of Belém's contribution to Portuguese snack heaven. For here are bakery-restaurants the size of churches where the *pastéis de Belém* – a crusty-topped custard tart guaranteed to make your eyes water – has been made since the 1830s. Hundreds of people occupy gilded dining rooms in the most popular of these institutions, the Confeitaria de Belém. Sprinkled with cinnamon and sugar, the tarts are every bit as addictive as everyone told me they would be.

My European journey has been long on culture but short on sport, and this will not do in the continent where the world game first flourished. Tonight Belém is at home to the most successful and famous Portuguese football club of all, Benfica – and it appears everyone who follows the game here is expecting a walkover. I, on the other hand, am expecting an uphill push, and wondering if it will all prove a waste of time. For one thing, it's chilly and I'm not wearing a jacket. What could I have been thinking? Outside the ground a public thermometer says it's 9 °C, but I know 4 °C when I feel it.

Stopping by a merchandise barrow that would be familiar to any footy fan back home, I ignore the mascots and assorted literature in favour of a wiser purchase, a scarf. But which scarf would that be? Belém the underdogs and whipping boys, or Benfica the league's success story? 'Oh, it doesn't really matter,' I tell the barrow lady whose quizzical look reminds me she can't possibly understand what I'm saying – and then, recollecting whose home turf I'm on, I point to a blue-and-white scarf and choose. 'Belém, *obrigado*.'

Beside me at the barrow, a Dutchman a long way from *his* home turf asks if I'd like help to complete the climb. 'Sure,' I say, in the knowledge that watching the game in company will be twice as much fun. Spectating in Europe – even in 'poor' Portugal – is a costly business these days. A ticket seller at the members' kiosk says as non-members we must pay €40 (A$67) each and, just as we're digesting this kick in the guts, a Belém club official marches up and asks if he can help. This official must have clout. He talks a couple of duty police officers into lifting me up a dozen steps, and gets us both a balcony spot in one of the grandstands.

Jos says the pre-match expectation round town has been of a 5-1 whitewash. But, for whatever reason, Belém has more of the ball in the first half and conventional wisdom no longer seems so wise. Twenty-five minutes into the second session, Belém's No. 7 – Weldon – boots the ball into the net from a wicked angle and the stand erupts. A beer-gutted drunken slob (but one of ours) tosses a plastic chair over the boundary fence and has no idea how lucky he is that the police react with self-restraint. The whole side lifts, and Benfica proceed to play like the losers they are. Leaving the ground after the match, Jos and I congratulate each other on our foresight in backing the winning team, and I wear my scarf proudly home – no fear.

1592–1601 km

Mario, one of the receptionists at my Lisbon hostel, looks a lugubrious Portuguese, but he's really a deep thinker, or what the French call *un homme sérieux*. So it's a great relief when his first response to my desperate request of him to drive me to the end of Europe is to smile. Otherwise, the last 40 km of my transcontinental voyage could only be bridged by a budget-busting taxi ride or sticking out my thumb and trusting to luck. No public transport goes there. I cannot believe my good fortune when Mario says that not only does he have Sunday morning and early afternoon off but he is a former tour guide at the hilltop resort of Sintra and would be pleased to take me there en route.

Sintra is a Portuguese Katoomba, with holiday houses, mansions and manors dotted throughout. But nothing can compare with the *folie de grandeur* known as Quinta da Regaleira. Quinta's centrepiece is an 18th-century palace in the Manueline style (named after a Portuguese king). Just over 100 years ago, a new owner with an unlimited interior and exterior design budget ordered a set of grandiose new structures, including a 'mini-cathedral', and lined the garden walks with his choice of classical statuary. I could have spent twice as long at Quinta but Mario understood my impatience to be off, with the end of my long road beckoning. So, after bidding a former colleague goodbye, Mario retook the wheel and aimed his car at the coast.

Having checked my speedometer before we hit the road, I now consulted my travel diary as the car headed west, and essayed some final computations. In seven-and-a-half months I had pushed 1600.8 km, half the distance from Sydney to Perth. My initial daily range of 4.5 km (in Russia) had surpassed 7 km a day by early December but the cobbled ways of Évora and old-town Lisbon ultimately brought this back to 6.97 km a day. Including the distance pushed, I had covered more than 26,000 km, or five-eighths the circumference of the globe. (That my pushing accounts for just one-sixteenth of this may sound puny, but my biceps beg to differ.) Turning to my accounts, I now saw that the French restaurants (and others) forgone had allowed me to come in 21 eurocents (a mere 35 Australian cents) a day under budget.

Calculations done, I looked up. My inner child wanted to yell, *When do we get there?* Sure, I set out to cross Europe the long way, but there shouldn't be as much of it as this. Europe is the smallest continent after all! And then, just when I was sure we must have taken a wrong turn, the bushes parted. We entered a gravel drive and parked. Since our destination was one of Europe's extremities, you'd expect a lighthouse – and so there was. From our car seats we could hear the pounding of waves, like the roar of distant cannon. A few 'steps' more and I'd have made it.

Directly I am back in the chair, we crunch our way across a stone path fringed by Hottentot fig – a South African gorse that has proliferated here without natural competitors (reverse colonisation, it occurs to me) – and the realisation dawns that we, too, are planted by the vast Atlantic. My eyes are drawn to a cairn that looks for all the world as if it's been waiting for me. Chiselled into it are the first two lines of the poem that has been tugging at my memory ever since Tarifa. By Camões, the poet whose tomb I saw less than 24 hours ago, it reads:

Here is where the land ends
And the sea begins.

This much leads on to words that have slumbered in memory for years beyond recall:

The land says to the sea
There is no more of me.

At some level I was always heading for this point, this resolution at the end of my long road. You may think it mystical if I say it was my Fate. But then you know, as we Portuguese say, there are no coincidences.

On 16 December 2007, my 230th day out of Tallinn, I sit on a slate fence at Cabo da Roca, Portugal, the *Ponta Mais Ocidentale do Continente Europeu* – the westernmost point of Europe (latitude 38° 47' N, longitude 9° 30' W). East to west, from Archangelsk, I've come almost one-seventh of the way around the globe. For ten minutes I survey the wild surf beaches north and south, and, in my mind's eye, the vast hinterland behind me which somehow I've managed to cross from another, even wilder sea. And gazing out at the Atlantic, visited by the ultimate epiphany, I become aware in an instant – and only after the voyage has ended – what its purpose, what my quest, has been.

Europilogue

It was a year – a journey – anyone could have had. The year I disappeared into the Russian Outback, snorted snuff in Murmansk, cruised the fjords and fished in one too, confronted a polar bear armed only with a sword (the bear, that is: I was defenceless), became a house guest to a family of bank robbers, tracked the Loch Ness monster down to a Swedish lake, and the Swedish sense of humour to its lair; missed out on all the Nobel Prizes (again); wrestled tigers;[52] rode the Vertical Death Drop; saw fireworks at Copenhagen's Tivoli (and more of them in Lisbon); went up the Rhine, down the Elbe and up the Eiffel Tower; was homeless in Paris when not at the Louvre; wheeled *sur le pont d'Avignon* but left the dancing to others; tried my luck at Monte Carlo; pushed it everywhere else; slept in a monastery on the Med and a nunnery at Lourdes; promenaded at Biarritz; drank cider with the Basques; scaled the Rock; was the man in the arena, no bull; and *Ode to Joy* was the soundtrack to it all.

From the Arctic to the Atlantic, this expanse of land is populated by Russians, Danes, French, Germans ... almost everyone *but* Europeans. The exceptions are worth noting, and I have done so in a spirit of tribute and admiration.

The ancients called it the 'known world', but what did they

know of themselves? Precious little, if Herodotus is right. Hear the great writer and pioneering traveller – who should have known about the place if anyone did – admit in exasperation, 'Clearly no one knows about Europe, neither about the parts lying to the East nor to the North, and whether it is surrounded by sea ... Nor can I find out the names of those who decided upon its boundaries.'[53]

I have followed Herodotus to those farthest shores. No one cried out when I trod on Europe's extremities – Gamvik, the Lofoten Islands, Skagen, the beaches of Etretat and D-Day, the Tower of Hercules at A Coruña, the Pillars of Hercules at Tarifa, and Cabo da Roca. Only there I found the one boundary marker on which everyone agrees, where 'the land ends and the sea begins'.

Maybe the Eurosceptics were wiser than they knew, and Europe doesn't really exist. *The Paperback Oxford English Dictionary* lists Eurasian, euro, Eurocentric, European, Europeanise (and its cognates), European Union, the element europium and, yes, Eurosceptic – but look for 'Europe' and it's not there.[54]

In general, I have discovered, people on either side of Europe's national borders regard their neighbours as significantly different from themselves. The 'bad neighbour' policy is in evidence all over the world. But in each nation there have always been voices who dared to speak up. 'They are no less human than we,' they say. 'Let us learn from the stranger at our gates.'

The European spirit is hostile to absolutism. It promotes diversity through the pairing of opposites. It is not a European trait to be 'of one mind'. The prevailing spirit is friendly to duality, keen to compare belief systems. In politics this is reflected in the European invention of democracy, which might begin with a duality – conservatism versus socialism – although more than two can play as each pairing attracts its own opposites until soon the public space (the ancient Greek *agora*) is a cacophony.

Pluralism in religion leads to alternative visions of 'ultimate truth': Protestant versus Catholic, and both separated from the Orthodox faithful. Having found what happens when governments try to compel belief, Europe now believes in 'live and let live'. But it learnt its lesson the hard way. In Lisbon I met a restaurateur who had left the Catholic faith in which she was raised, to become a Buddhist. Her former co-religionists might disagree, but her decision was surely in the European spirit.

As I suggested early on, the basic division of Europe is not between East and West but between North and South. In the standard typology, Northern phlegm – cold reserve – is opposed to the exuberant warmth of the South. But, as the reader may recall, I met with rudeness in France (where the rudest person of all was from Morocco). In the same country I encountered humanity (from an Algerian) and hospitality (from the member of an ethnic group Algeria had oppressed). I shared railway platforms with Germans mortified by late-running trains, an insult to Teutonic efficiency; and found that the trains in Spain run mainly on ... time (even if some no longer run on the tracks).

And yet nations do exhibit 'personality traits' – not invariably but often enough to make us say, 'How typically Dutch' or 'Just like the French'. The Swedes tend to adopt a quiet demeanour, as Andreas Edvardsson said in Archangelsk. (Though now I'm told young Swedes at parties really let themselves go. Obviously, I was hanging out with the wrong crowd.) In this house of many mansions it may help to think of each nation as a communicating apartment where each family lives by its own set of rules. It is a great strength of Europe that somewhere within this warren of apartments you will meet a cast of mind, or a national attitude, congenial to your own.

Yesterday Europe, today the world. The idea of Europe began with the Greeks, and spread from the Greeks via the Romans to the lands of the Goths. But Europe, as we know it, wasn't built from the South up. All along my route, from its Russian start to its Portuguese end, the Vikings had been before me. For all the nobility of Viking and Greek myths, both were warrior races. The hunger for dominance does not reside in one place, or one race – and has certainly not been banished from the human heart. Its presence 'so close to civilisation' prompted Ryszard Kapuscinski to call Europe, in a masterly phrase, 'a bright Arcadia that every few years overflows with blood'.[55]

Arcadia the idyll, whose ideal is 'the good life'. This Europe is not a piece of real estate but a mindset. The notion of Europe as a civilised place – by contrast with Asia, Africa or the Americas – has somehow survived two brutal world wars intact. The failure of that ideal state, Europia, to dawn quite yet – in Europe or beyond – has not dimmed a shared belief in 'the good life' as a goal worth striving for. Football, fireworks, flamenco and *fado*. The last leg of my Europe-wide slalom ride, touched by far too few glorious sunsets and far, far too much rain, has furnished some of its best memories. But what do all these have in common? They thrill the senses, tug at the emotions.

Throughout historical time the European region has been a garden beyond which you ventured into the wild and barren steppe of Asia. The garden is cultivated, the soil rich. Tilling it, or raising livestock on it, the European settles down and strives to tame the world – at first the world he can see, and later the world far over the sea. Blessed as the land is, Reason demands an explanation for luck. *Blessed by whom?* he aches to know. And the answer, spread by those with claims to special insight, is *Blessed by the gods* – Norse, Greek, Germanic – and, later, by God Himself.

Claiming God was on their side, and that they had a civilising mission, European-descended societies in Australia, and the Americas North and South (much later in Africa), came to dominate non-European communities. The justification claimed for this domination – a justification must always be found – was that the occupied races were sub-human or savage; like the plants in Europe's Eden or the beasts on its farms, they needed to be tamed ... for their own good, of course.

Europeanisation of the globe remains a work in progress. It was Mike Holland, my English fellow traveller in Bavaria, who pointed out that the little specks of purple on the obverse of euro currency notes represent French Polynesia, Réunion and French Guiana, making European currency legal tender in parts of the Pacific and Indian Oceans as well as in a corner of tropical South America. The European dream of a 'good life' could not be sustained without non-European immigrants or refugees – Iraqis, Egyptians, Algerians,

Bangladeshis – who work for the Club of Europe but can never hope to join. Many of the members, as it happens, aren't the least bit clubbable.

How many self-identifying Europeans are there in Europe? Several tens of thousands, it would appear, perhaps fewer. They could make up a small nation of their own – and, in the sense that they transcend national borders, they do. There was the Dutchwoman working in tourist information at a Brussels railway station; Eugenio, the Spanish restaurateur of French and Portuguese parentage; a Catalan receptionist in a Barcelona hostel; and an Englishman living in Portugal with his German wife. To say 'I am a European', where national sentiment remains so strong, requires much more bravery than to say 'I am an Australian'.

To be of a European mind in the 21st century is to lay claim to the world's most exciting and long-running story – the Norse word 'saga' applies – one that has not only run and run in Europe but provided a template for the way most of this vast globe is now run. If we are all Europeans now – and exploring my own family background bolsters the claim – we must have been so for a long time. When we appreciate the arts and sports Europe created, our own good life, which we have worked hard to achieve and enjoy, can only be enriched by tapping into the source.

* * *

Runyon's riddle can at last be answered. Which Europe would that be? *All of them*. The noble, the base; the kind, curt and rude; the unalterable fact of geography, the ever-changing mood. Even at the far end of Europe I feel oddly like Ulysses, long an exile, coming home.

The magic box, shaken vigorously, has yielded certain clues to its well-hidden mysteries. At the end of my road a final epiphany awaits. And so it falls out that the real purpose of this expedition, which has taken up the best part of my life's best year, was nothing other than a quest to capture Europe's soul.

Notes

1 *The World in 2008*, The Economist, London, 2007, p. 96

2 *Russia & Belarus*, Lonely Planet, 4th ed., March 2006, p. 36

3 Jared Diamond, in his book *Collapse: How Societies Choose To Fail or Survive*, dubs this expansion 'autocatalytic'. But the Norwegians at that point were pagans – not for another 50 years would their chieftains begin to adopt Christianity – so you could hardly call them 'autocatalytic converters'. Anyway, they lacked autos, preferring to get about in longships. Who said history can't be fun?

4 With *King's Men*, the first book of his Viking trilogy, Tim Severin sheds light on the oft overlooked connections between Norsemen and Normans. They have also been referred to, on occasion, as Northmen.

5 Not what you're thinking. To pronk, a word of Afrikaans origin, means to spring or prance in the manner of an antelope or a deer.

6 The pithy note Per pressed against the Forus Bank's window to attract the staff's attention read: *Han trener Kr. viersmill oe oi han pemer. Vaer en god norman.* (I cannot vouch for Per's spelling.) Which translates: 'I need money. The post office has no entrance for me. Please be human.' Interestingly, the word for 'human' is 'Norman'. So at least the English can be thankful they were invaded by humans.

7 Those who wish to pursue the tail further are invited to log on to www.storsjoodjuret.com

8 You can view *Vital Signs* at www.mosdeux.com

9 *Time for Celebration,* Jun Feng, Select Books Online @ www.selectbooks.com.sg/get Title 2000

10 The past is a foreign country, they do things differently there' are the opening lines of L.P. Hartley's novel *The Go-Between.*

11 Although Steen Thomsen himself points out that, as he is from the Bendixsen line of our far-flung family tree – a branch on the opposite side, as it were – he is technically a 'non-cousin' of mine.

12 *Intellectuals*, by Paul Johnson, p. 168

13 By John Kelly, 2001. Now on permanent display at Victoria Dock, opposite Docklands (renamed Etihad, 2009) Stadium, Melbourne

14 In 1861, when his long essay *Considerations on Representative Government* first appeared, the political economist John Stuart Mill could write without fear of contradiction, 'The Flemish and the Walloon provinces of Belgium, notwithstanding diversity of race and language, have a much greater feeling of common nationality than the former have with Holland, or the latter with France.' Today that would be begging the question. *On Liberty and Other Essays*, by J.S. Mill, p. 427

15 *The State of Africa*, Martin Meredith. Jonathan Ball Publishers, Johannesburg and Cape Town, 2006, pp 511-12

15 *Truth*, Felipe Fernández-Armesto, St Martin's Press, New York, 1997, p. 94

17 Several weeks later, on a bus from Germany to France, I will see the same thought is circulating in Belgium. A *Guardian Weekly* article quotes Flemish Party leader Bart de Wever as saying, 'Brussels is the last obstacle. We would have divorced years ago if it weren't for Brussels.'

18 *Brussels, Your Capital City, Your European Village*, available at Brussels Town Hall, Grand Place/Grote Markt, p. 53

19 *Gargantua and Pantagruel*, François Rabelais, Penguin, p. 663 (orig. 1532, 1534)

20 The qualification 'heavier-than-air' is often overlooked when giving the Wright Brothers credit for their pioneering flight at Kitty Hawk, North Carolina, twelve years later.

21 *Benedict – Church Leader*, published by the Rectory of St Oswald, Marktl am Inn

22 *Buchenwald – A Tour of the Memorial Site* by Sabine and Harry Stein, Buchenwald Memorial, 1993, p. 18

23 *Routes to Luther in Wittenberg*, booklet published by Luther-Forum, Lutherstadt-Wittenberg, undated, p. 21

24 It now seems doubtful if Luther posted his theses on any church door, at least initially. Around the time in question he is known to have sent them in a letter to the Archbishop of Mainz. Martin Luther's *95 Theses*, booklet published by Akanthus, 2005, p. 5

25 *Chronology of the History of France*, by Claude Lebédel, Editions Ouest-France, 1999 (reprinted in English translation by Angela Moyon, February 2007, p. 6)

26 *Louvre: The Pocket Louvre*, by Valérie Mittais, Musée du Louvre Editions/Artlys, 2006, p. 88

27 Natalie Vella presented Oz Music Radio from 2007 and early in 2010 moved on to film, presenting the Sexy International Paris Film Festival (sexyfilmfestparis.weebly.com)

28 Jason Burke, *The Observer*, 30 September 2007, pp 40-41

29 *Et elle coule, coule, coule; Et elle coule nuit et jour;*
Car la Seine est une amante; Et Paris est son amour.

30 *La Renaissance du Bessin*, Issue 6578, vendredi 19 octobre 2007, p. 37

31 Société Nationale des Chemins de Fer

32 Spoken to Pontius Pilate. John 18: 36

33 Neither French city was successful with its bid to be European Capital of Culture in 2013. And the winner is … Kosice, Slovakia.

34 The competitors, in descending order of size, were: Cyprus, Luxembourg, Andorra, Malta, Liechtenstein, San Marino, Monaco. Apparently, the Vatican is not very sporting.

35 15 March 1993 issue, *Diari d'Andorra*

36 For more information, visit www.museus.ad

37 The month before my arrival in Spain, some of the 21 accused over the Madrid atrocities were convicted but the alleged mastermind was still at large. In January 2008 he was arrested in Morocco and in December of that year the man – Abdelilah Ahriz – was sentenced in the Moroccan town of Scalé to 20 years in jail for his involvement in the bombings. But in Spain itself the apportionment of criminal responsibility for the atrocities remains an open question. In December 2010 a US cable released by WikiLeaks identified two Indian as having also been involved.

38 *The New Spaniards*, by John Hooper, p. 19

39 Alexander VI (Rodrigo Borgia)

40 *The New Spaniards*, ibid.,p. 238

41 *Europe on a Shoestring*, Lonely Planet, 4th edition, Feb. 2005, p. 954

42 Royal photo-burners fined €2700, *Catalonia Today*, 22 November 2007

43 It's That Man Again, *Catalonia Today*, ibid., p. 4

44 www.barcelonaworld.org

45 *Ghosts of Spain: Travels Through a Country's Hidden Past*, Giles Tremlett, Faber & Faber, 2006, p. 132

46 *The Great War for Civilisation – The Conquest of the Middle East*, by Robert Fisk, Harper Perennial, 2006, p. 1275

47 *Ghosts of Spain*, ibid., p. 249

48 *The Alhambra and Generalife: Official Guide*, p. 9

49 In an email, 13 March 2008

50 In a second email, 14 March 2008

51 The *muleta* is a stick attached to the red cloth called a veronica which is held by the toreador. It obscures the sword with which he will stab it to death.

52 That bit about the tigers was just to see if you're still paying attention: the rest is true.

53 *The Histories*, by Herodotus, Oxford University Press, p. 26

54 *Paperback Oxford English Dictionary*, pp 255-256

55 *Travels with Herodotus*, Ryszard Kapuscinski, p. 81

Bibliography

Some of these books are referred to in the text; they contain observations that shed light on the historical landscape through which I travelled. The others were no less inspiring or, in certain cases, of practical use. Note: Where no individual can be cited, titles are listed alphabetically by publishing house instead of by author.

Author unattributed, *Altötting City Guide*, St Antonius Buchhandlung, Munich, 2005

Bernaudez Lopez, J. and Calera Andreu, P., *The Alhambra and Generalife: Official Guide*, Patronato de la Alhambra y Generalife, Granada, 1999

Bronnikera, E and Seledkova, O., *Soberg, I.*, Gostiny Dvor Publications, Archangelsk (undated)

Carlyon, L., *The Great War.* Pan Macmillan, Sydney, 2006

Coates, L., *Ypres, 1914–18: A Study in History Around Us*, Self-published, Norwich, 1995

Davies, N., *Europe: A History*, Pimlico, London, 1997

Deutsches Museum, *Deutsches Museum: A Guide to the Museum.* 3rd revised ed., Munich, 1995

Diamond, J., *Collapse: How Societies Choose to Fail or Survive*, Allen Lane, New York, 2005

Feng, J., *Time for Celebration*, Select Books Online @www.selectbooks.com.sg/get Title, 2000

Fisk, R., *The Great War for Civilisation: The Conquest of the Middle East*, Harper Perennial, London, 2006

Flynn, N., *Another Bullshit Night in Suck City*, Faber & Faber, New York, 2004

Hardy, T., *Race Around the Sports World*, GSP Books, Melbourne, 2006

Hemingway, E., *For Whom the Bell Tolls*, Arrow Books, New York, 1941

Herodotus, *The Histories* (translation, introduction and notes by Dewald, C.), Oxford University Press, Oxford, 1998

Hooper, J., *The New Spaniards*, Penguin, London, 1995

Isherwood, C., *The Berlin Novels: Mr Norris Changes Trains and Goodbye to Berlin*, Vintage, London, 1998 (orig. 1935, 1939)

Johnson, P., *Intellectuals*, Weidenfeld & Nicolson, London, 2005 (orig. 1988)

Kapuscinski, R., *Travels with Herodotus.* Allen Lane, New York, 2007

Kuringova, T., *Sorbian Customs and Traditions in the Course of the Year*, Serbska Cultura Informacija, Bautzen, 2005
Lewis, E., *Left Bank Waltz: The Australian Bookshop in Paris*, Vintage, Sydney, 2006
Lonely Planet, *Europe on a Shoestring*, 4th ed., Melbourne, February 2005
Lonely Planet, *Russia & Belarus*, 4th ed., Melbourne, March 2006
Meredith, M., *The State of Africa*, Jonathan Ball Publishers, Johannesburg and Cape Town, 2005
Mill, J.S., *On Liberty and Other Essays,* Oxford World's Classics, Oxford, 1998
Mittais, V., *Louvre: The Pocket Louvre*, Musée du Louvre Editions/Artlys, Paris, 2006
Montefiore, S.S., *Prince of Princes: The Life of Potemkin*, St Martin's Press, New York, 2001
Orwell, G., *Down and Out in Paris and London*, Penguin Modern Classics, London, 1968 (orig. 1933)
Oxford University Press, *Paperback Oxford English Dictionary*, Oxford, 2006
Roberts, J., *A Sense of the World*,. Simon & Schuster, New York, 2006
Saramago, J., *The History of the Siege of Lisbon*, Harcourt Inc., London (orig. in Portuguese, 1989)
Scott, Sir W., *Ivanhoe*, Penguin Popular Classics, London, 1994 (orig. 1819)
Severin, T., *King's Man*, Vol. 3 of the Viking Trilogy, Macmillan, London, 2005
Taylor, F., *The Berlin Wall, 13 August 1961-9 November 1989*, Bloomsbury, London, 2006
The Economist, *The World in 2008*, London, 2007
Tremlett, G., *Ghosts of Spain: Travels Through a Country's Hidden Past*, Faber & Faber, Ipswich, England, 2006
Van Gogh Museum, *A Museum for Van Gogh: Vincent Van Gogh: Life, Work and Contemporaries*, Amsterdam, 2005

Maps of Europe consulted

Marco Polo map by Institut Géographique National, 1:4 500 000; 1st edition, 2005
GeoCenter map by MairDumont, 1: 2 500 000; 2007
LänderKarte map by Carto Travel, ADAC, 1: 2 500 000; 2007

Acknowledgements

Sponsors of the Journey

None of these people has asked for, or been given, any say in the opinions or emphases adopted in the text of *Europe @ 2.4 km/h*, all of which are my own. But I hereby record my gratitude for their contributions which eased the financial burden of my long journey.

Pentax Corporation (www.pentax.co.jp/english)
Graham Deacon, Elsternwick Camera Centre
Russia & Beyond (www.russiabeyond.com.au)
YHA Australia (Australian division of Hostelling International) (www.yha.com.au)
QBE Insurance (www.qbetravelinsurance.com.au)
Principal and partners, Selwyn Greenberg & Co.
Hurtigruten Steamship Company, Tromsø branch – with particular gratitude to communications consultant Stein Lillebo and team leader Eigil Molø. (www.hurtigruten.com)
Peninsula Star Cycles, Playne St, Frankston (www.peninsularstarcycles.com.au)
Eric and Liesbeth Dasbach, Hotel Campanile, Gaasperplas, Amsterdam (www.amsterdam@campanile.com)

Special recognition

(grouped according to where they were when they made their particular contributions)

AUSTRALIA

Mum and Dad: For being there when I wasn't – and even when I was.
Les Carlyon: Your letter of encouragement and challenge stayed on my desk from the first day of writing till the last.
Joye Oldham: For blazing the trail to our European family.
Stephanie Bunbury: Your globetrotting and work ethic remain exemplary. Note, I'm still obeying the international vagrancy laws.

Bob Weis: For sending me to Buchenwald.

Tony Hardy: For writing first and best about Café Oz's Grand Final knees-up.

Geoff Slattery: For putting me in touch with Tony and his rollicking *tour de force* of a book.

Bernard Whimpress, without whom I wouldn't have found a home for this book.

At Wakefield Press: Julia Beaven, for patience, precision and always keeping my focus where it needed to be; Michael Bollen for his quiet vigilance; Angela Tolley and Stephanie Johnston for getting the word out; Michael Deves for showing you where I went without telling me where to go; and Stacey Zass for making the journey look a picture.

NAMIBIA

Tangeni Amupadhi: For supplying the electronic wherewithal and immense patience.

Graham Hopwood: For drawing my attention to the provenance of my Chapter 4 title, and for the footnote explaining it. And, more than ever, for your friendship.

Viviane Scholz: Your hospitality put me in the right frame of mind to tame another Beast; and extra thanks to you, Günter and Renée, for creating good impressions.

Christelle and Jaco Reed, and Schalk, at Puccini: For giving me the best possible writing environment there is – yet again.

Marc Hofer: For your high resolution and technological genius in extracting the best photos from 2841 starters. (www.journalistpicture.de)

Chris Pate: For expert manuscript rescue beyond the call …

COSTA RICA

Linda Gray: *Viva* for your response to my unexpected Spanish inquisition. (www.ranchotranquilo.biz)

RUSSIA

Marina Smirnova, curator of St Isaac's Cathedral Museum, St Petersburg.

Angela and Rustig Rstislav, Petrozavodsk.

Alexei Surkov, Pavel Nevzorov and Dmitri Shapovalov, Moscow.

Technical University students met in Kem.

Nadezhda Pestovskaya and the Hotel Dvina, Archangelsk. (www.hoteldvina.ru)

Osmo Kolu, Flait Travel Agency, Murmansk.

Alexey Telegin, Muscovite translator: For casting a critical eye over Chapter 1.

NORWAY

Mayor Marius Nilsen, conqueror of the True North.

Odd Magne Johansen, Tromsø: For giving me house space and displaying generosity in a time of personal adversity.

Professor Kolbein Lyng, Faculty of Health Sciences, Molde University College: Good company, good fishing.

Tina and Per (Bonnie and Clyde): If any of my friends ever want a put-up job in Norway, I'll tell them to go to Hell.

SWEDEN

Captain Cook, Aussie pub and restaurant, Östersund. (www.captaincook.se)

Hotell Muttern, Uppsala. (www.hotellmuttern.se)

DENMARK

Jun Feng: Thanks for kind permission to reprint your 'European poem'.

Steen Thomsen: For sharing your home, and the road. Also for introducing a 'non-cousin' to both our families.

NETHERLANDS

To Gordon and all the resident felines at Poezenboot, the Cat Boat of Amsterdam. (www.poezenboot.nl)

Muhammad and Savash, service staff at Hollandspoor railway station, The Hague, and strongest porters in the Netherlands: For showing the rest of the nation how to do their job.

Hague Peace Palace tour guide, Natalie Westerkamp. (www.icj-cij.org)

The Stayokay hostel network throughout the country, but in particular my hospitable friends in at the Haarlem, Hague, Apeldoorn and Maastricht hostels.

Jurjen Toepoel, Nationaal Jeugd Orkest summer academy tour manager. (www.njo.nl)

Ken Ueno, composer. (www.kenueno.com)

Bert Smit, Apenheul Primate Park: For taking time out from your duties to explain your function and mission. (www.apenheul.com)

Emilie and Hans Binnerts: May our roads always meet up.

BELGIUM

Brugge Public Library: For letting me have a lend of you. (www.brugge.be/bibliotheek)

Svein Koningen, Australian Viking. (www.koningen.net)

Sharon Uyttenhove-Evans, authority on Ypres. (www.quasimodo.be)

My hosts Jean-Luc and Anne at Le Vieux Moulin, family-run guesthouse in Rochefort: For your adaptability and the free lift to Jemelles station. (www.giterochefort.be)

GERMANY

Sonja Pierach, information and assistance officer, Walle Friedhof, Bremen Free State municipal cemetery: For shedding light on my German family.

Birgit Dess: A long-lost cousin salutes your openness.

Herbert Böttger, general manager, Consul Hotel, Bonn. (www.consul-bonn.de)

Sylvie, Günter and Hans, of Koblenz' Pfälzer Hof hotel. (icontihotel@gmx.de)

Peter Jaeger, *Stars and Stripes*, Darmstadt.
Kaiser Tom and all the crew at Wombat Hostel, Munich. (www.wombats-hostels.com)
Mike Holland and Regina Nickel: Great to catch up with you, Mike; equally great to meet you, Regina, and for welcoming an unruly house guest (me, not him).
Tomasz Nawka of the Sorbian Museum, and the Sorbian Cultural Information Centre, Bautzen. (www.ski.sorben.com)
Stephan Schelhaas, director of tourism, Lutherstadt-Wittenberg: For the lift from the station, the Luther DVD viewing and all the Luther literature. (www.wittenberg.de)
Professor Emeritus Derek F. Abell, European School of Management and Technology, Berlin. (www.esmt.org)
Raffaele Sorrentino, chief concierge, Hotel Adlon, Berlin. (www.hotel-adlon.de)
Walking Berlin tour guide Jason Andrews.

FRANCE
Jean Cédric Menard, deaf cinematographer. (www.jcedricmenard@yahoo.fr)
Front desk, Hotel B.S., Avenue Parmentier, 11th *arrondissement*: My bags got better service than I did.
Nunzio: Who runs the best Italian restaurant in the twelfth *arrondissement* and, most probably, in all of Paris (*Trattoria da Nunzio e Nadia*, 134 bis, Rue de Charenton). *Grazie.*
Vicki-Marie, guide *par excellence*: You brought Sainte-Chapelle alive.
Francis Boussard, manager, Café de Flore, St Germain des Près.
Cyril, hotel manager, Hotel Belle Epoque, 12th *arrondissement.*
David and Pauline, proprietors, The Old Farm of Bellerive, Picardy: For your generosity, and rides to the Clearing of the Armistice, Compiègne, Villers-Bretonneux and Amiens.
Christophe Thomas, principal of Victoria School: Australia will never forget you either. (www.ecole.victoria.villersbretonneux@ac-amiens.fr)
Jacqueline Brunneval, the Hotel-Restaurant France Bourgogne (21 Cours de la République), Le Havre: Three cheers for two chairs.

Ed Guerin, D-Day Tours: You shone by comparison with the competition, but then again ... what competition?
Yann Scavarda, journalist, *La Renaissance*, Bayeux: A very professional write-up, young gun.
Jean-François and Annette at Hotel de Naples, Vichy. (hoteldenaples@orange.fr)
Frères Gilles, Pierre-Marie: Île St Honorat. (www.abbayedelerins.com)
Manuela and Yves Desjardin, and Hélène, Hotel d'Arlatan, Arles. (www.hotel-arlatan.fr)
Claude and Hubert: For treating me to Toulouse's finest *cassoulet*.
Frédéric Rodier and Cathérine de la Coussaye, pharmacists, Nîmes.
Sister Ghislaine de Clerq, Assumption Centre, Lourdes. (lourdes.assomption@wanadoo.fr)
Frédéric and the crew at Biarritz H.I. hostel. (www.fuaj.org/ai/biarritz/)

MONACO

Rod, Neville and Isabelle Smith. (www.vfsgroup.com)

ANDORRA

La patrona, Hostal dal Sol (Plaça Guillemó, 3).
Ms Roser Jordana, director of Andorran tourism.
Montse Buil and Meri Meritxell at Radio SER.
The curator, Museum of the Miniature. (www.miniaturamuseu.com)

SPAIN

Nerea, at Sidreria Donostiarra: Keep tapping cider in the Casque Country. (www.sidreriadonostiarra.net)
Francisco Fuentes, bagpiper at the Tower of Hercules, A Coruña.
Manuel Santos: You drove me out of Portugal but all is forgiven.
Eugenio Duarte, owner of El Zaguan restaurant, Salamanca.
Angel Hurtado and Soy de Carabanchel, Al Magro, Madrid hostel: *Gracias* for ensuring I didn't miss the Australian election coverage.

Benigno and Diana Calvo, and Leon Massouf: For sharing Alhambra. Especial thanks, Benigno: For translating de Icaza's beautiful poem.
Germán Gamarro, of Algeciras Port Authority: For telling me about the lighthouse – and the dark house. (www.apba.es)
Becky and Luli from Casa Caracol house. (www.caracolcasa.com)
Marian at Tavira Tower: Thanks for the CD. (www.torretavira.com)
Quadro Flamenco de la Carbonéria – Mauro Perego, Anna Japon, Juan Murube and Jordi Flores: For a magical performance.
Paco, true barber of Seville: You really made those scissors sing.

GIBRALTAR
Chief Minister Peter Caruana, and press secretary Francis Cantos: For talking to me.
Governor Sir Richard Fulton: For not talking to me.

PORTUGAL
Maria Teresa, Eduardo and Henrique Almeida: You showed me the smiling face of Portugal with an open-door policy typical of Braga.
David Policarpo, from Pensão Policarpo: *Munto obrigado.* (www.localnet.pt/residencialpolicarpo)
Pedro Souto de Castro, Ana Sofia Varela and Rita Almeida: It was no coincidence that we met, but *Fado.*
Nicholas McNair, Lisbonian, opera composer, Englishman, European: Perfect timing.
Jos Damen, Dutch football fanatic: Go Belém!
Mario Anágua: For seeing me through to the end.